A SPENSER
HANDBOOK

A SPENSER HANDBOOK

BY

H. S. V. JONES
Late of University of Illinois

APPLETON-CENTURY-CROFTS, INC.
NEW YORK

PREFACE

In preparing this *Spenser Handbook* I have tried, so far as practicable, to make conveniently available our present knowledge of Spenser and his poetry. It has been impossible, of course, to give credit in detail and at every turn to all those who have contributed to our understanding of the poet and his works. Nor within the limits of my undertaking could I very well present every contention on each side of every debatable question. However, among the chapter references will be found listed the articles and books I have used, and in controversial matters I have tried to be judicious where I had no space to be argumentative. Particularly have I been at pains to include whatever might give support to views that differ from my own.

I need hardly say that Carpenter's *Reference Guide* with Miss Parrott's supplementary bibliography has been of the greatest service. To titles derived from these sources I have added those of more recent publications, even when the articles in question appeared too late to be considered in the preparation of my text. This applies particularly to the studies just published by Professors Greenlaw, Padelford, Lemmi, and Bush on the problems of the *Mutabilitie Cantos*.

In quoting classical and Italian authors I have used the following translations:—Welldon's *Nicomachean Ethics* (Macmillan) ; Jowett's Plato ; Cockman's Cicero's *Offices* (Everyman's Library) ; Rose's *Orlando Furioso* (G. Bell

& Sons) ; and Wiffen's *Jerusalem Delivered* (G. Bell and Sons).

There remains the pleasant duty of acknowledging a debt to Professor R. E. N. Dodge, who has generously given me the benefit of his exact scholarship and critical acumen.

H. S. V. J.

Urbana, Illinois

CONTENTS

Contents

A SPENSER
HANDBOOK

A SPENSER HANDBOOK

CHAPTER I

THE AGE OF SPENSER

THE Age of Spenser was one in many ways calculated to stimulate and enlarge the imagination. Its love of amusement and display made splendid the surface of its life. Many of the "abuses" which the Puritan Stubbes undertook to "anatomize" must have fed the eye of the Puritan Spenser. Sumptuous costumes worn in public, royal progresses, princely pleasures such as those of Kenilworth, frequent masques and pageants lent color and drama to the daily life of Merrie England. But there was much in the age to give wider scope to the imagination. To the support of ancestral patriotism those spacious days brought first of all new horizons. Taking westward the course of empire, England turned away from outworn hopes of European conquest. At high cost in men and money she had learned the lesson of the Hundred Years' War. Now, following in the wake of Italian and Portuguese explorers or striking out along ocean ways of her own choosing, she gave play to those instincts of trade and dominion which are natural to every great maritime power. After having hung for centuries on the rim of the civilized world, she was now to find herself at a new geographical center, and, working out from this, she was in time to knit closely together the tough fabric of the British Empire.

Attending these new forces of expansion were fortunately others that made for organization and integration. For example, the Reformation, which precipitated civil war in France, consolidated with the aid of Elizabeth's realistic statecraft the patriotism of the English people. In 1559 the Acts of Supremacy and Uniformity proclaimed at one and the same time the independence and the solidarity of the English Church. Like the loss of Calais in the year preceding, these acts marked the change from the old order to the new; and the new order was truly national not only because it repudiated the authority of the papal see but because it in fact made the Church subject to the Queen and Parliament. In this manner England took her place as the chief Protestant power in Europe and, as a result, inevitably found herself opposed to Catholic and imperial Spain.

English exploration was in the service of English trade. For example, the search for the north-east passage to India by Challoner and Jenkinson led to the formation of the Muscovy Company, which included among its charter members such prominent statesmen as Cecil and Walsingham. Sailing from London some 2,250 miles to the mouth of the Dwina, its ships carried to Russia the products of English looms and brought back such Russian products as rope, tallow, whale and seal oil. Pushing on to Persia, the English traders established a contact with one of the chief arteries of Oriental trade, and, in spite of dangers and losses by the way, were able to bring back rich cargoes of silks and precious stones. Of less immediate importance to English commerce was that quest for the north-west passage with which the name of Frobisher is most closely associated, and in which both Walsingham and Raleigh were financially interested. The ore brought home by Frobisher proved to be worthless; but the enterprise of his successor, John Davis, did much to promote the fisheries on the Great Banks and to advance colonization in Newfoundland.

Less edifying than the expeditions just described were the voyages of John Hawkins and Francis Drake to the Guinea coast in quest of negro slaves. In three successive expeditions, on two of which he was accompanied by Drake, Hawkins with the support of the Queen bought hundreds of blacks on the African coast and then sold them in forcible or crafty ways to the Spaniards in the West Indies. To John Hawkins the profitable traffic in negroes was one with which no God-fearing Englishman would allow a Catholic prince or Spanish laws to interfere. Business of this kind and adventures in freebooting or piracy, such as Drake's plundering of Venta Cruz and Nombre de Dios in 1573, while increasing the wealth of England, constituted virtually a state of war and made only a matter of time the decisive conflict between the great Catholic and the great Protestant power of the Western World. Fundamental questions involved were those of trade monopoly and the freedom of the seas.

For the prosperity of English trade it was necessary that England should become mistress of the seas, an end of which there was some promise in Sir Francis Drake's circumnavigation of the globe (1577–1580). The undertaking was supported by the war party, including such men as Walsingham and Leicester, in opposition to the more cautious policy of Lord Burghley. Weathering storms and suppressing mutiny, the intrepid seaman pushed on into the Pacific through the Strait of Magellan and surprised and defeated the Spaniards off Valparaiso. With a rich cargo of silver in the hold of the Golden Hind he started for home. He rounded the Cape of Good Hope in June and in September he sailed into Plymouth Sound. The position of Elizabeth was at first difficult; for months she had been listening to representations from the Spanish Ambassador, and she could now hardly receive Drake publicly without provoking the hostility of Philip. When, however, it became known that Spanish soldiers had been landed in Ireland, she was able to break off all negotiations with Mendoza. In the following year she felt free to throw off the restraining hand of Burghley and upon the deck of the Golden Hind at Deptford to confer knighthood on the great popular hero, whom the Spanish Ambassador was pleased to describe as "the master thief of the unknown world."

In the wake of exploration followed attempts at colonization. Ignoring Pope Alexander's division of the New World between Portugal and Spain, Elizabeth granted in 1578 a charter to Sir Humphrey Gilbert, conferring upon him the right "to inhabit and possess at his choice all remote and heathen lands not in the actual possession of any Christian prince." Raleigh, associating himself with this enterprise, looked upon it as a means of finding a retreat for those loyal English Catholics whose presence in the home country was a constant embarrassment to the Queen. He had intended, indeed, to act as vice-admiral to the first of the expeditions; but this the Queen forbade. To Sir Humphrey Gilbert fell the high command of a fleet of six ships, including the Golden Hind, the Swallow, and the Squirrill.

which set forth on June 11, 1582 and on August 5 took possession in the name of the Queen of the harbor of St. John, where upon a wooden pillar Gilbert set the arms of England. But the story of this voyage, which, indeed, promised more than it performed, Sir Humphrey was never to recount to the Queen; for it was during his return journey in 1583 that he went down with the Squirrill not long after his voice had been heard above the storm calling to his comrades: "We are as near to Heaven by sea as by land."

Fortunately there were others to carry on to a fuller success the enterprise which Gilbert had begun. In the following year Raleigh had obtained a charter for "The College of the Fellowship for the Discovery of the Northwest passage," and under this charter he sent out to "fruitfullest Virginia" Philip Amadas and Arthur Barlow. Following a southerly course they sailed by the West Indies and then north to the Virginia coast. There it seemed to them they had reached an earthly paradise. They were particularly impressed by the fertility of the soil, the profusion of fruit, and the fragrance of the black cedars with which the island of Wohokon was thickly wooded. Moreover, they were astonished by the courtesy and hospitality of the natives, who brought them daily presents of fish, game, and vegetables. The new country was pronounced "the goodliest and most pleasing territory of the world."

Led further by his active imagination and his intrepid spirit of adventure, Raleigh more than ten years after the last of these Virginia voyages entered upon the famous "trial of Guiana" or quest of El Dorado. He left England in February, 1595 and returned in August of the same year. In less than seven months, he made the journey to the island of Trinidad, punished severely there the Spaniards who had betrayed an earlier party of English explorers, and then with the aid of a commandeered Spanish guide continued his explorations until the annual rainfall checked his progress. Taking careful observations of the fertility and beauty of the country through which he passed, Raleigh was also at pains to conciliate with justice and kindness the natives whom Spanish cruelty had antagonized. He gave them to understand that he had come to free them from the tyranny of Spain. What, however, as a vision led him on was the hope of new dominion for his Queen, which would "confirm and strengthen the opinions of all nations, as touching her great and princely actions. And where the south border of Guiana reacheth to the dominion and empire of the Amazons, those women shall hereby hear the name of a virgin which is not only able to defend her own territories and her neighbors', but also to invade and conquer so great empires and so far removed . . . I trust in God . . . that he which is King of all kings and Lord of all lords will put it into her heart which is Lady of ladies to possess it."

Along with the story of England's expansion in the sixteenth century goes that of its consolidation and centralization; and just as Catholicism menaced the former undertaking, so it interfered seriously with the realization of the latter. Happily, English statesmanship and diplomacy had a directing genius, whose achievement may properly be compared with what was accomplished by English explorers. To William Cecil, Lord Burghley, fell the anxious task of guiding the ship of state through seas as perilous as any encountered by Drake or Raleigh. Threatened by both Catholic France and Spain, with enemies in Scotland to the north and in Ireland to the west, and encompassed by repeated plots and stratagems at home, he maintained through almost half a century his own position and that of his Queen. Upon his loyalty there never rested the shadow of a doubt, at a time when nothing seemed more difficult in public life than to keep free of suspicion. "If he was austere in a frivolous court," writes his biographer, M. A. S. Hume, "if bribes failed to buy him in an age of universal corruption, if he was cool and judicious amidst general vehemence, it was because the qualities of his mind and his strict self-schooling enabled him to understand that his country might be thus most effectively served, and that it would be unworthy of William Cecil to act otherwise."

What in the past had made for disunion in England was the authority of the papacy and the strength of the feudal nobility. The year following the accession of Elizabeth it was sought to protect the country against the first of these dangers by the two famous acts of Supremacy and Uniformity (1559). After the reign of Mary Tudor it was necessary thus to reassert and reinforce the position and the claims of the national church established by Henry VIII but now opposed by Convocation and the ecclesiastical peers in the House of Lords. After not a little diplomatic hesitation, the Papacy about ten years later issued its famous Bull of Excommunication, releasing English Catholics from obedience to their Queen. From this time on the religious question became an acutely political one. To be a Catholic was almost enough to establish a presumption of treason. When about ten years after the publication of the Bull of Excommunication the Jesuit Mission under the leadership of Campion and Parsons arrived in England (1581) with the purpose of dethroning Elizabeth, the Catholic danger became highly critical. To meet the situation a number of repressive measures were necessary. Already in 1571 Parliament had passed an act declaring it high treason to call Elizabeth a heretic, a schismatic, or a usurper, and fixing death as a punishment for anyone who should bring a papal Bull into the country. Now in 1581 it was declared an act of treason to reconcile a person to the Church of Rome, and the convert himself became liable to capital punishment. In 1585 and 1593 even severer legislation was passed. Against Jesuits and seminary priests there was a decree of banishment, and Catholics refusing to conform to the Church of England were required to keep within five miles of their houses.

The cause of Catholicism in England was closely bound up with the claims of Mary, Queen of Scots, to the English throne. If the illegitimacy of Elizabeth were granted, Mary as the granddaughter of Margaret Tudor was the lawful sovereign; or waiving this question and supposing that Elizabeth should die without issue, Mary would be her successor. In such circumstances the Scottish Queen became the center of Catholic hopes. Unfortunately for Mary she had sacrificed her prospects to personal passion, and her dubious conduct had seriously compromised her reputation. Having married Lord Darnley, she not only exposed herself to the suspicion of complicity in his murder but confirmed this suspicion by marrying Bothwell, the murderer, soon after Darnley's death. Then, hard-pressed by those in rebellion against her, she was so indiscreet as to throw herself upon the mercy of Elizabeth. In England, although necessarily kept as a prisoner by her cousin, she attracted the support and nourished the hopes of English Catholics. Most prominent of these was the Duke of Norfolk, a representative of those northern earls who maintained the feudal traditions of the Middle Ages in the midst of a rapidly changing civilization. It was the ambition of Norfolk to marry Mary and with the support of Spain and such prominent English Catholics as the Earl of Northumberland to restore his country to the Mother Church. At the critical juncture Norfolk submitted, the Spanish help failed to arrive, and the conspiracy collapsed. However, soon afterward, in 1570–71, the plan to bring about a Catholic reaction involving the marriage of Norfolk with Mary was renewed by Ridolfi, an agent of the Pope. The Ridolfi plot, in turn, was quickly uncovered by the astute Burghley, and Norfolk in due course was brought to the block.

The danger of a Catholic rising in the north was thus greatly diminished by the fatal indiscretions of Mary, Queen of Scots. Of more positive advantage was the bulwark erected by the Scottish Reformation against the ambitions of France. The moving and directing spirit in this great religious upheaval was the Scottish peasant, John Knox. Having early identified himself with Protestantism, he preached in both Scotland and England, saw service for his faith on the French galleys, and during the reign of Mary Tudor was an exile at Geneva. In 1555 he was placed under sentence of death in Scotland. Nevertheless, he returned two years later to his native land in response to an invitation from the Lords of the Congregation. At once he became the leader of a great popular uprising, which set about the destruction of church property and the establishment of a theocratic state after the model of Geneva. In 1560, not long after the death of Mary Guise, Elizabeth and the Scottish Lords signed the Treaty of Edinburgh, which provided at once for the independence of Scotland and the protection of both Scotland and England against

French ambitions. Along with this, the adoption in the same year by Parliament of the Scottish Confession and the passing of stringent laws against the authority and the practices of the Roman Church obviously opened the way for the ultimate union of the two countries.

While the cause of Mary, Queen of Scots, was largely the cause of Catholic France, the sixteenth century Irish question was rendered acute by the ambitions of Spain. To weaken the hand of her enemy in that quarter Elizabeth lent aid to the Dutch Protestants, just as her French policy entailed assistance to the French Huguenots. On the other hand, Ireland had no body of reformers comparable to the Scotch Covenanters. Thanks to the Reformation policy of Henry VIII and the activity of the Jesuits the country was more thoroughly Romanist than ever, and, in the words of Holinshed, it "was thoroughly concluded between the Pope and King Philip to make a thorough conquest of all Ireland; and so consequently as time should serve to do the same with England."

Indeed, the excommunication of Elizabeth in 1570 had brought Ireland in Catholic opinion directly under the authority of the Pope. As a result, after the abortive expedition of Thomas Stukely, which had set out in 1578 with the approval of Gregory XIII, there were landed in Ireland successively two detachments of Spanish soldiers, the first of which, having constructed Fort del Oro on Smerwick bay, was destroyed before Grey reached Ireland. It was the second and more formidable of these invasions that Spenser's patron, the Lord Deputy Grey, had to meet. With the coast blockaded with English ships, Grey bombarded the fort for two days, and after the surrender of the garrison, it was concluded, as Camden says, "against the will of the Deputy who wept thereat, that the leaders should be saved and all the rest put to the sword for an example and that the Irish should be hanged; which was presently done."

But it was not only with armed forces that Elizabeth undertook to solve her Irish problem. Under the Lord Deputy she set up Presidencies and Councils in Munster and Connaught, whose responsibilities were similar to those of the Presidencies and Councils of the North and the Welsh border. It was to one of these Councils, that of Munster, that Spenser for a period acted as Secretary. Furthermore, to secure her hold upon the disaffected country she gave to English colonizers, called undertakers, large estates, one of which at Kilcolman fell to Spenser. These undertakers were expected to take over in large measure the defense of the counties in which they were settled and to give allotments to farmers varying in number with the size of their seignories. The hopes entertained from the undertakers remained largely unfulfilled. Lord Roche, with whom Spenser had legal difficulties, said that whereas the Irish had had "great expectation of justice with favour and expedition," they "were left entangled and subject to the suppression and heavy hand of the undertakers without redress as before and every one discontented." To this judgment others bring confirmation. For example, Sir William Herbert said:—"Our pretense in the enterprise of plantation was to establish in these parts piety, justice, inhospitation, and civility with comfort and good example to the parts adjacent. Our drift now is being here possessed of land, to extort, make the state of things turbulent, and live by prey and by pay."

While Elizabeth and Burghley were dealing as best they

might with the Catholic peril in Scotland, in Ireland, and on the high seas, Protestantism in England was a house divided against itself. In the early years of Elizabeth's reign there was active criticism of the vestments and the images of the English Church. Such accessories, it was contended, were but the trappings of Papistry. Those who set themselves up as precisians in such matters came to be known as Puritans. Their voice more than once was heard in Convocation with reference to such matters as the proper posture for communicants, the playing of organs, and the use of the sign of the cross. Before long, however, vestiarian and similar controversies made way for issues of a different kind. In 1572 the Puritans sought through parliamentary action to do away with the *Book of Common Prayer,* in which they found many passages contrary to God's word. They petitioned, too, for a reorganization of the church, whereby ministers, instead of being appointed by the bishops, would be elected by congregations, and, instead of joining living to living, would be set over a single flock. They objected, further, to the manner in which the sacraments were administered, and to "the filthy quagmire" of the Archbishop's court. Two years after this famous *Admonition to Parliament* Cartwright and Travers issued their *Book of Discipline.* Here it was contended, chiefly, that in the Bible might be found not only precepts for righteous living but direction, as well, for the organization and administration of God's church. For example, in St. Paul's Assembly of Elders they found warrant for their Consistory of Pastors, Doctors, and Elders, that had powers of both suspension and excommunication.

Having failed to accomplish anything through parliamentary channels, the Puritans opened a campaign of abuse.

From secret printing presses they issued a flood of pamphlets, which sought to bring into ridicule and discredit the whole episcopal organization. The assault proceeded from the Presbyterian camp, but it did not carry the approval of representative men like Cartwright. Strictly speaking, the first broadside of the Martinists, who took their name from Martin Marprelate, the best known of the pamphleteers, was an *Epistle to the right puisante and terrible Priests my cleargie Masters of the Convocation house.* The bishops, it was here maintained, were "no better than anti-christian popes and popelings," who arrogated to themselves an authority "gainsaid and accounted anti-christian generally by all the churches in the world for the most part." Furthermore, these bishops were as open to attack in their private lives as in their priestly callings. Martin declared that "he understood all their knavery and it may be he keeps a register of them." The *Epistle* was followed by the *Epitome,* professedly offering a digest of John Bridges' *Defence of the Government established in the Church of England,* but devoted in large measure to an attack upon Aylmer, Bishop of London, in whose case it is shown that "beetle-headed ignorance" did not "live and die with him [Bridges] alone." Subsequently appeared *The Minerall Conclusions,* wherein is "laid open the very quintessence of all catercorner divinities," *Hay any worke for a Cooper* in answer to *An Admonition to the People* written by Thomas Cooper, bishop of Winchester, and other pamphlets more or less similar in purpose and style. The answer in kind to the Puritan lampoons was made by two men whose names are much better known than those of any of the Puritan protagonists. In his *Pappe with a Hatchet,* Lyly described himself as "one that dares calle a dog, a dog," and announced that his book was to be sold "at the sign of the crab tree cudgel in thwackcoate lane." That Thomas Nashe co-operated with Lyly in "thwackcoate lane" we know from his own declaration, and it has been assumed, though without any positive evidence, that *Pasquil's Apology* and *The Return of Pasquil* came from his pen. Whoever were the authors of these and the other anti-Martinist pamphlets, such as *Plaine Percevall* and *A Whip for an Ape,* the tone adopted is obviously much more caustic and scurrilous than that of their Puritan opponents.

In the midst of the conflict and controversy between Catholics and Protestants, Anglicans and Puritans, one sometimes hears the voice of tolerance. For example, Francis Bacon, in his *Advertisement Touching the Controversies of the Church of England,* published in 1589, thought the religious wound "was in no way dangerous, except we poison it with our remedies." He thought, too, the controversies were "not of the highest nature," and he deprecated the "immodest and deformed manner of writing lately entertained, whereby matters of religion are handled in the style of the stage." Similarly, Hooker, the author of the *Ecclesiastical Polity,* declared that his "meaning is not to provoke any but rather to satisfy all tender consciences." In harmony with these tolerant opinions are those of Spenser's friend, Gabriel Harvey, and those which Spenser himself has expressed in the Fifth Book of the *Faerie Queene.* Harvey says that nothing could come out of the controversy except a general contempt of all good order, in saying or doing, a "universal topsy-turvy." "Had it not been," he continues, "a better course to have followed Aristotle's doctrine: and to have confuted levity with gravity, vanity with discretion, rashness with advice, madness with sobriety, fire with water, ridiculous Martin with reverend Cooper."

That Spenser was deeply interested in the political and ecclesiastical questions of his day the following chapters will make abundantly clear. Nor is the evidence far to seek that the imagination of Raleigh's poet friend was stirred by the tales that travelers told of their adventures overseas. Let the man, says Spenser, who thinks the *Faerie Queene* but "painted forgery" remember—

> That of the world least part to us is red:
> And daily how through hardy enterprize
> Many great regions are discovered,
> Which to late age were never mentioned.
> Who ever heard of th' Indian Peru?
> Or who in venturous vessell measured
> The Amazons huge river, now found trew?
> Or fruitfullest Virginia who did ever vew?

REFERENCES

Bagwell, Richard. *Ireland Under the Tudors.* London, 1885–1890.

Creighton, M. *The Age of Elizabeth.* N. Y. 1891.

Frere, W. H. *The English Church in the Reigns of Elizabeth and James I, 1558–1625.* London, 1904.

Froude, James A. *History of England.* N. Y., 1890.

Inness, A. D. *England Under the Tudors.* London, 1905.

Mullinger, J. Bass. *History of the University of Cambridge.* London, 1888.

Pollard, A. F. *History of England from the Accession of Edward VI to the death of Elizabeth.* (*Political History of England,* Vol. VI.) London, 1915.

Shakespeare's England. *An Account of the Life and Manners
of his Age.* 2 vols. Oxford, 1916.

Traill, H. D. and Mann, J. S. *Social England,* Vol. III,
Section II.

CHAPTER II

THE LIFE OF SPENSER

O N the basis of a rather indefinite passage in a poem of uncertain date, 1552 has been accepted as approximately the year of Spenser's birth. In any case the great Protestant poet of sixteenth century England was born about the time of the accession in 1553 of Mary, the Catholic Queen. Although only a lad of some six or seven years when Elizabeth succeeded her half-sister on the throne, he had lived long enough to receive impressions of religious persecutions and bigotry. Throughout his boyhood, no doubt, he had heard in his father's house much talk of the martyrs who had suffered death under Mary. It was in London that the martyrs were burnt, and it was in London that Spenser, according to his own testimony, was born. To him, he declares in his *Prothalamion,* she had proved a "most kindly nurse."

Born according to legend in the eastern quarter of the city, not far from the Tower, the future poet matriculated in due course at the Merchant Taylors School, which had been founded on the twentieth of September, 1561 by the worshipful and ancient Guild of the Merchant Taylors. On that day statutes were framed, a master was chosen, and it was decided that the school should be housed in an old mansion called the Manor of the Rose, in the parish of St. Lawrence-Pountney. The statutes stipulated that the number of pupils in the school should not exceed two hundred and fifty. Of these as many as one hundred might be poor men's sons, to whose expenses their parents would make no contribution, and fifty others would be accepted at half the regular fee of five shillings a quarter. The remaining one hundred would be "rich or mean men's children."

To which of these groups Spenser belonged we cannot be absolutely sure; but the facts that while still at school he was presented a gown from the estate of Robert Nowell and that from the same source he received ten shillings on going to Cambridge, would lead us to conjecture that he was not among the rich or mean men's children who paid the fees in full. In any case, before entering the school he had to present himself for an examination in the catechism in either English or Latin and to demonstrate that he could "read perfectly and write competently." Once enrolled, he became subject to exacting rules. The school day began at seven in both winter and summer and, with an intermission from eleven to one, lasted until five in the afternoon. In the morning, at noon, and in the evening, Spenser and his fellow-pupils, "kneeling on their knees," said their prayers, "appointed with due tract and pausing." They might "bring no meat, nor drink, nor bottles, nor use in school no breakfasts, nor drinking in the time of learning in no wise." Nor might they engage in "cock-fighting, tennis-playing, nor riding about of victoring nor disputing abroad, which is but foolish babbling and loss of time." Once a week, on Tuesday or Thursday afternoon, the pupils had leave for recreation; but this privilege was withdrawn whenever one or more holidays occurred during the week. The restrictions imposed by the school statutes were no doubt patiently borne by so good a pupil as Spenser seems to have been; and we may be sure that he profited from such wise provisions as that whereby the rent of the school cellar was in part expended on "wood, coals, billets, faggots or other good fuel for such of the scholars as in the extreme cold time of winter may have need to warm them by," and in part used for the purchase of "wax candles or other lights of wax, for the poor children to read in their books by in the winter mornings or evenings."

From time to time the routine of Spenser's school-life was interrupted by the visitation of public examiners. In many cases these were men of distinction. At eight o'clock one November morning Spenser and his fellow-pupils presented themselves, certainly with fear and trembling, before a board of examiners, among whom was no less eminent a person than Miles Coverdale, famous for his work on the translation of the English Bible. We should like to think that the future poet was among those who on this occasion, after "a pythye and eloquent oration in the midst of the school" by a boy named King, delivered copies of verses and epistles into the hands of Bishop Grindal, the admired Algrind of the *Shepheardes Calender*. On that November morning in 1564, there also appeared among the visitors at the Merchant Taylors School Alexander Nowell, the Dean of St. Paul's, who is described as "a learned man and charitable to the poor, especially if they had anything of the scholar in them." It was Robert Nowell, a brother of this Dean of St. Paul's, who established a fund for poor scholars, of which Spenser, as noted above, was a beneficiary both at school and on proceeding to the University. All the evidence at our disposal points to the conclusion that our poet while still a school-boy earned the goodwill and respect of distinguished and influential men.

During this period there were, further, relations of another kind which had an important effect upon Spenser's development as a poet. These were the relations of master and pupil. It was our poet's good fortune to attend the Merchant Taylors School while its head-master was Richard Mulcaster, a teacher justly esteemed by both his contemporaries and posterity. In 1562 the visitors reported that he was "worthy of great commendation." He was, indeed, much more than a pedagogue. Himself an excellent scholar, he not only taught his pupils Hebrew, Greek, and Latin, but insisted upon a study of English also, and provided instruction in vocal and instrumental music and the art of acting. He was, thus, an advocate of the Renaissance ideal of a broad, liberal education. Not only was he a man of his time but he was also forward-looking. One of the first to advocate a democratic education, he insists that the subjects taught should be within the capacities of the pupil. Education, but not the same education, should be for all. The fundamentals should be within the reach of everybody, but only the specially capable should be given the benefits of a grammar school and university course. Together with the Spaniard Vives, Mulcaster was among the first advocates of a training school for teachers. His patriotism, which will explain his emphasis here and there, is expressed in the frequently quoted sentence:—"I love Rome, but London better, I favour Italy, but England more, I honour Latin, but worship English." One aspect of his patriotism, particularly noteworthy for students of Spenser, appears in his attitude toward the native speech. Like Du Bellay, speaking for the *Pléiade,* he combined a respect for his mother tongue with a recognition of the need for enriching it with borrowings from other languages.

As his school-days approached their term, Spenser must have recognized with some anxiety that without the aid of others he could never acquire a University education. No doubt he was ambitious to hold one of the two Merchant Taylors scholarships established at Cambridge and Oxford respectively; and, in view of Bryskett's testimony to his knowledge of Greek, we may suppose that his thoughts turned also to the Greek scholars maintained at Pembroke Hall, Cambridge, through the munificence of Thomas Watts, one of the Merchant Taylors examiners. Unfortunately the thirty-seven fellowships founded by Thomas Watts for Merchant Taylors boys at St. John's were not being filled at this time. As things turned out, it was from Robert Nowell's fund, from which the poet had received a gown while still a school-boy, that he was granted on going to Cambridge an initial allowance of ten shillings. Later on, from the same fund, he with other boys received "sick pay" repeatedly.

Entering Pembroke as a sizar, Spenser was required to perform more or less menial services in return for free commons. He may have acted as porter at the college gate or as valet to some student more fortunately situated. Whatever the disadvantages of his position, he was on the whole fortunate in matriculating at Pembroke Hall. There he must have been keenly aware of new forces that were stirring in all England; for his college was, indeed, a hotbed of Puritanism, which, beginning with a criticism of the forms of service and the vestments of churchmen, advanced to a much more dangerous assault upon the organization of the Church. Though Spenser, so far as we know, took no prominent part in this movement, students of his poetry need not be told that it left its mark upon him.

A score of years before Spenser entered Cambridge the mediæval curriculum, based upon the trivium (grammar, logic, and rhetoric) and the quadrivium (music, arithmetic, geometry, and astronomy), had been largely recast. The subjects in the new course of study were mathematics, dialectics, philosophy, perspective, astronomy, and Greek; and although by 1569 mathematics were neglected and Greek was studied little if at all, Spenser upon entering Pembroke was in the way of an education very different from that of the Middle Ages. For one thing, the Aristotelian logic, which was at the foundation of the older education, had been subjected to vigorous criticism by Peter Ramus in his thesis for the Master's degree at Paris. The aim of this famous attack was to substitute for mediæval formalism the natural light of reason, or the dialectic of the Platonic dialogues for the logic of Aristotle. Cambridge, the home of Puritanism, became also in contrast to Aristotelian Oxford, the center of this radical movement in education. In general, then, it may be said that the spirit of revolt against the old order, now yielding place to new, was what Spenser encountered when he went up from the Merchant Taylors School to Pembroke Hall, Cambridge.

Among Cambridge progressives was Gabriel Harvey, probably the poet's closest friend at the University. Harvey became a confirmed Ramist, an anti-Ciceronian, and an enthusiastic advocate of a reform of English versification. A record of the friendship between Spenser and Harvey is preserved in a group of letters which during the lifetime of the correspondents attained to the dignity of publication. Couched in a style more labored than felicitous, they are of first-rate biographical interest. They discourse upon the perennial themes of college friends: their verses submitted to each other for criticism, their affairs of the heart, their aspirations to achieve some notable reform. In this case "the new famous enterprise" was the "exchanging of barbarous and balductum rymes with artificial verses." To the end of achieving "infallible certainty in English prosody and bringing our Language into Art and framing a grammar or rhetoric thereof," the ambitious young men experimented in classical meters and sought, like Mulcaster, "universal agreement upon one and the same orthography in all points conformable and proportionate to our common natural prosody." At Pembroke, indeed, the new was in vogue. "All inquisitive after Newes," writes Harvey to Spenser, "newe Bookes, newe Fashions, newe Lawes, newe Officers, and some after newe Elementes, and some after newe Heavens and Helles to." And along with the new fads went foreign influence: "The *French* and *Italian* when so highly regarded of scholars? The *Latine* and *Greeke* when so lightly?"

Letters in a different key reveal the young men boasting to each other about the favor real or imaginary into which they have come. In a communication from Leicester House, Spenser says he is "in some use of familiarity" with Sir Philip Sidney, speaks of having been with the Queen herself, and alludes mysteriously to some confidential mission abroad. He finds that Master Sidney and Master Dyer are in sympathy with the literary reforms which he and his friend have at heart, and writes humorously of a more or less imaginary organization. "And nowe they have proclaimed," he says, "in their ἀρειωπάγῳ a generall surceasing and silence of balde rymers, and also of the verie beste to: in steade whereof, they have, by authoritie of their whole senate, prescribed certaine lawes and rules of quantities of

English sillables for English verse: having had thereof already great practise and drawen mee to their faction." Harvey, not to be outdone, would have his friend imagine him extemporizing verses on a bay tree "in a goodly Kentish garden of your old Lords or some other Noble man."

The theme of ambition alternates with that of love. Spenser has not been so occupied with ambitious schemes that he has found no time for Mistress Rosalind—not to speak of an *Altera Rosalindula*—who thought that the poet had "all the intelligences at commaundement," and who christened him "her Segnior Pegaso." From another college friend, Edward Kirke, we learn, in a gloss on the April eclogue, that Rosalind was "a gentlewoman of no meane house, nor endewed with anye vulgare and common gifts both of nature and manners."

But who was Rosalind? The question has been variously answered. Aubrey, writing in the seventeenth century, maintained that she was a kinswoman of Sir John Dryden's and lived among the Cotswold Hills. Church, one of the eighteenth century editors of Spenser, thought, in Edward Kirke's words, that the letters of Rosalinde "well ordered" "bewrayed" the name Rose Linde, a name frequently met with in Kentish records. Making the anagram more difficult, Malone produced an Eliza Horden, also of Kent. Quite as dubious as the preceding suggestions was that of Halpin, who in 1850 suggested that Rosalind was John Florio's wife, whom in the absence of all evidence he supposed to be the sister of the poet Samuel Daniel. None of the above solutions of the anagram, it should be said, has gained wide currency. On the contrary the identification of Rosalind with one Rose Dinley, first suggested by Fleay and later supported with geographical changes by Grosart, has acquired almost the authority of a tradition. Fleay thought that Rose belonged to the Dinleys of Worcestershire; but the placing of the poet's family near Pendle Hill in North-East Lancashire by R. C. Spencer, Craik, Collier, and Church, which had traditional support, and the assumed Lancastrian dialect of the *Calender,* led Grosart to transfer Rosalind from Worcestershire to Lancashire. This would then be the "North countrye" alluded to by E.K. in his Gloss to June. Now that it has been shown that neither the dialect nor the scenery of the *Calender* is disinctively Lancastrian, Grosart's theory need no longer be credited. Nor has Dr. Long's conjecture that the "widow's daughter of the glen" is Eliza North, daughter of the translator of Plutarch, met with much favor. To any of these highly conjectural identifications some students of Spenser will perhaps prefer the view, first expressed by Keightley and later approved with modifications by Professor J. B. Fletcher, that Rosalind is a creature of the poet's imagination; but it is wiser to conclude with Professor Draper that "the Rosalind problem is unsolved, and seems likely to remain so."

On account of what E.K. calls "speciall occasion of private affayres and for his more preferment," Spenser, perhaps in 1577, goes south. In July of the same year, to judge from a passage in the *View of Ireland,* he witnessed at Limerick the execution of Murrogh O'Brein. It is supposed that he was at this time in Ireland either as secretary to Sir Henry Sidney or on a visit to Bryskett. He may have been the bearer of despatches, as suggested by the Dictionary of National Biography, from Leicester to Sir Henry. In the following year, 1578, we know from an inscription in a copy of Turler's *Travailer* given to Harvey by Spenser, that he was acting as secretary to Dr. John Young, who, having been successively the chaplain of Grindal, while the latter was Bishop of London and an examiner at the Merchant Taylors School, and then Master of Pembroke Hall while Spenser was a student there, had now risen to the position of Bishop of Rochester. From his school-days to the period that followed his withdrawal from Cambridge, Spenser had obviously attracted the favorable notice of two of the influential churchmen of his time. In 1579 he seems to be in the way of enjoying the patronage of an even greater man. Under date of the fifth of October of that year, he writes in high spirits and indeed somewhat loftily to Harvey from Leicester House that he had hoped to send him some verses but that he had had "no spare time in the world to thinke on such toyes." He is just then on the point of departing to some unnamed destination "to his Honours service"; Sir Philip Sidney has promised to write him, and he hopes that Harvey will send him the news. It seems that nothing came of these bright prospects. We know only that the poet departs for Ireland in the following year, 1580, as secretary to Lord Grey.

It should here be recalled that Spenser before his departure for Ireland in 1580 had already made his mark as a poet. Not to speak of his early contribution to the *Theatre for Worldlings,* he had during these years written the *Shepheardes Calender,* most of the works now lost, the *Hymnes to Love and Beauty,* probably a first version of *Mother Hubberds Tale,* and certainly a part of the *Faerie Queene.*

From the time of his going to Ireland as secretary to Lord Grey until about 1588, Spenser was a resident usually in or near Dublin. As early as 1582 he had leased a house in that city for a period of six years, and in the same year he took out a lease for the New Abbey in County Kildare, where he served as Commissioner of Musters in 1583 and 1584.

The Irish or young London, as Dublin was called in the sixteenth century, was a city "not in antiquity inferior to any city in Ireland" and "in pleasant situation, in gorgeous buildings, in the multitude of people, in martial chivalry, in obedience and loyalty, in the abundance of wealth, in largeness of hospitality, in manners and civility it is superior to all other cities and towns in that realm." To the eye of the poet it offered hills and the sea on the south and open fields on the west; and "if you be delighted with fresh water, the famous river called the Liffie runneth fast by." In Spenser's time the city was surrounded with strong walls of hewn stone through which the city could be entered by any one of the many gates, such as New Gate, St. Nicholas Gate, or the Dame's Gate. On his arrival in Dublin, Spenser, as a matter of course, would have repaired with Grey to the Castle, where the Lord Deputy had his official residence and where one might suppose the secretary remained until he leased his Dublin house in 1582. Dublin Castle, which had been renovated and enlarged by Sir Henry Sidney, was well protected by a moat, a drawbridge, and towers. It was there that the High Court of Parliament met and sometimes the Courts of Law. Upon entering the Castle, Spenser would have had his attention attracted to the heads of traitors stuck on pikes, as they appear in an illustration to John Derrick's *Image of Ireland* representing Sidney's entrance to the Castle.

As soon as he had time to look about, we might imagine the poet interesting himself in the customs and traditions of the city. He would have learned at once of the abundant hospitality of the Mayor, and of the military musters of the Dublin youth four times a year. He might well have witnessed, too, a ceremony described by Richard Stanihurst in which the Mayor of the Bull Ring, a kind of captain or guardian of the unwedded youth of the city, conducted with his crew some "bridegroom upon his return from church to the market-place and there with a solemn kiss for his *ultimum vale,* he doth homage unto the bull ring." Of the buildings in Dublin famous in his day, Spenser would have noticed particularly Christ Church, in which was entombed its builder, Gerald Fitz Thomas, Earl of Kildare, and the more impressive St. Patrick's, and St. Stephen's Hospital for "poor, lame, and impotent lazars." One can imagine, too, what interest the author of the *Faerie Queene* would have taken in the current story of a thief named Scaldbrother, who lived, like Malengin, in a labyrinth reaching two large miles under the earth. Here he would hide all that he could steal and he was so swift of foot that he could outrun the swiftest and lustiest young men. Now and then in derision of those who pursued him he would take his course under the gallows, which stood near his cave. "A fit sign," exclaims the chronicler, "for such an inn!"

From residents of the city the poet would have heard with interest of the Chapel of St. George, which, to be sure, had been razed before he went to Dublin but at which in earlier days before the Mayor and officials of the city had been enacted the Pageant of St. George. For this the Mayor had to find St. George a horse; the elder master of the guild, a maiden well attired to lead the dragon; and the clerk of the market, a golden line for the Dragon.

In surroundings so suggestive to the imagination, Spenser found himself, also, in the way of congenial associations. Prominent among the men of letters who shared with him the "luckless lot" of banishment to Ireland, was Geoffrey Fenton, famous for his *Certaine Tragicall Discourses* translated from Boisteau and Bellforest's *Histoires Tragiques* and dedicated to Mary Sidney, the Countess of Pembroke. Possibly we have evidence of a close friendship between the two men in a copy of Fenton's translation of Guicciardini's *Wars of Italy* (1579), which bears on its cover the initials E.S. stamped in gold. Have we here a gift to the poet from the translator? We need not dwell upon the interest that Spenser would have taken in still another work of Fenton's; namely, his *Monophylo, A Philosophical Discourse and Division of Love,* translated in 1572 from the French of Pasquier. Geoffrey saw service with his brother Edward in the Irish campaign under Sir William Pelham and, like Spenser, he held a secretaryship under Lord Grey. In 1585–86 he was a member for Carlow County in the Irish Parliament.

Another and perhaps closer friend of Spenser in Dublin was Lodowick Bryskett. After a short residence at Trinity College, which he left without taking a degree, we find him in 1571 in the position of temporary Clerk of the Council in Ireland under Sir Henry Sidney. Evidently he was on terms of intimacy with the Sidney family; for during three years he toured Germany, Italy, and Poland as a companion of Sir Philip. To the volume commemorating Sidney's death Bryskett contributed two poems. His duties in Ireland must have been very similar to those of Spenser.

In 1577 he preceded Spenser as Clerk of Chancery for the faculties in Ireland, and in 1582 he was appointed by Grey secretary of the Munster Council.

This "ancient servitor of the realm of Ireland," as he is described by Sir Robert Cecil in 1600, wrote a book of special interest for students of Spenser entitled *A Discourse of Civil Life, Containing the Ethic Part of Moral Philosophy*. Though the book drew heavily upon Italian sources, and although "it is not at all clear that the conversations Bryskett described ever took place," it is nevertheless a valuable memorial to the friendship of Spenser and Bryskett. Its Introduction tells of a gathering at Bryskett's cottage near Dublin, in which were numbered Dr. Long, Archbishop of Amagh, Captain Thomas Norris, and Edmund Spenser. To this group of friends their host, according to the *Discourse,* made the followings remarks:— "There is a gentleman in this company whom I have had often a purpose to intreate, that as his liesure might serve him, he would vouchsafe to spend some time with me to instruct me in some hard points with which I cannot of myselfe understand; knowing him to be not only perfect in the Greeke tongue, but also very well read in Philosophie, both morall and naturall. Nevertheless such is my bashfulness, as I never yet durst open my mouth to disclose this my desire unto him, though I have not wanted some hartning thereunto from himselfe. For a love and kindnes to me, he encouraged me long sithens to follow the reading of the Greeke tongue, and offered me his helpe to make me understand it." Spenser is thereupon requested to declare "the great benefits which men obtaine by the knowledge of Morall Philosophie, and in making us to know what the same is, what be the parts thereof, whereby vertues are to be distinguished from vices; and finally that he will be pleased to run over in such order as he shall thinke good, such and so many principles and rules thereof, as shall serve not only for my better instruction, but also for the contentement and satisfaction of you al." The poet is accordingly requested to open "the goodly cabinet, in which this excellent treasure of vertues lieth locked up from the vulgar sort." Though thus earnestly urged, Spenser begs to be excused from acceding to this request since he had "already undertaken a work tending to the same effect, which is in *heroical verse* under the title of a *Faerie Queene* to represent all the moral vertues, assigning to every vertue a Knight to be the patron and defender of the same." Finally the poet suggests that in lieu of his discourse Bryskett himself should entertain the company with his translation of Giraldi Cinthio's *Tre Dialoghi della Vita Civile,* which serve as a preface to Part II of the *Hecatommithi.* This suggestion meeting with the approval of the company, Bryskett devotes three successive meetings on as many days to reading aloud his English version of the Italian dialogues.

Among the other literary men in Ireland whom Spenser probably knew are Barnabe Googe (1540–1594) and Barnabe Riche (1540–1620). Both of these men were associated with the efforts of Walter Devereux, first Earl of Essex, to colonize Ulster. Googe, who in 1563 had been appointed one of the Queen's gentlemen-pensioners, was in 1574 sent by Cecil to Ireland, probably with a view to keeping the latter fully informed of the conduct of the Earl of Essex. Since Googe remained in Ireland until 1585, Spenser would have had ample opportunity to meet him there. He is remembered now not for his translation of *The Zodiac of Life* by Marcellus Palingenius but for a small volume of original poems which was published in 1563 under the title of *Eclogues, Epitaphs, and Sonnets.*

From 1588 to 1598 Spenser resided chiefly in Munster, a large province in the southwestern part of Ireland. For a time, acting as Bryskett's Deputy, he was Clerk of the Council of Munster, Bryskett himself holding the chief title to the office from 1588 to 1600. This, however, was a mere incident in the poet's official career. What kept him in Munster for ten years was his estate at Kilcolman, which, roughly speaking, lay midway between Limerick to the north and Cork to the south. It was pleasantly situated between hills and rivers. Just to the north was the curving range of the Ballyhoura Hills, familiarly named Old Father Mole in the poet's verse; to the west and south ran in circular course the Awbeg, and on the east the Bregog went to meet its sister river, flowing with it into the Blackwater on the south. Within these boundaries the poet had been assigned 3,028 acres from the forfeited lands of the Earl of Desmond, which amounted in all to 574,645 acres. Spenser's grant was one of the smallest, the allotments ranging from 12,880 to 1,304 acres. Thirty miles and more to the southeast of Kilcolman lay the seignories of Sir Walter Raleigh and Sir Christopher Hatton, the former about four times as large as Spenser's. It seems likely that Spenser took up his residence on his estate in 1589.

When Spenser settled at Kilcolman he found that the country round about had been almost depopulated by war, disease, and famine. Within half a year 30,000 men, women, and children had perished there. According to the Articles for the Undertakers, each holder of a seignory was required to establish English farmers upon his land, the number varying with the size of the allotment. Of these house-holds Spenser had set up six, and it is to be noted that un-like most of his fellow-undertakers he had no Irish tenants on his estate. Unlike Hatton, Raleigh, and many other un-dertakers Spenser lived on his seignory. Prominent among the events of his residence was Raleigh's visit of 1589, commemorated in *Colin Clouts Come Home Againe,* the poet's protracted litigation with Lord Roche, and the Ty-rone rebellion, which broke out in Munster in 1598.

Raleigh's visit to Spenser in 1589 was not of course a mere literary pilgrimage. Supplanted at court by the Earl of Essex, he no doubt considered the time opportune to visit his estate near Youghal. The two men had certainly met before; perhaps at court and probably at Smerwick, where Raleigh as a captain had done rough work for Lord Grey. Now there was leisure, within sight of the hills and the rivers, to talk of poetry and the poet's prospects. Perhaps in the circumstances the two might be mutually helpful if, as poet and patron, they were to appear at court with three books of the *Faerie Queene.* This at any rate they did, and to the three books, with their dedication to the Queen, Spenser added a letter to the Right Noble, and Valorous, Sir Walter Raleigh, Knight, etc., "expounding his whole intention in the course of this work."

What the poet thought of the life of the court is re-corded in *Colin Clouts Come Home Againe,* with its dedica-tory letter dated from Kilcolman, 1591, and in *Mother Hubberds Tale,* which was included in the volume of *Complaints* bearing the same date. No doubt his views of the court were colored by his disappointment over the de-gree of recognition accorded him there. Raleigh was, in-deed, not a likely patron where Burghley was still a controlling influence. With the former's exuberant nationalism, the cautious Burghley could have no sympathy, and Spenser's epic, while it set out to illustrate the golden mean, was touched by the patriotic ardor of the Shepherd of the Ocean. Everything considered, it is, then, not surprising that the fruit of that hopeful journey to London was no more than a pension of £50 a year.

To the poet's disappointment in these years, there was added much anxiety and annoyance arising out of differences with his Anglo-Irish neighbor Maurice, Lord Roche, Viscount Fermoy. The difficulties were of a kind inseparable from the Irish situation. What with confiscations by the crown and confusions arising from different systems of land tenure, questions of property rights would inevitably arise. Whether Spenser's embroilment might have been avoided by a stricter sense of equity on either side, it is now impossible to determine. His case might have been made more difficult in English courts by the fact that Lord Roche during the Desmond rebellion had remained loyal to the crown. The trouble, beginning in 1589, continued more or less intermittently until 1595. The first legal step was taken by Lord Roche, who in 1589 brought suit against Edmund Spenser, Clerk of the Council of Munster, and others, charging that Spenser had seized Lord Roche's land, despoiled his tenants, beaten his bailiffs, and so on. Thereupon Spenser retaliated with a counter-suit charging that Lord Roche had imprisoned his men, that he had killed "a beef" of a man who had mended a plough-iron belonging to Mr. Pier, and that he had further killed "a fat beef" belonging to Teig Olyves because Teig had received Spenser in his house. Other articles in the rather long bill of complaints are that Roche "relieved his foster brother, a proclaimed traitor, that he had spoken ill of Her Majesty's government, and that he had uttered words of contempt of Her Majesty's laws, calling them unjust." Neither in this case nor in a later one which involved the ownership of three ploughlands, does it appear that Spenser was granted a favorable judgment. Today the cases are of interest chiefly on account of the light they throw upon the troubled conditions in the midst of which the poet lived and worked.

In spite of disappointments and untoward circumstances Spenser continued his literary activity from the time of his first going to Ireland until his death. To 1589–91 belong many of the poems in the *Complaints,* the *Daphnaïda,* the *Astrophel,* and the *Colin Clouts Come Home Againe.* In spite of some good reasons for an earlier dating, the *Amoretti* are for the most part more safely assigned with the *Epithalamion* to 1591–1594, and the last three books of the *Faerie Queene* were no doubt mainly written in Ireland during the period 1591–96. In the matter of publication, the years 1595–96 are most noteworthy in Spenser's life. In the first of these years, appeared *Colin Clouts Come Home Againe* and the *Amoretti-Epithalamion* volume ; and in the second, the first edition of the *Faerie Queene* IV–VI with a second edition of I–III, the *Foure Hymnes,* a second edition of *Daphnaïda,* and *Prothalamion.* It was probably in this same year, 1596, that Spenser wrote the *View of Ireland,* which, however, was not published until 1633.

This brings us to the final years of the poet's life. In 1597 he had made provision for his son Peregrine by the purchase of the lands of Renny, County Cork for £200. In August of 1598 came the outbreak of Tyrone's rebellion. By October it had spread to the south, and Kilcolman lying in its course was "spoiled." The story told by Jonson to

Drummond that Spenser lost an infant during the sack of his estate is not now generally credited. We are sure, however, that Spenser with the other undertakers and the Council of Munster fled south and took refuge from the enraged insurgents in the walled town of Cork, to which supplies might be brought them by water. There he remained the greater part of two months, occupying a part of his time in the preparation of a "Briefe Note of Ireland," which describes the wretched state to which the English had been reduced by the rebellion and makes certain recommendations for crushing the rebels. Those who had escaped to Cork and other port towns were, he says, "most pitiful creatures, naked and comfortless, lying under the town walls and begging about all the streets, daily expecting when the last extremity shall be laid upon them."

On January 16, 1599, within a month after his return to England, Spenser died. No credit is now given to the oft-repeated story, for which Jonson is responsible, that he died of starvation in a garret. This is incredible, seeing that Spenser held a pension and that he had just come from Ireland bearing official despatches to the Queen. Perhaps we should also consider apocryphal the story that he "refused twenty pieces from my lord of Essex, saying that he was sorry he had no time to spend them." We know, however, that Essex met the expense of his funeral, to which many poets and men of noble rank came to pay their last tribute of respect and affection. It was in Westminster Abbey not far from his beloved Chaucer that Spenser was buried, his poet friends throwing into his grave the elegies they had composed in his honor and the pens with which they had written them. Though the Queen gave orders that a monument should be erected to Spenser in the Abbey, her orders were either rescinded or neglected; and it was not until 1620 that an appropriate memorial was provided, through the generosity of Anne, Countess of Dorset.

REFERENCES

Carpenter, F. I. *Reference Guide to Edmund Spenser,* II. The Life. Chronological Outline of the Life; 11 ff.

Carpenter, F. I. *The Marriages of Spenser.* Modern Philology, XXII (1924), 97–98.

Church, R. W. *Spenser.* London, 1879.

Covington, F. F. *Biographical Notes on Spenser.* Modern Philology, XXII (1924), 63–66.

Dunlop, Robert. *The Plantation of Munster, 1584–1589.* English Historical Review, III (1888), 250–269.

Fletcher, J. B. *Spenser. Encyclopedia Americana.* N. Y. XIV

Garrod, H. W. *Spenser and Elizabeth Boyle.* London Times Literary Supplement (May 10, 1923; May 24, 1923).

Greenlaw, Edwin. *Spenser and the Earl of Leicester.* Publications of the Modern Language Association, XXV (1910), 535–561.

Grosart, A. B. *Works of Spenser,* I. Introduction. London, 1882.

Hales, J. W. and Lee, Sidney. *Spenser.* Dictionary of National Biography, XVIII, 792 ff.

Harrison, T. P., Jr. *The Relations of Spenser and Sidney.* Publications of the Modern Language Association, XLV (1930), 712 ff.

Henley, Pauline. *Spenser in Ireland.* N. Y. 1928.

Landrum, Grace Warren. *Spenser's Use of the Bible and his Alleged Puritanism.* Publications of the Modern Language Association, XLI (1926), 517–544.

Légouis, Émile. *Edmund Spenser.* Paris, 1923.

Long, P. W. *Spenser and Lady Carey.* Modern Language Review, III (1908), 257–267.

Long, P. W. *Spenser and Sidney.* Anglia, XXXVIII (1914), 173–193.

Long, P. W. *Spenser and the Bishop of Rochester.* Publications of the Modern Language Association, XXV (1910), 535–561.

Maynadier, H. *The Areopagus of Sidney and Spenser.* Modern Language Review, IV (1909), 289 ff.

Padelford, F. M. *Spenser and the Puritan Propaganda.* Modern Philology, XI (1913), 85 ff.

Padelford, F. M. *Spenser and the Theology of Calvin.* Modern Philology, XII (1914), 1 ff.

Padelford, F. M. *Spenser and the Spirit of Puritanism.* Modern Philology, XIV (1916), 31 ff.

Selincourt, E. de. *Poetical Works of Spenser.* Introduction. Oxford, 1912.

Smith, J. C. *Spenser. Encyclopedia Britannica.* Fourteenth Edition.

Tolman, A. H. *The Relation of Spenser and Harvey to Puritanism.* Modern Philology, XV (1918), 49 ff.

Weepley, W. H. *Spenser and Elizabeth Boyle.* London Times Literary Supplement, May 24, 1923.

Weepley, W. H. *Edmund Spenser. Some new discoveries and the corrections of some old errors.* Notes and Queries, CXLVI, No. 27 (1924), 445; CXLVII, No. 1 (1924), 35.

Winstanley, Lilian. *Spenser and Puritanism.* Modern Language Quarterly, III (1900), 6–16; 103–110.

Wilson, Harry B. *The History of Merchants Taylors School.* London, 1812–1814.

Wilson, I. P. *Spenser and Ireland.* Review of English Studies. II (1926), 456 ff.

CHAPTER III

THE SHEPHEARDES CALENDER

THE *Shepheardes Calender,* first issued in 1579 from the press of Hugh Stapleton and republished by John Harrison in 1581, 1586, 1591, and 1597, stands at the beginning of that remarkable development of English literature which marks the last two decades of the sixteenth century. Dedicated to "the noble and vertuous Gentleman, most worthy of all titles both of learning and chevalerie, Maister Philip Sidney," it was praised successively by Sir Philip himself in his *Defence of Poesie,* written about 1583, by William Webbe in his *Discourse of English Poetrie* (1586), and by Thomas Nashe in the Preface to *Menaphon* (1589). The commendation of the new poet ranges from Sidney's carefully qualified comment to Thomas Nashe's extravagant praise. The former, while recognizing "much Poetry in the *Eclogues:* indeed worthy the reading if I be not deceived," dared "not allow that same framing of his style in an old and rustic language"; the latter would set "the divine Master Spencer, the miracle of art, line for line for my life in the honor of England gainst Spaine, France, Italie, and all the world." Somewhat more quietly Webbe proclaimed him "the rightest English poet that ever I read." Recognition of a different kind came from Abraham Fraunce and George Peele. Fraunce in his *Lawiers Logicke* (1588) pays Spenser the

39

compliment of quoting extensively from the *Calender,* and Peele in his *Arraignment of Paris* (acted in 1580) and in the *Eclogue Gratulatory* of 1589 adopted the names of some of Spenser's shepherds.

The work thus acclaimed bore the signature Immerito, and was edited by E.K., probably Edward Kirke, a fellow-collegian of the poet. Besides an introductory epistle to Spenser's college friend Harvey, an argument for the whole book, and individual arguments for the several eclogues, Kirke contributed a large body of notes. According to this contemporary editor, the author who had concealed his name would also conceal "the generall drift and purpose of his Æglogues." The sense of mystery created by all this concealment, E.K. deepens here and there by professing his inability to fathom the poet's meaning in particular passages. For example, in a note to the September eclogue, he writes: "This tale of Roffy seemeth to coloure some particular action of his. But what I certainelye know not." Elsewhere the editor would have us understand that his repeated questioning of the poet did not avail to penetrate the mystery. Of Dido in the November eclogue he writes: "The personage is secrete, and to me altogether unknowne, albe of him selfe I often required the same." Further on, in a note on "the great shepheard," Dido's father, he writes: The person both of the shephearde and of Dido is unknowen, and closely buried in the authors conceipt." E.K. has, indeed, after feigning ignorance in a note on "January," satisfied our curiosity by identifying Hobbinol with Gabriel Harvey in a note on September, but he sets us guessing again when he writes that "by the names of other shepheardes he covereth the persons of divers other his familiar freendes and best acquayntaunce."

The veil of mystery that hangs about the *Shepheardes Calender* has been lifted here and there. Already in the sixteenth century the poet's name through his own declaration and that of others became generally known. In spite of efforts to identify E.K. with Spenser himself, the identification with Edward Kirke is now universally accepted. This Edward Kirke, possibly related to the "Mistress Kirke" mentioned in one of Spenser's letters, had, like the poet, entered Pembroke Hall as a sizar, though later he transferred to Caius, where he took both the B.A. and the M.A. About other identifications we can be either absolutely or reasonably certain. Colin Cloute is of course Spenser himself; Hobbinol, as we have seen, is Harvey; and Algrind is a transparent anagram for Bishop Grindal. The proud shepherd Morell of July may well be Bishop Aylmer, and perhaps Roffy, though very similar to Marot's Raffy, is the pastoral name of Dr. Young, Bishop of Rochester, who, as already noted, was Master of Pembroke while Spenser was a student there. About Rosalind's identity it has been noted in the previous chapter that nothing is known.

Though ignorant of the identity of Rosalind, we have some evidence for her character and station. The description of her in "April" as "the widow's daughter of the glen" is rather said, according to E.K., "to coloure and concele the persone then simply spoken." More positively we are assured by the same authority that Rosalind was a "gentlewoman of no meane house, nor endowed with any vulgare and common gifts both of nature and manners: but suche indeede, as neede nether Colin be ashamed to have made knowne by his verses, nor Hobbinol be greved, that so she should be commended to immortalitie for her rare and singular vertues." Furthermore, from one of Harvey's letters to the poet, as already noted, comes a pleasant suggestion of the poet's relations with his mistress.

The plan of the *Shepheardes Calender* is original with Spenser. Only in its title does it bear any resemblance to the French *Kalendrier des Bergers,* which, translated into English, was widely known in the sixteenth century. The French book has been described as "a sort of popular almanac, encyclopedia of popular science, and handbook of devotion." Sommer thought that in its Protestant doctrine and polemics the *Shepheardes Calender* tried to counteract the influence of this popular manual, written "by a member of the Church of Rome in the interest of his church." However that may be, we must turn to other quarters for anticipations of Spenser's plan. The earliest pastoral poets naturally made some mention of the seasons. Thus Daphnis in the ninth idyl of Theocritus alludes to the "scorching summer," and Cornix in the sixth eclogue of Mantuan makes mention of the winter winds and the sleeping earth. Turning to Spenser's predecessors in the English pastoral, we may call attention to the slight indications of the seasons in the eight tedious eclogues of the Puritan, Barnabe Googe. But the most definite suggestion for his plan doubtless came to the English poet from Marot's *Eglogue au Roy,* the source of "December." Here Marot had developed a comparison between the course of human life and the progress of the year. It is not only in his final eclogue that Spenser, following the French poet, has carried out this parallel. He has used it also at critical points in the *Calender,* so that it was evidently an idea fundamental to his plan. In "January" the plaintive lover is young, in "June" he has attained to the middle years, and in "December" he is old.

Crossing their arrangement according to the months is E.K.'s classification of the eclogues as Plaintive, Recreative, and Moral. The distinction between the first two classes he has failed to make clear, because, after listing as plaintive the first, the sixth, the eleventh, and the twelfth, he goes on to describe as recreative those which "containe matter of love, or commendation of special personages." Clearly some of the plaintive eclogues would come within this definition. In the class of Moral eclogues, "which for the most part be mixed with some satyrical bitternesse," he includes "the second, of reverence dewe to old age; the fift, of coloured deceipt, the seventh and ninth, of dissolute shepheards and pastours, the tenth, of contempt of poetrie and pleasaunt wits."

Of the four plaintive eclogues, the "January," "June," and "December" may profitably be considered together. Marking the beginning, the middle, and the end of the *Calender,* they also follow, as has been said, a progression from the youth to the old age of Colin with particular reference to his love for Rosalind and his friendship for Hobbinol. In "January" the shepherd's boy is according to E.K. "but newly (as seemeth) enamoured of a countrie lasse called Rosalinde." In the winter landscape he complaineth him of his unfortunate love, comparing "his carefull case to the sadde season of the yeare." Set humorously against Colin's unsuccessful wooing of Rosalind is Hobbinol's "dayly suit" of the shepherd poet. The clownish gifts of his friend—"his kiddes, his cracknelles [biscuits], and his early fruit"—Colin passes on to Rosalind. By "June" the little drama of friendship and love has been complicated by the entrance of a rival, Menalcas,

> that by trecheree
> Didst underfong my lasse to wexe so light;

and Hobbinal has developed from the hopeless suitor into the sympathetic counsellor, actively interested in his friend's poetry and advising him to "forsake the soil that so doth thee bewitch," and to repair to the dales

> where shepherds ritch,
> And fruictfull flocks, bene every where to see.

Hobbinol laments Colin's disappointment in love and blames Rosalind as faithless and void of grace. As for the poet's "rymes and roundelayes," these delight Hobbinol more than "larke in sommer dayes." It should be observed that Hobbinol is here more than a guide and a friend. He is, further, as we shall find him in the moral eclogues, the philosopher of the *Calender*. With many echoes of Virgil's first eclogue, Hobbinol, rejoicing in his pleasant site, applies to the troubled state of Colin's heart a mellow Horatian epicureanism—the philosophy, one might say, of the Sabine farm. His theme is the familiar one of sweet content and the tried estate, which received classic expression in an epigram of Martial, which the Earl of Surrey translated as follows:—

> Martial, the things for to attain
> The happy life be these I find:
> The riches left not got with pain;
> The fruitful ground; the quiet mind;
> The equal friend; no grudge, nor strife;
> No charge of rule nor governaunce;
> Without disease, the healthful life.

In "December," Colin has grown old:

And in my face deepe furrowes eld hath pight:
My head besprent with hoary frost I fynd,
And by myne eie the crow his clawe dooth wright.

No longer does he seek to please Rosalind,—it is enough
if he please God; and, at last, it is Hobbinol, the rejected
one of "January," who is preferred. In contrast with "the
loser lasse" is "Hobbinol that was so true."

The remaining eclogue of the plaintive group is "November." But here the plaint is not of love but of death. To
the Rosalind theme we have only a passing allusion in the
lines:—

Thy Muse to long slumbreth in sorrowing,
Lulled a sleepe through loves misgovernaunce.
Now somewhat sing, whose endles sovenaunce
Emong the shepeheardes swaines may aye remaine,
Whether thee list thy loved lasse advaunce,
Or honor Pan with hymnes of higher vaine.

Beside this allusion to Rosalind, "November's" praise of
Colin's poetry serves to connect it with the other plaintive
eclogues. Further, the autobiographical interest is developed in the elegy commemorating Dido, whose identity,
in the words of E.K., is "closely buried in the author's conceipt." The Lobbin of the Elegy, who, E.K. says, "seemeth
to have bene the lover and deere frende of Dido," has been
conjecturally identified with Leicester, whom Elizabeth
was wont to call her Robin. Lobbin might then be considered a contraction for Lord Robin. In view of Leicester's
residence in the south, the apostrophe to the Kentish shepherds would support this identification, and, remembering
Spenser's relation with the Earl, the allusion in line 78 to

the songs that Colin made in praise of Dido would not be inconsistent with it.

Of the recreative eclogues—"March," "April," and "August"—the last two connect with the previous group through their praise of Colin's poetry, and "April" through the presence of Hobbinol. "March," though it makes "purpose of love," contains no mention of either Colin or Hobbinol. On the other hand, "April" is woven into the pattern of the plaintive sequence by the introduction of Colin's friend recalling the gifts with which he had tried to win his wanton heart and lamenting that "fayre Rosalind hath bredde hys smart." The hymn of praise addressed to Elizabeth gives us another example of the poet's art. Likewise, "August" repeats the theme of "January" in the love lament of Colin recited by Cuddie.

From the eclogues dealing with love and friendship we may now turn to those designated Moral, "which for the most part be mixt with some satyrical bitternesse." It should be remembered that while E.K. declares that the *Calender* was composed to mitigate the poet's passion, he likewise hints mysteriously at a "generall dryft and purpose" of which he minds not to say much, and that the professed intention of the work as stated in the Epilogue is—

> To teach the ruder shepheard how to feede his sheepe,
> And from the falsers fraud his folded flocke to keepe.

The quotation, of course, has special application to the Moral eclogues, that is to say to "February," "May," "July," and "September." With these four E.K. groups the less obvious case of "October."

Taken as a group, the Moral eclogues show no such clear progression as the plaintive-recreative series, but for all that they achieve a kind of unity by centering interest in such traditionally contrasted themes as youth and age, pride and humility, restless ambition and contentment. In this group, as in the other, criticism has overlooked the importance of Harvey's place in the *Calender*. As in his constancy and wise counsels he marked as it were the center of gravity of the Plaintive-Recreative series, so here in "September" he appears as the moral philosopher of the second group, who

> Sitting like a looker-on
> Of this worldes stage, doest note with critique pen
> The sharpe dislikes of each condition.

"February," like "May," "July," and "September," begins with a debate and concludes with an illustrative fable. Here as elsewhere in the series it would be a mistake to suppose that the conduct of the argument is determined solely by Spenser's moral convictions. Though these doubtless enter in, the tradition of the debate, that had long been accommodated to the pastoral, was all in favor of a well-balanced rather than a one-sided argument. We are particularly reminded of this in the case of "February." Clearly something is to be said for and against both youth and age. While we respect the sober wisdom of Thenot, we know that Cuddie has some reason in his *ad hominem* argument:—

> But were thy yeares greene as now bene myne,
> To other delights they would encline.

In the ensuing fable the honors, though perhaps not quite even, are obviously divided. On the one hand, the oak was

brought to misery by such "foolerie" as being "crost with
the preestes crewe," and "hallowed with holy water dewe";
but, on the other hand, after the oak is felled, the brier,
lacking its protection, is beaten upon by "blustering
Boreas," and "naked left and disconsolate"—

> The byting frost nipt his stalke dead,
> The watrie wette weighed downe his head.

Unable to stand longer, the briar is trodden into the mud
by the cattle. Evidently there is a pride of youth as well
as a pride of age; but in maintaining that youth needs the
protection of age, the new poet would seem to argue that
new and radical movements need the shelter of old traditions. If the fable may be taken as expressing the poet's
own views, it would place him as a low church Anglican.
As Mr. Herford says: "Spenser as the disciple of the old
poet and the lover of his archaic speech, defends the reverence for antiquity, of which all his own poetry is a monument."

Carrying on appropriately in the older language and
meter his traditional moralizing, Spenser in "May" really
develops still further the theme of "February." Evidently
Palinode is only another Cuddie and speaks very much like
the brier in the fable; while Piers may be compared with
Thenot and the oak. Nevertheless, "May" does not dupli-
cate "February." In its treatment of the theme of sobriety
and worldliness, it marks a distinct advance over the earlier
eclogue. For one thing, it differs from "February" in developing the ecclesiastical allegory. Unlike Cuddie and
Thenot, Piers and Palinode are pastors as well as shepherds; and the reason of the eclogue is its pointed and
somewhat detailed criticism of the corruption of the Church.

Unlike Cuddie, Palinode, as Piers remarks, is a man of elder wit, who should have outgrown the follies no doubt suitable for younkers. The issue would seem to be one of decorum, and therefore less absolute in its terms than that posed by "February." Furthermore, there is no question here of the authority of tradition and the claims of new movements. The sobriety of age is associated with the Puritan cause and not with the Catholic tradition. Nevertheless, it would hardly do to say that Piers is Spenser. Palinode's weakness is his delight in the pleasant May games of Merrie England, for which the pastoral poet betrays his sympathy in the attractive verses of Palinode's description. It is to be noted, too, that the worldly shepherd advances an opinion that Hobbinol elsewhere expresses and that is to be found in Harvey's *Pierces Supererogation,*— an opinion obviously in accord with the policy of the Queen. In lines 162-3, Palinode prudently declares:—

> Let none mislike of that may not be mended:
> So conteck soone by concord mought be ended.

Quite in harmony with this tone of moderation is the note of E.K. to line 121:—"Nought here spoken, as of purpose to deny fatherly rule and godly governaunce (as some maliciously of late have done, to the great unreste and hinderaunce of the Churche) but to displace the pride and disorder of such as, in steede of feeding their sheepe, indeede feede of theyr sheepe."

Though "July" offers a clear-cut issue of pride and humility, its lesson is once more that of moderation. Here the poet reveals his sympathies more clearly than in either "February" or "May" by his praise of Grindal, the moderate Anglican, whom Piers in "May" had incidentally alluded to. After Thomalin has more than once respectfully quoted the opinions of Algrind, Morrell is moved to ask:—

> What is Algrin, he
> That is so oft bynempt?

Then when he has been answered in the fable of the eagle and the shell-fish, he says in conclusion:—

> Ah, good Algrin! his hap was ill,
> But shall be bett in time.

Whatever might be their differences, the shepherd of the mountain and the shepherd of the valley agree in their sympathy for Grindal. Here at least is a kind of accord in line with that suggested by the fable of the oak and the brier; for Grindal's ideal was that of reform within the communion of the Established Church. Finally, Thomalin's emblem, the text of the eclogue, *in medio virtus,* states explicitly the principle of the golden mean, which is as much the theme of the moral eclogues as it is of the *Faerie Queene*.

Now moderation was not only the moving spirit of Bishop Grindal's ecclesiastical policy but also the informing principle of Gabriel Harvey's philosophy of life, as expressed in his *Pierces Supererogation* and commemorated in Spenser's complimentary sonnet. Moreover, the dedication of E.K.'s letter to Harvey and the prominence of Hobbinol among the shepherds of the *Calender* should lead us to expect some recognition of Harvey's opinions in that work. Leaving aside the "October," which stands apart from the other Moral eclogues on the score of its general structure as well as of its meter, we may say that "September" fitly brings to a term the sequence written in the old accentual verse and introducing in each case an illustrative fable after a debate. It is climactic, too, in that it conveys the most sweeping indictment of the bad shepherds; and in its criticism of restless ambition it offers the most persuasive statement of the philosophy of moderation, which in the earlier eclogues had been variously set against the vice of pride in its different manifestations. In a sense we might say that "September" points the moral to be drawn from the whole series. The remedy for overweening ambition, says "the philosophical looker-on of this world's stage," is "sweet content" :—

> Content who lives with tryed state
> Neede feare no chaunge of frowning fate;
> But who will seeke for unknowne gayne,
> Oft lives by losse, and leaves with payne.

In response to Diggon Davie's gloomy picture of corruption in the Church, he answers, echoing Palinode's opinion in May :—

> Better it were a little to feyne,
> And cleanly cover that cannot be cured.

Further, when Diggon in the manner of Piers in "May" says that it sits not with shepherds to play, Hobbinol rather in the tone of Palinode replies :—

> thilke same rule were too straight,
> All the cold season to watch and waite:
> We bene of fleshe, men as other bee:
> Why should we be bound to such miseree?

Finally, with slight anticipation of the *Mutabilitie Cantos,* he adds :

> What ever thing lacketh chaungeable rest,
> Mought needes decay, when it is at best.

The philosophy of the tried estate, which stands as we have seen at the central point of the plaintive sequence, here serves for the climax of the moral ecologues; and it is Harvey who in each case philosophizes the theme. We may conclude, then, that in the opinions of Harvey we find a principle of unity for the *Shepheardes Calender* as a whole.

It remains to consider the position of "October" in the organization of the *Calender*. It is included by E.K., it will be remembered, among the Moral eclogues. But from these, as has already been noted, it stands apart both in structure and in metrical form. On the other hand, a justification of E.K.'s classification might be found in the treatment of the poet-patron theme in October. As Diggon Davie had maintained in "September" that the falling off in the priesthood was to be charged in some measure against the "Bulles of Basan," so here the decline in poetry is due to its neglect by princes :—

> But ah ! Mæcenas is yclad in claye,
> And great Augustus long ygoe is dead.

After the bad priest there naturally comes in the bad poet, Tom Piper with his ribald rhymes; for the world is far removed from that golden age, alluded to by Sidney in his *Apologie for Poetrie* and perhaps by Spenser in his lost *English Poet,* when the poet and the priest were one. Poetry, as E.K. says, is a matter of "celestiall inspiration." But besides its treatment of the poet-patron theme the "October" philosophizes the poet-lover theme in the Platonic speeches of Piers. The poet's love has not after all blighted his poetry—but has raised his mind "above the starry skie." With respect to both poetry and love Piers takes high ground in maintaining that it is not the reward or the attainment that counts but the glory of true fame and the inspiration of ideal love. Uniting as it does both the critical and romantic vein of the two series of eclogues, the "October" then has an important structural place in the organization of the *Shepheardes Calender;* it is, as it were, the keystone of the arch.

The tradition of poetry to which the *Shepheardes Calender* belongs goes back to Theocritus, a Syracusan poet of the third century B.C. Of his life very little is known. We can hardly say more than that he was born in Syracuse and seems to have written some of his poetry there. In his *Idyls* we find not only the outlines of the Sicilian landscape but much of the simple character of the Sicilian folk, which is still preserved in their peasant songs. Such was the vitality of Theocritus's work that he determined most of the forms that pastoral poetry was to take in the following centuries. It seems altogether likely that he did not write all of the pastorals that bear his name, but we may nevertheless gather from the collection of thirty eclogues the chief elements of his genius. The poems are notably dramatic as well as idyllic. By a shaded spring or on upland pastures overlooking the sea, the shepherds meet to sing songs or to contend in debate. Their homely and sometimes ribald talk is now enlivened with dramatic action and again yields to a quick and faithful observation of beauty in the natural world. In the tenth idyl Milon is plying the scythe while he taunts Battus for his laziness. Having failed to move with his song the heart of Amaryllis, the goatherd of the third idyl impulsively throws himself on the ground with the wish that he might never rise again. In the fifth idyl we have the familiar singing-match, in number seventeen the hymn of praise, and in one the lament for the dead.

Of the two successors of Theocritus in the Greek pastoral, Moschus is particularly remembered for his elegy in commemoration of Bion, and Bion for his lament for Adonis. Students of Spenser turn with special interest to the fourth idyl of Bion on account of the parallel that it offers with the March eclogue of the *Calender*.

The difference in this case between Spenser's poem and its source is instructive. Clearly the charm of the Greek idyl arises from its pointed and delicate treatment of a pretty theme. An innocent lad, quite without knowledge of love, spies one day the winged god perched on a box-tree bough. Having tried in vain to kill the fine bird, he returns to the old man who had taught him the art of hunting, relates his experiences, and then points out the nimble god of love sitting for a moment quietly on his perch. Smiling and shaking his head, the old teacher advises his pupil to flee rather than to seek the evil creature. "Some day," he says, "the bird that flees you now will come and perch upon your head." In Spenser the charm of the Greek poem is largely sacrificed by making the young shepherd scornful of love, by removing the old husbandman from the story, and by giving a burlesque account of Thomalin's encounter with the little god. After Thomalin has exhausted his supply of arrows, he throws pumice stones at Cupid, who adroitly catches them as he hops from bough to bough. Then E.K. thus heavily explains the charming fancy of the Greek idylist:—"I thinke, in the person of Thomalin is meant some secrete freend, who scorned Love and his knights so long, till at length him selfe was entangled, and unawares wounded with the dart of some beautifull regard, which is Cupides arrow."

We may notice a similar lowering of effect if we compare the singing match in the tenth of Theocritus with that in Spenser's "August." The contest, it should be observed, is similarly conceived in the two cases. One of the shepherds is making fun of the other's love. But instead of the English poet's rollicking roundelay with its reiterated phrases and exclamations, Theocritus offers, as in the following quotation, finished sentences and pointed wit:

Battus: Then it never befell thee to lie awake for love.
Milon: Forbid it; 'tis an ill thing to let the dog once taste of pudding.
Battus: But I, Milon, am in love for almost eleven days!
Milon: 'Tis easily seen that thou drawest from a wine-cask, while even vinegar is scarce with me.

The next important writer of pastoral poetry is Virgil. Born near Mantua in 70 B. C., he repaired to Rome when about thirty years of age and there won fame and the patronage of Mæcenas through the publication in 37 B. C. of his ten *Eclogues*. In these we find an important development of the personal and political type. For example, in the first eclogue Tityrus, representing Virgil himself, declares his gratitude to the emperor for opposing the confiscation of the poet's farm; in number four he flatters Augustus with a vision of the golden age to be realized under the emperor's reign; in five, giving an account of the deification of Daphnis, he seems to allude to Julius Cæsar. Eight refers to Pollio's return from a military campaign, and ten deals with the unhappy love affair of the poet's friend,

Cornelius Gallus. The allegory, it will be seen, ranges from broadly national themes to those of merely personal interest; just as Spenser's pastorals are now concerned with the praise of the Queen or the corruption of the Church, and now with the circumstances of his love for Rosalind and his friendship for Hobbinol. The new emphasis, which was to influence to a marked degree the later development of the pastoral, no doubt involved some loss of what lent special charm to the Greek idyl; but Virgil's gift of felicitous phrasing atones in large measure for what might be felt to be the misconceptions of his allegorical method.

The relation between the Virgilian and the Spenserian pastoral may be illustrated by comparing Spenser's "June" with Virgil's first and his "August" with Virgil's third. In Virgil I, Meliboeus, about to leave his country, felicitates Tityrus upon the delights of life on the farm, amid familiar streams and sacred springs. At any rate, Tityrus has here been liberated from Galatea. With the comforts of this retired life Meliboeus contrasts his own hard lot, which takes him from his "humble cottage with its turf-clad roof" to "the thirsty Africans" or to the Britons "wholly sundered from all the world." The occasion of the Virgilian eclogue was Octavian's successful efforts to prevent the confiscation of the poet's farm. Spenser's "June" has no such occasion: but the relation between Hobbinol and Colin is like that between Meliboeus and Tityrus. Here it is Hobbinol, the Horatian philosopher of the tried estate, who enjoys the sweet content of Virgil's Tityrus and who takes delight in "the simple ayre, the gentle warbling wind," "the grassye ground," and the bird notes in tune with the waterfall. It is only the plaintive melancholy of Colin, combining his praise of Chaucer with his love complaint, that interrupts the rural peace of Hobbinol, "the happy above happiest men." Here is how Virgil describes the happy estate of Melibœus: "Happy old man! Here, amid familiar streams and sacred springs, you shall court the cooling shade. On this side, as aforetime on your neighbour's border, the hedge whose willow blossoms are sipped by Hybla's bees shall often with its gentle hum soothe you to slumber; on that, under the towering rock, the woodman's song shall fill the air; while still the cooing wood-pigeons, your pets, and the turtle-dove shall cease not their moaning from the skyey elm."

Spenser's "August" has already been compared with the tenth idyl of Theocritus; we may now compare it with Virgil's third.[1] Unlike Spenser's friendly introductory dialogue between Perigot and Willie, Virgil's pastoral begins with a quarrel between Damœtas and Menalcas. In the song-contest itself Virgil's studied and graceful rhetoric is far above the rapid informality of Spenser's dialogue. Then, too, although Cuddie in his own estimation is an umpire fit for a king, he is no such dignified judge as Virgil's Palæmon. "Gynne when you lyst," is Cuddie's way of starting the contest, giving no indication as to whether it is Perigot or Willie who is to begin; whereas Palæmon delivers himself of this formal introduction:—
"Sing on, now that we are seated on the soft grass. Even now every field, every tree is budding; now the woods are green, and the year is at its fairest. Begin Damœtas; then you, Menalcas, must follow. Turn about you shall sing;

[1] Professor Hughes has argued that the classical influence is here transmitted to Spenser by the poets of the *Pléiade*—Baïf & Ronsard.

singing by turns the Muses love." Compare further with the rough and tumble speeches of Spenser's roundelay the following quotations from Virgil:—

Damoetas: Gifts I have found for my love; for I have myself marked where the wood-pigeons have been building high in the air.

Menalcas: Sweet to the corn is a shower, to the new weaned kids the arbute, to the breeding flock the bending willow, and to me Amyntas alone.

To the Virgilian tradition of the allegorical pastoral belong in the fourteenth century the eclogues of Petrarch and Boccaccio, and in the sixteenth, those of Baptista Mantuanus (1448–1516). For the present purpose the first two may be passed over; but the third ranks with Virgil as a source of the *Shepheardes Calender*. Entering the Carmelite monastery at Mantua when about eighteen years of age, Baptista acted as its prior in 1479–80. After he had served as vicar general of the Congregation from 1483 until 1513, he became general of the whole Carmelite order. Thus honored by the monastic brotherhood to which he belonged, he was also well known as a scholar, as a master both of Latin and of Greek. He was even mentioned for his interest in Hebrew. His *Eclogues* were widely used as a school-book. It will be remembered that Holofernes, the schoolmaster in *Love's Labour's Lost,* quotes the opening line of the first eclogue as one might now quote the beginning of the *Gallic War.*

It is as a rough satirist of ecclesiastical abuses, the corruption of the Papal court, and the vices of women that Mantuan is now chiefly remembered. With a heightened realism Alexander Barclay translated two of his pastorals into English early in the sixteenth century. As might be surmised, it is the moral eclogues of the *Shepheardes Calender* that are indebted to Mantuan; particularly "July" (compare Mantuan, VII and VIII) with its assault upon the pride of the clergy and "October" (compare Mantuan, V) with its complaint of the neglected poet.

In "July," while borrowing from the Latin satirist such details as his list of sacred hills (S.C. 39 ff.), the blending of the Endymion story with that of the Earthly Paradise (S.C. 57 ff.; Mantuan, VIII, 45 ff.), and the wording of the allusion to the story of Abel (S.C. 125 ff.; Mantuan VII, 14 ff.), Spenser has modified his source in a manner to be compared with the modifications already noted. Whereas in Mantuan, Candidus, the shepherd of the mountain, bears the burden of the dialogue and wins an easy victory over his opponent Alphus, the shepherd of the plains, it is in Spenser the shepherd of the valley, representing Christian humility, who is the victor in the debate. Mantuan's version can be understood only with reference to the narrative setting of his seventh and eighth eclogues. In the Latin poet the story is that of the youthful Pollux, who, his life made miserable by a hard father and a proud step-mother, resolves on flight; it was only his love for his girl that had made him delay. But if love is strong, violence is stronger. And so he departs. On Mount Carmel Pollux has a vision of the Queen of Heaven, who gives him a list of the pastoral blessings in her power to bestow and a calendar of her feast days. He is cured of his mortal love, and Cupid, who had shot all his arrows at him, departs. He could say with Spenser:

> The loser lasse I cast to please nomore;
> One if I please, enough is me therefore.

Given this introduction, there was clearly no reason for Mantuan to introduce the theme of pride and humility, and it was only natural that his Pollux should prefer the mountain to the valley.

Again, in "October," Spenser, while borrowing many details from Mantuan's fifth eclogue, recasts that poem as a whole. Whereas in the Latin pastoral the parties to the dialogue were the malcontent poet Candidus and the potential patron Silvanus, the conversation in Spenser is carried on between two friends who hold different views on the inspiration and the function of the poet. However, the two eclogues get under way in a similar manner. In Mantuan, Silvanus says: "You were wont to feed your flocks and to play your shepherd's pipe with us in the cool shade; you would, too, exchange jests and engage in wrestling matches." In adapting this, Spenser gives a homely English quality to the passage by his mention of rhymes, riddles, and bidding-base as amusements of the shepherds. Then, Mantuan's Silvanus tries to persuade Candidus to be contented with his lot. God has made the wisest division of all things. To kings have fallen riches and power; to poets, genius, eloquence, and the art of song. So Spenser's Piers would have his Cuddie contented with the praise which is better than the price. But the peacock, moralizes Cuddie, for all the praise of his tail, is not fuller by a grain. As the argument in Mantuan progresses, there is set in realistic contrast the lot of the poet as it is and as it ought to be. As a matter of fact, his coat is threadbare, his knees are uncovered, his skin is scabby, and he goes unshaven. On the contrary, how fine it would be if he might have full garners, a well-stocked cellar, and brimming jugs,—if he might pass the long

December evenings before the fireplace, roasting chestnuts, quenching his thirst, and laughing over stories among the spinning-girls. Omitting all this, Spenser's eclogue passes on to the advice that Cuddie should change the subject of his poetry. Both poets cite the example of Tityrus (Virgil), who first sang of the fields and the cattle and then of the more lofty subject of war until his song reached the stars. "Go to Rome," says Silvanus to Candidus; "there you will find those who will raise you from your low estate, if you will only narrate wars, the deeds of heroes, and the battles of kings." "Turn," says Silvanus, in words that are very like those of Piers, "turn to those who wield the sceptre and govern kingdoms." Observe, too, the likeness of the following passages. Mantuan says:—"Since strong men and masculine vigor have decayed, eloquent poets have found nothing to write about; the genius of our ancestors perishes and lofty poetry declines." And Spenser: —

> But after vertue gan for age to stoupe,
> And mighty manhode brought a bedde of ease,
> The vaunting poets found not worth a pease
> To put in preace among the learned troupe.
> Tho gan the streames of flowing wittes to cease,
> And sonnebright honour pend in shamefull coupe.

In the following the Latin is more circumstantial than the English poet:—"Kings," says Mantuan, "who have turned to pleasure and sloth, like the poets to praise what they practise; so our songs are now concerned with devotion to Venus, now with scurrility, or eating houses, or with infamous deeds that it is wrong for a chaste poet to celebrate. . . . Lofty poetry has fallen into decay." Compare with this the following speech of Spenser's Cuddie:—

> And if that any buddes of poesie
> Yet of the old stocke gan to shoote agayne,
> Or it mens follies mote be forst to fayne,
> And rolle with rest in rymes of rybaudrye,
> Or, as it sprong, it wither must agayne:
> Tom Piper makes us better melodie.

The next writer of pastorals to whom Spenser is indebted is Clément Marot. Born in 1495, he was admitted while still a young man to the court of Margaret of Valois in the capacity of *valet de chambre*. There he found himself one of that group of artists, poets, and scholars who were in sympathy with the Reformation. His enthusiasm for the new religion carried him so far beyond the bounds of prudence that, coming under a charge of heresy, he was committed to prison. Not long after his release he was saved from a second imprisonment only through the intercession of Marguerite and her husband, the King of Navarre. Being at Blois at the time of the "Affair of the Placards," he was denounced as a Calvinist and saved his life only by taking refuge in Italy. Once more through the kind offices of Marguerite he was permitted to return to France; then, finding himself again in difficulties, following his publication of a Protestant version of the Psalms, he took refuge at Geneva. Thence he passed into Lombardy, where he died in 1544.

In the work of this Protestant poet of France the Puritan Spenser found sources for his last two eclogues. In "November" he follows the *Complaincte de ma Dame Loyse de Savoye* and in the "December" the *Eglogue au Roy soubs les noms de Pan et Robin*. In both the "November" and the *Complaincte* the shepherds have the same names and defer to each other in similar fashion, but

Marot's Thenot opens the dialogue less abruptly than the English shepherd by commenting upon the brook, the shade, the grass, and the gentle winds. Without wishing in any way to diminish the glory of Pan, the French Thenot maintains that the woodland god has something to learn from Colin. These compliments Colin graciously repays in kind, declaring that his friend could be victor in a singing contest with Calliope. Each of the shepherds urges the other to sing, Thenot modestly remarking that he should keep silent as the wood-pecker does before the nightingale. In due course Colin is persuaded to lament the death of Lois. As a reward for his song he is promised six yellow and six green quinces; and should his verses be as well composed as those he had written in honor of Isabel, he will be given a double pipe made by Raffy Lyonnois. In Spenser the prizes are different:—Thenot offers first a cosset, i. e., a lamb reared apart from its mother, and then should his rhymes be as good as those he had made for Rosalind, he will get a much greater gift.

In the Dido elegy Spenser, following Marot, adopts the general plan of the pastoral elegy that derives from Virgil's fifth eclogue. That is to say he divides the poem into two parts, the first expressive of sorrow for the loss of Dido, the second voicing a joyful assurance of her happiness in heaven. Passing from the first to the second part Spenser makes a less abrupt transition than does Marot. Like Milton in *Lycidas,* Marot suddenly admonishes the mourners to be silent :—

Be silent you have mourned enough ;
She has been received into the Elysian fields.

Apart from this traditional structure, the two poets conform in other ways to the mode of the conventional pastoral. For example, each elegy opens with an apostrophe to the poet's verse, and each illustrates what Ruskin called the "pathetic fallacy." Here Marot goes farther than Spenser. On the death of Lois of Savoy, the King's mother, leaves and fruit fell from the trees, the sun no more gave warmth, the meadows were divested of their green mantle, and the heavens shed tears; further, many streams went dry, the sea was troubled, and all animals except the wolf of evil nature were plunged in grief. The lily and even the wool of the sheep turned black. With this passage we may compare Spenser's poem at 1, 125 ff. In place of Marot's nymphs of Savoy, Spenser introduces the shepherds of the Kentish downs. The decking of the hearse, which takes many lines in the French poem, Spenser barely alludes to in lines 98–99. On the other hand, in the comparison of nature and mankind with respect to life and death, Spenser's eclogue echoes very definitely its source:—

> D'ou vient cela qu'on veoit l'herbe sechante
> Retourner vive alors que l'este vient,
> Et la personne au tumbeau tresbuchante,
> Tant grande soit, jamais plus ne revient?

Compared with Spenser, the French poet offers a much more circumstantial description of the joys of the other world. In that happy land, says Marot, there are ambrosial odors and eternal springtime. There Lois will eat fruit of priceless worth, drink liquors which quench all thirst, and be conversant with a thousand noble spirits. Among the countless birds and animals, the Queen will find her pet "papegay," that died before her. This personal touch marks also the more definite characterization of Lois as compared with Dido. At line 99 ff. Spenser praises Dido for having entertained the shepherds with "cakes and cracknells and such country cheere," and for calling home the simple shepherd's swain and giving him "curds and clouted cream." Much more circumstantially and picturesquely Marot tells of the shepherds' daughters, whose fathers wished to have them of the retinue of Lois. Gathering these maidens about her under a great elm to give them good advice, Lois was wont to tell them that it is not everything to have beauty and wealth. They should take care that their flowering time is not disfigured by idleness. She then sets them to work:—one plants herbs, another feeds the doves; and while one embroiders, still another makes chaplets of flowers.

Even more important than his influence upon "November" is Marot's contribution to Spenser's final eclogue. "December," indeed, derives in large measure from the French poet's *Eglogue au Roy soubs les noms de Pan et Robin* (1539). This eclogue perhaps helped to suggest the general arrangement of the *Calender*. An important difference between the two poems is that whereas Marot takes his retrospect from the autumn of the year, Spenser looks back from the winter season. At the close Marot sounds a note of optimism:—"Arise, my sheep, little thin flock, leap about me with merry heart, for already Pan (i. e. the king) from his green house has done me the honor of listening to my prayer." On the other hand, Spenser's poem concludes with a melancholy farewell to his sheep, his Hobbinol, his Rosalind, and indeed all his delights. To this melancholy strain, in which the poet describes the blackness and bleakness of winter, is devoted rather more than the last third of his poem. In his treatment of the earlier seasons Spenser borrows many details from his French source. For example, like Marot he compares his youth to a swallow flitting here and there, recalling the time when he wandered through the forest without fear or anxiety; and both poets make mention of stealing birds' eggs and of nutting parties. To Marot's mention of the good Jannot, his father, who had trained him as a poet, corresponds Spenser's praise of Wrenock, a good old shepherd, and both poets speak of making cages and of weaving baskets. Here, as in other passages, Marot, when compared with Spenser, shows a more circumstantial treatment of his theme and not infrequently more grace of style.

At the conclusion of the *Shepheardes Calender* Spenser, addressing his book, wrote:—

> Goe, lyttle Calender! thou hast a free passporte:
> Goe but a lowly gate emongste the meaner sorte:
> Dare not to match thy pype with Tityrus his style,
> Nor with the Pilgrim that the Ploughman playde awhyle:
> But followe them farre off, and their high steppes adore:
> The better please, the worse despise; I aske no more.

In a sense we may say that Spenser did dare to match his style with that of Chaucer and of *Piers Plowman*. That is to say, in the verse of "February," "May," and "September" we have his contribution to that tradition of accentual, alliterative verse of which *Piers Plowman* is the best exemplar in the fourteenth century. Though not an alliterative poet, Chaucer was no doubt associated during the sixteenth century with the writers of free accentual verse on account of the general neglect of the final *e* in the reading of his poetry. Whether or not we wish to derive the popular four-stressed verse from Anglo-Saxon poetry, we may study early examples of it in Layamon's *Brut* and such a poem as the Middle English *Genesis and Exodus*. For a later period not only the alliterative poems of the fourteenth century but the Miracle and Morality plays may be cited. Coming down to the period of the Renaissance, the accentual verse reappears variously; as, for example, in Wyatt's *The Recured Lover* and Thomas Tusser's *Five Hundred Good Points of Husbandry*. The best known modern example is the line of Coleridge's *Christabel*.

This accentual verse was not only practised in Spenser's time but was described by contemporary critics. For example, King James wrote in his *Reulis and Cautelis of Scottish Poesie*:—"Let all your verse be Literall (i. e. Alliterative), as far as may be, quhatsamever kynde they be of, bot speciallie Tumbling verse for flyting;" and then he gives as an example of the literal, tumbling verse:—

Fetching fude for to feid it fast furth of the Farie.

George Gascoigne, too, in his *Certain Notes of Instruction Concerning the Making of Verse* (1576) writes:—"Commonly now a dayes in English rimes (for I dare not call them English verses) we use none other order but a foot of two syllables, whereof the first is depressed or made short and the second is elevate or made long: and that sound or scanning continueth throughout the verse. We have used in times past other kindes of Meeters: as for example this following:

No wight in this world that wealth can attain,
Unlesse he beleve, that all is but vayne.

Finally Puttenham says in his *Arte of English Poetry* (1589) :—"Your ordinarie rimers use very much their measures in the odde, as nine and eleven, and the sharpe accent upon the last sillable, which therefore makes him go ill favouredly and like a minstrels musicke. Thus said one in a meter of eleven very harshly in mine eare, whether it be for lacke of good rime or of good reason, or of both, I wot not.

Now sucke childe and sleepe childe, thy mothers owne joy,
Her only sweete comfort, to drowne all annoy;
For beauty surpassing the azured skie,
I love thee, my darling, as ball of mine eye.

Besides the four stressed alliterative line rhyming in couplets Spenser used a variety of stanza forms. Among these are stanzas of four, six, and eight lines; and the verses which constitute the stanzas are sometimes of equal and again of different length. Among the familiar forms employed are the two ballad stanzas of "March" and "July," the sixain of "January" and "December," and the elegiac quatrains in the dialogues of "April" and "November." Of these the sixain, which was employed in the *chansons* of both Marot and Ronsard, is of particular interest on account of the concluding couplet, which was to be the mark of both the Spenserian sonnet and the Spenserian stanza. These inventions of our poet are further anticipated in part by the linked quatrains of "April" and "November," a device for which French poetry had again furnished a precedent. When, as in the case of Hobbinol's speeches in "April," the linked quatrains make a unit, we have actually the eight-line stanza of Chaucer's *Monk's Tale*, which is commonly regarded as the basis of the Spenserian stanza. Furthermore, the linking of three quatrains in "April" (9–20 inclusive) gives all of the Spenserian sonnet except the final couplet. From the metrical point of view, then, the *Calender* is interesting not merely on account of its variety, but because it shows the poet reaching out for metrical forms which were later to be closely associated with his name.

There remain to be noted the unrhymed sestina of "August" and the forms of the ode or hymn in "April" and "November." The sestina, invented by Arnaut Daniel in the thirteenth century, is so called because it includes six stanzas, each of which consists of six lines; upon these there follows an envoy of three verses. In the original sestina as illustrated for example in Sidney's *Arcadia,* the final words in the initial strophe were repeated in following strophes according to the following arrangement:— abcdef faebdc cfdabe ecbfad deacfb bdfeca; in the envoy with the original words appearing at the cæsura as well as at the end of the line, we return to the order of the first stanza. Spenser here shows his independence as a metrist. Instead of following a swinging pendulum in placing the repeated words, he in each strophe preserves the sequence of the one which precedes, except for the initial linking rhyme. The arrangement is therefore:—abcdef fabcde efabcd defabc cdefab bcdefa; and then in the envoy, with internal as well as final rhyme, there is a return to the original sequence as in the orthodox sestina.

The idea of combining in a single stanza the principles of adjacent and interlaced rhymes, already noted in "October," is again adopted in the nine-line stanza of the "April" hymn with its varying line length. Furthermore, we have here employed to singularly good purpose the *rime couée* or tail-rhyme, which early found a place in popular and religious verse, came to be used in the metrical romances, and was parodied by Chaucer in the *Rime of Sir Thopas*. Elements of Spenser's stanza will be recognized in the following examples from the hymns of the Church:—

> Omni die—dic Mariæ—mea laudes anima;
> ejus festa—ejus gesta—cole devotissima.

(Compare these with the last three lines of Spenser's stanza.)

> Nam quis promat summæ pacis—quanta sit lætitia,
> ubi vivis—margaritis—surgunt ædificia.

(Compare these with the last five lines of Spenser's stanza.)

For the first four lines we have the septenary with leonine rhyme, broken into fives and twos instead of the fours and threes of the ballad stanza. These opening lines Professor Saintsbury has happily described as an overture; and the stanza as a whole affects him as more stately than easy in its grace. "But," he continues, "it is admirably graceful; and its very stateliness has got rid of the buckram which had so long pressed and compressed formal lyric in English." Remembering the song and dance in which the lyric had its origin, we are in the stanza of the "April" hymn reminded more of the dance than of the song.

It is different with the "November" dirge. Here we are near the province of music. With it one might be tempted to compare the *Lamentations* of Palestrina, who in Spenser's time was giving a new meaning to church music. Beginning with the full volume of the alexandrine, the stanza by a descending scale of pentameters and tetrameters reaches at the end the plaintive note of the dimeters. In the words of Professor Herford, "it well conveys the expression of a recurring access or wave of emotion, marked at the outset (in a highly original manner) by the energetic and resonant Alexandrine, then gradually subsiding through verses of diminishing compass, until just before the close it rises in one expiring palpitation."

REFERENCES

Herford, C. H. Ed. *Shepheards Calender*. London, 1907.

Baskervill, C. R. *The Early Fame of the Shepheards Calender*. Publications of the Modern Language Association, XXVIII (1913), 291–313.

Bhattacherje, Mohinimohan. *Studies in Spenser*. Calcutta, 1929; Chapter III, Theory of Poetry.

Brunner, K. *Die Dialektwörter in Spenser's "Shepherds' Calender."* Archiv. f.d. Studium d. neueren Spr. u. Lit., CXXXII (1914), 401–404.

Draper, J. W. *The Glosses to Spenser's "Shepheardes Calender."* Journal of English and Germanic Philology, XVIII (1919), 556–574.

Draper, J. W. *The Colonnade*. N. Y. 1922; XIV, 38–40. On the Rosalind question.

Erskine, John. *The Elizabethan Lyric*. N. Y. 1903; 104–116.

Greenlaw, Edwin. *The Shepheards Calender*. Publications of the Modern Language Association, XXVI (1911), 419–51.

Greenlaw, E. *The Shepheards Calender*, II. Studies in Philology, XI (1913), 1–25.

Greg, W. W. *Pastoral Poetry and Pastoral Drama*. London, 1906.

Higginson, J. J. *Spenser's Shepherd's Calender in Relation to Contemporary Affairs*. N. Y. 1912.

Hughes, Merritt Y. *Virgil and Spenser*. University of California Press. Berkeley, 1929.

Hughes, Merritt Y. *Spenser and the Greek Pastoral Triad*. Studies in Philology, XX (1923), 184 ff.

Kluge, F. *Spenser's Shepheard's Calendar and Mantuan's Eclogen*. Anglia, III (1880), 266–741.

Long, P. W. *Spenser's Rosalind*. Anglia, XXXI (1908), 72–104.

Long, P. W. *Spenser and the Bishop of Rochester*. Publications of Modern Language Association, XXXI (1916), 732 ff. Interpretation of February eclogue.

Padelford, F. M. *Spenser and the Puritan Propaganda*. Modern Philology, XI (1913), 85–106. Satire in the Sh. Cal.

Reissert, O. *Bemerkungen über Spenser's Shepheards Calendar und die frühere Bukolik*. Anglia, IX (1886), 205 ff.

CHAPTER IV

COMPLAINTS

IN 1591, about twelve years after the publication of the *Shepheardes Calender,* there appeared from the press of William Ponsonby a volume entitled *Complaints Containing Sundrie Small Poemes of the Worlds Vanitie.* In a prefatory address to the "gentle reader," the printer professes to explain the occasion and the character of the volume. Encouraged by the favorable reception of the first three books of the *Faerie Queene,* Ponsonby endeavored "by all means to get into his hands such small poems of Spenser's as he heard were dispersed abroad in sundry hands and not easy to be come by, by himself, some of them having been stolen from him, since his departure over sea." The poems are described as all containing "like matter of argument" and are recommended as being "very grave and profitable." The printer has heard, moreover, of sundry other poems, which, to judge from the titles listed, must have been even more "grave and profitable," and which he hoped later to publish. Like the *Complaints* these poems, which are now all lost, were dedicated to ladies.

No one now takes this explanation of Ponsonby at its face value. Spenser had certainly more to do with the publication than the printer's address to the reader would lead us to suppose. It is important to remember that the poet was still in England when the volume was entered on the Stationers' Register, December 29, 1590; and, as Mr. Renwick observes, "he had too keen a sense of his own dignity and of the value of his work to leave the collection and arrangement even of minor poems to chance and the taste of his publisher." The probabilities are all in favor of the assumption that Ponsonby's *Address* was either a convenient blind behind which Spenser the satirist might take refuge, or a conventional attitude which suggested an aristocratic indifference to publication.

If Spenser had any misgivings about the publication of *Complaints,* these, according to pretty clear contemporary evidence, were justified in the event. There is reason to suppose that the volume was "called in." The most explicit evidence is found in the following epigram by John Weever, that was written and published in 1599:—

> *Colin's* gone home, the glorie of his clime,
> The Muses Mirrour, and the Shepheards Saint;
> *Spencer* is ruined, of our latter time
> The fairest ruine, Faëries foulest want:
> Then his *Time-ruines* did our ruine show,
> Which by his ruine we untimely know:
> *Spencer* therfore thy Ruines were cal'd in,
> Too soone to sorrow least we should begin.

To like purpose is the testimony of Middleton's *Black Book,* 1604:—"a health half as deep as mother Hubburd's cellar—she that was called in for selling her working bottle-ale to bookbinders, and spurting the froth upon courtiers' noses"; and of his *Father Hubburds Tales,* also of 1604: "Why I call these *Father Hubburds Tales,* is not to have them called in again, as the *Tale of Mother Hubburd.*" With these quotations should be associated the following from Gabriel Harvey and Thomas Nashe. In a letter of 1592, Harvey wrote: "Mother Hubbard in heat of choler . . . wilfully overshot her malcontented selfe"; and Nashe in his *Strange Newes,* 1593, attacked Harvey for doing Spenser a disservice by citing *Mother Hubberd's Tale.* "Who publikely accusde or of late brought Mother Hubbard into question," asks Nashe, "that thou shouldst by rehearsall rekindle against him the sparkes of displeasure that were quenched?" The evidence for the "calling in" Mr. Renwick is disposed to discount. He remarks that "the number of copies extant would not lead any one to suspect suppression"; and he is "inclined to believe that—unless a reprint was suppressed—Weever and Middleton are retailing gossip."

To judge from the above allusions, the objectionable poems in the *Complaints* volume were the *Ruines of Time* and *Mother Hubberds Tale.* However, it seems reasonable to suppose that the whole volume, if anything, was "called in." At least no one has discovered a copy of the Quarto which omits either poem; whereas the existence of several copies of the *Complaints* in manuscript might be interpreted to mean that the printed edition was quickly exhausted. On the other hand, the Folio of 1611 not only omitted *Mother Hubberds Tale* but it made inoffensive the passage in the *Ruines of Time,* ll. 447–454, which pointedly satirized Burghley. This seems to have been done out of deference to Sir Robert Cecil, since after his death in 1611 the *Mother Hubberds Tale* again appears, the title page in some of the issues being dated 1612, in others 1613.

Another matter of interest is the "make-up" of the *Complaints* volume. The constitution of the Quarto, as

Professor Emerson pointed out, favors the hypothesis that the printer's first intention was to issue the constituent poems in four separate booklets, each consisting of a multiple of four pages and each supplied with a separate title-page and dedication. The distribution of the type bears out this hypothesis. In the case of the third booklet including *Prosopopoia* and the *Ruines of Time,* the type had to be crowded to get all the matter in; on the other hand, there is so much space to spare in the fourth part that the matter has been "somewhat spread out in order to fill the last twenty pages."

This interesting book, whatever might have been its history, is marked by a striking uniformity in subject matter. All of the poems "are complaints and meditations of the worlds vanitie, verie grave and profitable." Still other productions, listed in Ponsonby's address to the reader but no longer extant, no doubt illustrated further the poet's vein of melancholy reflection. These are his translations of *Ecclesiastes* and the *Canticum Canticorum, A Senights Slumber, The Hell of Lovers,* and *The Sacrifice of a Sinner.* One can judge from these titles and from the prevailing tone of *Complaints* what somber themes occupied our poet during the first three decades of his literary career; for, although not published until 1591, the volume of *Complaints* contains poems belonging to the poet's University years and those immediately following (1570–1576), to the time that Professor Dodge has called the first London period (1576–80), and finally to the years from 1580 to 1589 that constitute his first Irish period, immediately followed by his brief visit to London.

Like Van der Noot's *Theatre,* "wherein be represented as well the miseries and calamities that follow the voluptuous worldlings as also the greate joyes and pleasures which the faithfull do enjoy," Spenser's *Complaints* appealed to a taste for melancholy, moralizing literature which was well developed in sixteenth century England. The taste was satisfied in some measure by the "tragedies" and complaints which are in line of descent from Boccaccio's *De Casibus Virorum Illustrium,* Chaucer's *Monk's Tale,* and Lydgate's *Fall of Princes,* and which are best exemplified for the sixteenth century by the *Mirrour for Magistrates.* Sackville's famous *Induction* to the last-mentioned work realizes in its unrelieved gloom and passionate melancholy the artistic potentialities of this literature of sorrow. But we cannot miss illustrations of it elsewhere. To every one will occur the Senecan tragedies and the *Dances of Death,* and such lyrics as Watson's "Come, Gentle Death." No more cheerful is the *Zodiake of Life,* written by Palingenius and translated by Googe, *wherein are conteyned twelve Bookes disclosing the heynous Crymes and wicked vices of our corrupt nature,* or Gascoigne's *Droomme of Doomes day, wherin the frailties and miseries of man's life are lyvely portrayed, and learnedly set forth.*

REFERENCES

Renwick, W. L. Ed. *Complaints. Edmund Spenser.* The Scholartis Press. London, 1928.
Selincourt, E. de. Ed. *Spenser's Minor Poems.*

———

Davis, Bernard, E. C. *The Text of Spenser's "Complaints."* Modern Language Review, XX (1925), 18 ff.
Emerson, O. F. *Spenser, Lady Carey, and the Complaints*

Volume. Publications of the Modern Language Association, XXXII (1917), 306 ff.

Long, P. W. Review of de Selincourt's *Minor Poems of Spenser.* Englische Studien, XLIV (1912), 263 ff.

Palgrave, F. T. *Essay on the Minor Poems of Spenser.* Grosart's Works of Spenser, IV, p. ix ff.

CHAPTER V

THE RUINES OF TIME

THE *Ruines of Time,* the first poem in *Complaints,* is dedicated to Lady Mary Countess of Pembroke, sister of Sir Philip Sidney. The appropriateness of this dedication appears in the dedicatory letter and in the poem itself. Friends of the poet had remonstrated with him because he had shown no "thankful remembrance" to Sir Philip, "the patron of his young Muses," who had died in 1586, or, indeed, to any member of Sir Philip's family. In the words of the poem,

> Ne doth his Colin, carelesse Colin Cloute,
> Care now his idle bagpipe up to raise.

To "quite him of this guiltie blame," Spenser composed the *Ruines of Time.*

The dedication of the *Ruines of Time* is not quite accurate. As early as 1580 the poet had shown "thankful remembrance"to the Dudleys by writing his *Stemmata Dudleiana,* a poem which must have resembled very closely the *World's Ruins* or the *Ruines of Time.* It is clear from the following quotation that Spenser had some misgivings about its publication. In a letter to Harvey he says: "Of my *Stemmata Dudleiana,* and especially of the sundry apostrophes therein, addressed you knowe to whome, muste more advisement be had, than so lightly to sende

them abroade." It is possible, too, that there were other
considerations than those of piety to his patron's family
that persuaded Spenser and Ponsonby to include the
Ruines of Time and to give it the initial position in the
Complaints volume. At the time of publication of Spenser's book the literary world was taking new interest in
Sidney. In 1590 there had appeared an unauthorized edition of the *Arcadia* and in 1591 three editions of *Astrophel and Stella* had come off the press.

Whatever the special reasons for its publication, the in-
clusion of the *Ruines of Time* in *Complaints* is clearly
justified on the score of its subject matter and its style.
The poem falls easily into four main divisions:—(1) a
patriotic lament; (2) a necrology of the Dudley and Bedford families; (3) a eulogy of poetry; and (4) a complaint of the world's vanity.

In its first division, Spenser's poem is an English counterpart of Du Bellay's *Antiquitez de Rome*. Its opening
stanzas, reminiscent of Sackville's *Induction* to the *Mirrour for Magistrates,* introduce us to the ancient city
Verulam in the guise of an afflicted woman lamenting the
splendor of her prime. As Rome was the empress of the
whole world, she was the princess of "this small Northern
world." The lament of Verulam, largely occupied with the
traditional themes of the vicissitudes of fortune and the
fall of the mighty, which had interested both Chaucer and
Lydgate, is colored like the poem of Du Bellay by a modern and romantic sentiment of ruins. All that remains of
the ancient city is now overgrown with weeds and grass
and "black oblivion's rust." Furthermore, this section of
the poem is also touched by that antiquarian enthusiasm of
the sixteenth century to which the works of Leland and

Camden testify. Apostrophizing the latter, Spenser
writes :—

> Cambden, the nourice of antiquitie,
> And lanterne unto late succeeding age,
> To see the light of simple veritie
> Buried in ruines, through the great outrage
> Of her owne people, led with warlike rage,
> Cambden, though Time all moniments obscure,
> Yet thy just labours ever shall endure.

In the elegy or necrology, which is the second part of
this largely lugubrious poem, Spenser commemorates first
of all the Earl of Leicester; and the eulogy of his dead
patron led him into what we may judge from Weever's
epigram was indiscreet criticism of Burghley, the fox.
Speaking of the spite that "bites the dead," the poet says—

> He now is gone, the whiles the foxe is crept
> Into the hole the which the badger swept.

From the great earl he passes to his brother Ambrose,
Earl of Warwick, and the latter's wife, Anne Russell, the
Theana of *Colin Clouts Come Home Againe;* to Mary Dudley, Sir Philip's mother, who had died in 1586; to Anne's
father, Francis, the second Earl of Bedford, and her
nephew, Edward Russell, the third Earl, rising to a climax
in exalted praise of Sir Philip and his sister, the Countess of
Pembroke. The elegy on Sidney, here incorporated, Mr.
Renwick conjectures might have been originally written
for the Sidney memorial volume, to which Spenser later
contributed *Astrophel.* First, Spenser's failure to make
a contribution, and then his diversion to the *Ruines* of what
was originally intended for the coöperative enterprise

"would account for the tardy appearance of the Sidney elegies (headed by *Astrophel*) nine years after his death, and also for the disjointed state of the *Ruines of Time.*"

In what we have called the third division of the *Ruines of Time,* Spenser discourses on the familiar Renaissance themes of fame and the poet's power to confer it. Here the poem will remind us of the October eclogue and of the *Teares of the Muses.* The boast of ancient poets, exemplified in Horace's *Exegi monumentum ære perennius,* was proudly repeated by the humanists and made an argument for princely patronage. Particularly was the subject affected by the poets of the *Pléiade* in their attempt to enhance the dignity of the poet's calling. We may say, too, that it is agreeable to the genius of Spenser's verse; so that the *Ruines of Time* seems to reach its highest level when it sings of Fame flying with golden wings above the "reach of ruinous decay," and "beating with brave plumes the azure sky," or when, as in the following stanza, it pays tribute to the power of poetry :—

> For deeds doe die, how ever noblie donne,
> And thoughts of men do as themselves decay,
> But wise wordes taught in numbers for to runne,
> Recorded by the Muses, live for ay,
> Ne may with storming showers be washt away;
> Ne bitter breathing windes with harmfull blast,
> Nor age, nor envie, shall them ever wast.

As in his lament of the Dudleys, so in his praise of fame, Spenser contrives to attack Burghley. This was not difficult, inasmuch as it was generally known that the Lord Treasurer was no friend of the poets. He was, of course, hostile also to the war party to which Spenser was attached.

Our poet could therefore write, at l. 440 ff., that since the death of Walsingham (Melibœ)

> learning lies unregarded,
> And men of armes doo wander unrewarded.
>
> .   .   .   .
> .   .   .   .
>
> For he that now welds all things at his will
> Scorns th' one and th' other in his deeper skill."

In the stanza immediately following the lines last quoted there are significant differences between the readings of Quarto and Folio. The original text is as follows :—

> O griefe of griefes! O gall of all good heartes!
> To see that vertue should dispised bee
> Of him that first was raisde for vertuous parts,
> And now, broad spreading like an aged tree,
> Lets none shoot up, that nigh him planted bee.
> O let the man of whom the Muse is scorned,
> Nor alive nor dead, be of the Muse adorned!

In a figure of speech reminiscent of the February eclogue, the poet here evidently glances at Burghley. By changing throughout to plurals the singular nouns and pronouns the editor of the later text cancels the allusion. "Of him that first was raisde" is altered to read "Such as first were raisde"; "nigh him planted" becomes "nigh them planted"; and "O let the man" is changed to "O let not those."

The final section of the *Ruines of Time* belongs to the *genre* of vision poetry that is fully illustrated by *Visions of the Worlds Vanitie,* the *Visions of Bellay,* and the *Visions of Petrarch.* The type will be considered in connection with these other poems. Here it should be remarked that this portion of the *Ruines* reverts to the elegiac, obituary theme of the second division, dealing symbolically with what was there treated directly; for it is clear that of the two sets of visions the first commemorates Leicester, the second Sidney. Having in mind the coat-of-arms of the Dudleys, we can have no doubt about the allusion to Leicester and his brother the Earl of Warwick in the sixth vision of the first series; and the second vision of the second series points none the less clearly to Sidney. The two sets of visions are further related as the two main sections of the conventional elegy; that is to say, the first voices a great and unrelieved sorrow while the second expresses a faith in heavenly compensation. The Envoy, in which Sidney and his sister are addressed, returns quite properly to the theme of the Dedication.

Although the *Ruines of Time* achieves a certain unity in its uniform tone and in its occupation throughout with the themes of fame and mortality, treated both directly and symbolically, the poem shows obvious defects of structure. Every one has noted the anachronism of Verulam's lament for Leicester. While the poet is detailing his necrology of the Dudleys, the allegorical figure certainly fades from our consciousness, only to speak at l. 461 as though she had never been absent. With the disappearance of Verulam in the stanza beginning at l. 470 the poem might properly end. The appended visions certainly produce the effect of an afterthought. The general looseness of structure, which becomes apparent on even a rapid reading, has led Mr. Renwick to the conjecture that the poem was "written in fragments," that "some of the fragments were originally intended for other purposes," and that "the scheme we have is an afterthought." The *Ruines of Time,* in its present form, is compounded, he thinks, of "a poem commendatory of Camden's *Britannia,* an elegy on Sidney, the place of which was eventually taken by *Astrophel,* and bits of the old *Dreames* or *Pageants."*

REFERENCES

Emerson, O. F. *Spenser, Lady Carey, and the Complaints Volume.* Publications of Modern Language Association, XXXII (1917), 306 ff.

Hales, J. W. *Spenser and Verulam.* Middlesex Notes and Queries. London, 1896 (July), 127–134.

CHAPTER VI

THE TEARES OF THE MUSES

THERE is no general agreement upon the time when
Spenser wrote his *Teares of the Muses*. In his "Complaint of Thalia" he alludes, indeed, to one of his contemporaries as "dead of late," but unfortunately the commentators are not of one mind with respect to the identity of "our pleasant Willy." If we take the first quoted phrase in its literal sense, as no doubt we should, we cannot accept the suggested identifications of Willy with Shakespeare, T. Wilson, or Alabaster, who were all living when *Complaints* was published. Other suggestions are Sir Philip Sidney, who died in 1586, and the comedian Richard Tarleton, whose death occurred in 1588. If we accept the very recent guess of Mr. Renwick that "Willy" is George Gascoigne, who died in 1577, we may suppose, if we will, a very early date for the *Teares of the Muses*.

Whether "that same gentle spirit" (l. 217) is or is not the same person as "our pleasant Willy" is another bone of contention. Those who take what seems to be the more probable position that Spenser here alludes to a second contemporary, have been inclined to identify him with John Lyly, whose inactivity as an author from 1584 to 1590, would explain line 220:

Doth rather choose to sit in idle cell.

Other guesses are the Earl of Oxford (B. M. Ward) and Spenser himself (Renwick).

Whatever the identity of "pleasant Willy" and the "gentle spirit," it is possible of course to assume with Professor Dodge that the *Teares of the Muses* is "early work revised." We are then free to suppose that the allusions in Thalia's lament were interpolations in the second version. The whole matter is, however, highly conjectural. More definite considerations are that the poem's description of the low state of literature has more applicability to 1580 than 1590, and that if it applies to conditions in the latter year, it fails to agree with Spenser's praise of Elizabethan poets in *Colin Clouts Come Home Againe,* which was published in 1591. Again, the stanza form here employed might point to an early date. It is the same six-verse form that Spenser borrowed from French poetry for the January and December eclogues. His title he may have derived from Gabriel Harvey's *Smithus, vel musarum lachrymæ pro obitu T. Smith,* 1578.

The *Teares of the Muses* appeals to us principally as a kind of manifesto of the new poetry in England. As such it is in line with the October eclogue and the *Ruines of Time* and inevitably suggests comparisons with the doctrine of the *Pléiade.* That group of young progressives in French literature who adopted this designation and whose most brilliant representatives were Ronsard and Du Bellay came out for the divinity of the poet and his power to confer immortality upon his patron. Though the poet was born, not made, and though poetry, in the words of E.K.'s argument to the October eclogue, was "a divine gift and heavenly instinct, not to bee gotten by laboure and learning," it was nevertheless "adorned with both." The string upon which the Muses harp, therefore, is the prevailing ignorance against which they have to contend.

The poet's power to confer immortality, his need of a patron, and the contrast between the virtue and wisdom of the true poets and the vice and ignorance of the false ones, are themes common to Joachim Du Bellay's *La Deffence et Illustration de la langue francoyse* and Spenser's *Teares of the Muses.* "Certainly," writes Du Bellay, "if we had Mecænases and Augustuses, the Heavens and Nature are not such enemies of our time that we should not still have Virgils. Honor nourishes the arts, we are all fired by glory to study the sciences, and never are those things exalted which one sees are depreciated by everybody. Kings and princes should remember, it seems to me, that great emperor, who preferred that the ancient might of the laws should be broken than that the works of Virgil, condemned to the flames by the testament of their author, should be burned. What shall I say of that other great monarch who preferred the rebirth of Homer to a great victory? Once when near the tomb of Achilles he cried out: 'Oh, happy youth to have found such a trumpeter of your praises!' In truth, without the divine Muse of Homer the same tomb that covered the body of Achilles would also have overwhelmed his renown. And this, indeed, happens to all who put the assurance of their immortality in marble, bronze, colossi, pyramids, buildings constructed with great labour, and other things which are not less subject to the injuries of the skies and the seasons, of fire and sword, than they are the source of excessive expense and perpetual anxiety. The pleasures of Venus, gluttony, and sloth have banished from among men all desire of immortality; but it is an even more unworthy thing that those who set their chief glory in ignorance and all sorts of vices make sport of those who employ in laudable labour the hours consumed by others in games, baths, banquets, and other similar minor pleasures." The true poets are advised to look for the fruit of their efforts to an incorruptible and not envious posterity. "Glory is the only ladder by whose rungs mortals with a light step mount to heaven and make themselves companions of the gods."

That Spenser, speaking perhaps for a largely fictitious *Areopagus,* shared such ideas with Du Bellay, speaking for the *Pléiade,* the *Teares of the Muses* makes abundantly clear. For example, Calliope describes herself as the "nurse of vertue,"

> And golden trumpet of eternitie,
> That lowly thoughts lift up to heavens hight,
> And mortall men have powre to deifie:
> Bacchus and Hercules I raisd to heaven,
> And Charlemaine, amongst the starris seaven.

In contrast to the "brood of blessed Sapience," described by Clio as "secretaries of my celestial skill," is the brood of Ignorance "begotten of fowle Infamy," says Terpsichore:

> Blind Error, scornefull Follie, and base Spight,
> Who hold by wrong that wee should have by right.
> .   .   .   .
> All places they doo with their toyes possesse,
> And raigne in liking of the multitude;
> The schooles they fill with fond newfanglenesse,
> And sway in court with pride and rashnes rude;
> Mongst simple shepheards they do boast their skill,
> And saye their musicke matcheth Phœbus quill.

The noble hearts to pleasures they allure,
And tell their Prince that learning is but vaine;
Faire ladies loves they spot with thoughts impure,
And gentle mindes with lewd delights distaine;
Clerks they to loathly idlenes entice,
And fill their bookes with discipline of vice.

Sir Philip Sidney, another spokesman of the new poetry in England, expressed in his famous *Apology for Poetry* the same ideas. For him "the ever-praise-worthy Poesie is full of vertue-breeding delightfulness, and voyde of no gyfte that ought to be in the noble name of learning." Those who hold another doctrine are, he says, not poets but poet-apes. "In the name of the nyne Muses," he conjures all who read his book, "no more to scorne the sacred misteries of Poesie, no more to laugh at the name of Poets, as though they were next inheritours to Fooles, no more to iest at the reverent title of a Rymer"; rather to believe that they are the "Treasurer of Divinity," the "bringers in of all civilitie." Repeating a doctrine which Spenser had in mind in *The Faerie Queene,* Sidney further maintains that "there are many misteries contained in Poetrie, which of purpose were written darkely, least by prophane wits it should bee abused"; and, with E.K. in the argument to October, he holds that poets "are so beloved of the Gods that whatsoever they write proceeds of a divine fury." Again, we should believe the poets when they tell us that they will make us "immortall by their verses." Finally we might note that Polyhymnia agrees with the *Apology* in declaring that the early poets were high priests who put in verse their sacred laws and deep oracles.

From Polyhymnia we learn, too, that the new poets in England, like the poets of the *Pléiade* in France, concerned themselves not only with the theory of poetry but also with its vocabulary and metrical form. We need not suppose that Polyhymnia is here an advocate, like Ascham and Harvey, of classical meters; she merely expresses impatience with what Harvey calls "barbarous and balductum rymes." Perhaps she was thinking of Skelton or more generally of those alliterative poets whom E.K. in his Preface to the *Shepheardes Calender* describes as the "rakehellye route of our ragged rymers (for so themselves use to hunt the letter) which withoute learning boste, without judgement jangle, without reason rage and fume." In the uninspired and unregulated poetry of the period, "one verse," says Sidney, "did but beget another"; it is "a confused masse of wordes, with a tingling sound of ryme, barely accompanied with reason,"—such verse as we find in some of the Elizabethan anthologies; e. g., *A Gorgeous Gallery of Gallant Inventions*. With so-called poetry like this in mind Polyhymnia complains:—

> For the sweet numbers and melodious measures,
> With which I wont the winged words to tie,
> And make a tunefull diapase of pleasures,
> Now being let to runne at libertie
> By those which have no skill to rule them right,
> Have now quite lost their naturall deiight.

With a pointed allusion to the alliterative poets in the opening line of the following stanza, she continues:

> Heapes of huge words uphoorded hideously,
> With horrid sound, though having little sence,
> They thinke to be chiefe praise of poëtry;
> And thereby wanting due intelligence,

> Have mard the face of goodly poësie,
> And made a monster of their fantasie.

Having in mind a similar situation in France, Du Bellay in the eleventh chapter of the second book of the *Deffence* had prayed to Apollo for a poet whose well-sounding lute would silence the raucous bagpipes, much as a stone thrown into a swamp silences the voices of the frogs.

The declaration of his poetic faith that Spenser offers us in the *Teares of the Muses* was dedicated to the youngest of

> the sisters three,
> The honor of the noble familie
> Of which I meanest boast my selfe to be,
> And most that unto them I am so nie. (C.C.C.H.A., 536 ff.)

These were the daughters of Sir John Spencer of Althorpe. To the oldest, Elizabeth (Lady Carey), Spenser dedicated *Muiopotmos;* to the second, Anne (Lady Compton and Mountegle), *Mother Hubberds Tale;* to the third Alice (Lady Strange), the *Teares of the Muses.* In 1600 Alice took as her second husband Thomas Egerton, Lord Ellesmere, the Lord Chancellor. As further evidence of her interest and that of her family in literature, it should be noted that Milton's *Arcades,* according to the poet's own note in the 1645 edition of his works, was "part of an entertainment presented to the Countess Dowager of Derby at Harefield by some noble persons of her family"; and that the same poet's *Comus* was written for her stepson, Sir John Egerton, Earl of Bridgewater, who married Alice's daughter by her first marriage. According to Professor Hanford, "it is probable that Henry Lawes, then musical tutor in the Egerton family, who later superintended the production of *Comus,* was also the deviser of this masque." Alice, who was a young matron of thirty when she was honored by the dedication of the *Teares of the Muses,* was an old woman of seventy when the *Arcades* was produced before her. "It was perhaps," writes Professor Hanford, "the rounding out of her three score years and ten that gave occasion for the celebration."

REFERENCES

Gabbett, H. S. *Spenser's "Pleasant Willy."* Athenæum, LXVI (1875), 507–8.

Grosart, A. B. *Works of Spenser,* I, 89 ff., 185–189; lxiii–lxv.

Long, P. W. *The Date of Spenser's Earlier Hymns.* Englische Studien, XLVII (1913), 197–208.

Malone, E. *Works of Shakespeare,* 1821, II, 167 ff.

Ward, B. M. *The Seventeenth Earl of Oxford.* London, 1928. Appendix D.

CHAPTER VII

VIRGILS GNAT

THE approximate date of Spenser's translation of the pseudo-Virgilian *Culex,* that he entitled *Virgils Gnat,* may be inferred from its dedication and its prefatory sonnet. "Long since dedicated," he tells us, "to the most noble and excellent Lord, the Earle of Leicester, late deceased." The poem as interpreted by the poet himself clearly belongs to the period and probably to the final years of the period of Spenser's relations with Robert Dudley, that is to say 1577–1580. From the explanatory sonnet, which follows the *Amoretti* rhyme arrangement, we learn that the poet has been wronged by his patron in a manner to which only the Earl is privy. To Leicester, it seems, the Gnat's complaint may be easily known. Any one else who "reads the secret" of the "riddle rare" must be an Œdipus, indeed, with "power of some divining spright." With a seeming implication that the meaning of some other allegory had been made public by some indiscreet commentator, the poet requests that the chance Œdipus should "rest pleased with his own insight" and seek no further "to glose upon the text";

> For griefe enough it is to grieved wight
> To feele his fault, and not be further vext.

In the light of this explanation no one will hesitate to identify the Gnat in the poem with Spenser and the sleeping shepherd with Leicester. For whom or for what the serpent stands must for the present remain conjectural.

The interpretation of the poem which seems most likely is that which was long ago advanced by Professor Edwin Greenlaw. Professor Greenlaw, regarding *Virgils Gnat* as a sequel to *Mother Hubberds Tale,* thinks that it records the effect upon Leicester of the poet's attempt to warn him of the very serious danger to his personal prospects in the proposed marriage of Elizabeth to the Duke d'Alençon. In return for what the Earl considered an officious service on Spenser's part, the poet is punished by his patron, just as the gnat was killed by the shepherd. The gnat's descent to the infernal regions, described in l. 369 as a "waste wildernesse," is interpreted to mean Spenser's "banishment" to Ireland in 1580. If we accept this explanation, we may agree with Professor Greenlaw that Spenser wrote *Virgils Gnat* "after he had been long enough in Ireland to give up all hope but the hope that Leicester might bring him back." The date, he thinks, must have been prior to 1585, when Leicester went to the Netherlands. The two poems interpreted together in this way "give the history of that mistake of overboldness," says Greenlaw, "which Spenser wished so pathetically, in his letter to Harvey, to avoid." The passage in question from the letter to Harvey runs as follows:—"I was minded for a while to have intermitted the uttering of my writings; leaste by over-much cloying their noble eares, I should gather a contempt of my self, or else seeme rather for gaine and commoditie to doe it, for some sweetnesse that I have already tasted."

In criticism of Professor Greenlaw's dating of *Virgils Gnat* it might be remarked that the poem furnishes no evidence that the translation was made with special reference to the poet's relations with his patron. Nowhere does it seem to be in any way influenced by an ulterior purpose. It might, therefore, have been made in the poet's youth, when he was actively translating other authors, and later turned to an allegorical purpose. One should not, of course, forget that the Latin poem itself, addressed to Augustus, might have been a personal allegory.

Whatever may be the hidden meaning of *Virgils Gnat,* it is significant as illustrating Spenser's interest in a kind of poetry widely cultivated in classical times. As an example of Alexandrianism in Spenser's work, it should be grouped with the Cupid story in the March eclogue and with the so-called epigrams that were printed in the *Amoretti* volume. It shares with those other poems that prettiness of fancy that was affected by Alexandrian Greeks and which is a mark of some of the minor poems of the Greek anthology. More definitely, it belongs with the *Muiopotmos* to a type of literature which makes its appeal by giving unexpected worth or importance to apparently insignificant things. To the non-narrative forms of this type the term adoxography has been applied. Like certain varieties of the modern essay these compositions exhibit much ingenuity in praising the trivial, the ridiculous, or even the vicious. Such a writer as Synesius, for example, undertook to praise baldness, and others were the champions of gout and deafness. More to our purpose are the essays of Isocrates, Dio Chrysostom, and others in praise of the smaller animals and insects, such as the parrot, the ant, the bumblebee, flies, gnats, fleas, and lice. Similar productions in narrative form, that go under the name of epyllia or little epics, are best illustrated by the famous Greek mock-epic, the *Batrachomyomachia,* and the Latin *Culex.*

Spenser's translation of the *Culex* might in the first instance have been due to his love of Virgil and his ambition to try his hand at another form of Virgilian poetry. Moreover, he would have known the poem as one that had attracted no little attention in the sixteenth century. Published as early as 1471 in the second printed edition of Virgil, it appeared again in the first Aldine edition, printed at Venice in 1505. Worthy of note are the many illustrated editions from 1502 onward, "one of which," it has been suggested, "may have been responsible for some of the verbal embroidery which adds more than three hundred lines in Spenser's paraphrase to the length of the original poem." In 1530 the poem was made by the famous Cardinal Bembo the subject of a dialogue, entitled *De Virgilii Culice et Terentii Fabulis,* in the course of which the Cardinal undertook to emend the text in many passages. Many of Bembo's emendations must have been incorporated in the text from which Spenser translated, as Professor Emerson has abundantly demonstrated.

The translation of the Latin hexameters into Ariosto's stanza, the *ottava rima,* necessarily involved a considerable enlargement of the original. The result is that *Virgils Gnat* is half as long again as the *Culex.* Professor Emerson has shown how far Warton was wrong in characterizing *Virgils Gnat* as "a vague and arbitrary paraphrase." On the contrary, after we have made allowance for the stanza form of Spenser's translation, we may well praise the fidelity of his rendering. Mr. Renwick finds that "the spirit of his version is impeccably just," and that "his unmistakably personal style reproduces the soft glow of Virgil—the mark both of temperamental sympathy and of early training in the humanist school."

In producing his English version of the *Culex,* Spenser characteristically expands descriptive passages while he keeps his narrative well within the limits of his Latin original. In a typical passage he uses only forty-seven lines of narrative as compared with the forty-four of his original, whereas he expands 156 lines of description at the beginning of the *Culex* to 236 in the corresponding passage of his English version. Elsewhere the descriptive passages double or more than double the Latin lines upon which they are based. Apart from this altered proportion between the descriptive and purely narrative elements of the poem may be noted the felicity with which Spenser often renders his original. Enlarging upon a single word in his Latin text he writes—

> He shall inspire my verse with gentle mood
> Of poets prince.

Again, the emended reading *plaudente* of the *Culex* corresponds to "dancing all in company" in *Virgil's Gnat.*

REFERENCES

Emerson, O. F. *Spenser's Virgil's Gnat.* Journal of English and Germanic Philology, XVII (1918), 94 ff.

Greenlaw, Edwin. *Spenser and the Earl of Leicester.* Publications of the Modern Language Association, XXV (1910), 535 ff.

Hughes, Merritt Y. *Virgil and Spenser.* University of California Press, Berkeley, 1929; 309 ff.

Pease, A. S. *Things Without Honor.* Classical Philology, XXI (1926), 27 ff.

CHAPTER VIII

MOTHER HUBBERDS TALE

PROSOPOPOIA or *Mother Hubberds Tale* Spenser dedicated to Anne, daughter of Sir John Spencer of Althorp, who in *Colin Clouts Come Home Againe* is

> Phyllis, the floure of rare perfection,
> Faire spreading forth her leaves with fresh delight,
> That, with their beauties amorous reflexion,
> Bereave of sence each rash beholders sight.

Anne was three times married: first, to William Stanley, Lord Mounteagle; then, to Henry, Lord Compton, who died in 1589; and finally to Robert Sackville, son of the poet who wrote the *Induction* to the *Mirrour for Magistrates,* and who became on his father's death the second Earl of Dorset.

The dedication of *Mother Hubberds Tale* is dated 1591, but, in his prefatory letter to Lady Compton, the poet says of his *Tale* that it was composed long ago in the time of his youth, that lately he had lighted upon it among other papers, and that he "was by others, which liked the same, mooved to set them foorth." The poet himself thus bearing testimony to the early composition of *Mother Hubberds Tale,* the critics have endeavored to assign it more definitely to 1579–1580. With respect to the place of the plague in the setting of the poem, it is pointed out that these were plague years in both England and France. Furthermore, as Professor Greenlaw has reminded us, "the entire poem reflects the hatred of French gallantry and intrigue especially characteristic of these years." We should note, too, the parallels between the *Tale* and the *Shepheardes Calender,* which was published in 1579. For example, l. 78—"And from my beard the fat away have swept"—echoes "September," l. 123; the description at l. 392 ff. of the priest who having read his homilies might attend his plays reminds us of Palinode in "May"; and the story at l. 909 ff. of the ambitious man who leaves his mean estate and assured safety to seek his fortune elsewhere is like the theme of "September." More definitely, l. 628—"But his late chayne his Liege unmeete esteemeth"—is generally thought to allude to the Queen's displeasure upon learning from the French ambassador Simier in 1579 of Leicester's secret marriage to the Countess of Essex. The passage containing this line in its abrupt transition from plural to singular (623–625) shows signs of alteration, made rapidly perhaps just before publication. The curious description in l. 624 of the beasts "enchaste with chaine and circulet of golde" was thought by Professor Child to allude to the Queen's gift of gold chains to Sir Walter Raleigh and the other leaders of the Portugal expedition of 1589. If this is correct, the whole passage was probably revised not long before the publication of the poem. Professor Dodge's account of this revision may be accepted:— "In the text of 1579, the question 'Who now in court doth beare the greatest sway?' (l. 616) was probably answered by an allusion to Leicester. In 1590 this was made over into the allusion to the commanders of the Portugal expedition (l. 620 ff.);

yet not so carefully but that the original intent still showed." (l. 625 ff.)

The interpretation of the allegory of *Mother Hubberds Tale* offered some time ago by Professor Greenlaw has been generally accepted. According to this, the poem was written to warn Leicester of the dangers of Elizabeth's marriage with the Duc d'Alençon. This match, which seemed to be favored by Burghley and to which the Puritan party of Leicester and Sidney was strongly opposed, was apparently on the point of being realized in 1579. Early in that year Simier, the representative of the Duke, arrived in England and was at once received with great favor by the Queen. She called him her "monkey." When in August, in spite of Leicester's opposition, the Duke himself arrived, he became forthwith her "frog." The Queen's subjects generally, but particularly the Puritans, were alarmed. Stubbs published his protest entitled, "The discovery of a gaping gulph, whereunto England is likely to be swallowed by another French marriage, if the Lord forbid not the banns, by letting her Majesty see the sin and punishment thereof," and was duly punished by the loss of his right hand. Sidney, too, incurred the Queen's displeasure by writing a courageous letter in opposition to the match. No doubt Spenser's poem, like Stubbs's pamphlet and Sidney's letter, was resented by both Leicester and Elizabeth. Evidence of the Earl's irritation is found, as has been pointed out, in the prefatory sonnet to *Virgils Gnat;* and the Queen, as we have already noted, probably had *Mother Hubberds Tale* "called in." The poet, it has been supposed, was still further punished by "banishment" to Ireland, which he and others probably regarded as a kind of Siberian land of exile.

It has been felt by many critics of *Mother Hubberds Tale* that its political and personal allegory has been grafted upon the stock of a fable which was at first turned only to the account of general satire. In its opening passage, reminiscent of the setting of Boccaccio's *Decameron,* the fable develops along the lines of the social satire of the *états du monde.* The vagabond soldiers, the gullible rustics, the priests, and the courtiers come in successively for attention. With the satirical treatment of social abuses is united, as in such mediæval satires as the *Speculum Stultorum,* the *Architrenius,* and the *Roman de carité,* the motif of travel. The combination of these elements had already been made in familiar mediæval fables which represented the fox as a pilgrim. Other features common to Spenser and the Renard cycle are the disguise of the fox as a soldier, a priest, and a courtier. The final episode of *Mother Hubberds Tale,* the usurpation of the throne, has its analogue in the episodic *Couronnement de Renard.* Most of this matter Spenser might have found in two English translations of the French *Roman de Renard,* the Caxton translation of 1481, or that of Thomas Gualtier, printed in London in 1550.

In the final episode, recounting the usurpation of the throne and Jupiter's punishment of the usurpers, the more or less general social satire of the earlier episodes becomes pointed and personal. The change of technique is here noteworthy. Whereas up to this point the animals in disguise move usually among men, we have here wholly a beast world. Besides the ape and the fox, there are the sheep, the ass, the tiger, the boar, the camel, and the wolf introduced as minor characters. There are changes, too, in rank and character. The lion, who was previously a courtier, is now a sovereign; and the ape who before was masterful is now a mere creature of the designing fox. Noting these discrepancies as well as the impression one gets at l. 949 that the poet is making a fresh start, we might suspect that the final episode in *Mother Hubberds Tale* is in the nature of an afterthought.

In any case its satire upon Alençon, his representative Simier, and Burghley can hardly be missed. If Alençon had indeed married Elizabeth, he would certainly as king consort have been surrounded at the English court by a large company of French retainers. This danger Spenser has not overlooked:

> Then, for the safegard of his personage,
> He did appoint a warlike equipage
> Of forreine beasts, not in the forest bred,
> But part by land and part by water fed;
> For tyrannie is with strange ayde supported.
> Then unto him all monstrous beasts resorted
> Bred of two kindes, as Griffons, Minotaures,
> Crocodiles, Dragons, Beavers, and Centaures:
> With those himselfe he strengthned mightelie,
> That feare he neede no force of enemie. (l. 1117 ff.)

At l. 1151 ff. an allusion has been detected to the charge brought against Burghley that he used the influence of his office to advance the members of his family and particularly his son Robert Cecil. Further, the Lord Treasurer's hostility to the old nobility and his aggrandizement at their cost may well be assailed at l. 1172 ff., and his lack of consideration for scholars may have inspired l. 1191—"For men of learning little he esteemed." Earlier in the poem, at l. 219, Spenser had prayed that shame might light on the Ape because he turns

> the name of souldiers to abusion,
> And that, which is the noblest mysterie,
> Brings to reproach and common infamie.

With the double charge of hostility to both soldiers and scholars the Lord Treasurer's name has been already connected in a passage quoted above from the *Ruines of Time,* l. 440 ff.

However interesting may be the allegory of *Mother Hubberds Tale,* an even greater interest attaches to its ideas and its style. In more than one respect it may be compared with *Colin Clouts Come Home Againe.* Both poems written under the influence of Chaucer succeed in reproducing in some measure the familiar and leisurely style of the master. On this level they also anticipate somewhat the facility of Dryden in fable and satire. Like the work of the other two poets, Spenser's verse, though chiefly in the lower key of prose, rises here and there to a pitch of eloquence that has the energy and ardour of great poetry. Both the *Tale* and *Colin Clout* are fuller growths of what had already taken root in the *Calender.* Spenser here attempts a more sustained if not a higher flight in both the fable and the pastoral. With little factitious archaizing and without the *Calender's* frequent changes in the *tempo* and pitch of the verse, the two poems maintain from beginning to end a combination of ease and simplicity for which we can find no parallel elsewhere in Spenser's poetry.

In terse and balanced phrases, in the forms of proverb and epigram, Spenser here clearly stands between Chaucer and Dryden in the tradition of poetic wit and satire. The following passages have a flavor of Augustan verse :—

whose onely pride
Is vertue to advaunce and vice deride.

To speed to day—to be put back to morrow;
To feed on hope—to pine with feare and sorrow.

Justice he solde injustice for to buy.

Be you the souldier, for you likest are
For manly semblance, and small skill in warre.

And yet (God wote) small oddes I often see
Twixt them that aske, and them that asked bee.

Occasionally a pun is permitted to enliven the style :—

But tidings there is none, I you assure,
Save that which common is, and knowne to all,
That courtiers as the tide doo rise and fall.

But he so light was at legier demaine,
That what he toucht came not to light againe.

The higher style of the poem will be found in the *loci classici* that every critic quotes: the description of the perfect courtier, l. 717 ff., voicing the poet's enthusiasm for the ideal; and the description of the suitor's life, which is charged with such deep resentment and bitter indignation that many readers have felt that it must commemorate the poet's own experience.

REFERENCES

Alden, R. M. *The Rise of Formal Satire in England.* Philadelphia, 1899; 74 ff.

Gollancz, I. *Spenseriana.* Proceedings of the British Academy, 1907–1908; 99 ff.

Greenlaw, Edwin. *Spenser and the Earl of Leicester.* Publications of the Modern Language Association, XXV (1910), 535–561.

Greenlaw, Edwin. *The Sources of Spenser's "Mother Hubberd's Tale."* Modern Philology, II (1905), 411 ff.

Greenlaw, Edwin. *The Influence of Machiavelli on Spenser.* Modern Philology, VII (1909), 187 ff.

Long, P. W. *Spenser and the Bishop of Rochester.* Publications of the Modern Language Association, XXXI (1916), 725 ff.

Padelford, F. M. *Spenser and the Puritan Propaganda.* Modern Philology, XI (1913), 100 ff.

Russell, I. Willis. *Biblical Echoes in Mother Hubberds Tale.* Modern Language Notes, XLIV (1929), 162–164.

CHAPTER IX

THE RUINES OF ROME

ALTHOUGH there has been some disposition to deny Spenser's authorship of this translation of Du Bellay's *Antiquitez de Rome,* it is now generally accepted as authentic. It probably belongs to the same period as the translation of Du Bellay's *Songe,* which in the original is a sequel to the *Antiquitez;* that is to say, the translation was in all likelihood made when Spenser was still a University student. It has been argued that an allusion in the *Envoy* to Du Bartas's *Sepmaines* makes necessary a later dating, since the *Sepmaines* was not published until 1579; but "heavenly Muse," as Mr. Renwick points out, alludes rather to *L'Uranie,* a work of the poet's youth. Further this original sonnet might have been added long after the translation was completed.

In producing his translation, Spenser did not adhere to the metrical form of his original. The sonnets of the *Antiquitez* are of the Italian type, observing the division of octave and sestet and rhyming abba abba ccd eed (or, ede).[1] For this Spenser has substituted the Elizabethan form, consisting of three unlinked quatrains with alternating rhyme followed by a couplet—abab cdcd efef gg. The only exception to this rule is the Envoy, in which

[1] The sestet of the sonnet translated by Du Bellay from Castiglione rhymes cd cd ee.

according to the Italian practice there is a shifted point of view after the eighth line and in which the rhyme arrangement is partly Elizabethan and partly Spenserian.

Spenser's translation, though often competent, is not always accurate. Koeppel thought it showed a rather superficial acquaintance with French. In evidence he pointed out the following mistranslations:—
Sonnet I:—

> Trois fois cernant sous le voile des cieux
> De voz tombeaux le tour devotieux,
> A haulte voix trois fois je vous appelle.

Spenser:—

> Thrice having seene, under the heavens veale,
> Your toombs devoted compasse over all,
> Thrice unto you with lowd voyce I appeale.

Here the word *cernant* which means surrounding is mistranslated *having seen*. There is a curious misunderstanding in the second line of Sonnet II:—

> Le Babylonien ses haults murs vantera
> Et ses vergers en l'air.

Spenser renders this:

> Great Babylon her haughtie walls will praise,
> And sharped steeples high shot up in ayre.

As a result of confusing the verb *feindre* (to simulate) with *fendre* (to cleave) he gives a ridiculous translation of the following passage from Sonnet XVII:—

> Alors on vid la corneille Germaine
> Se deguisant feindre l'aigle Romaine
> Et vers le ciel s'elever de rechef.

Spenser's translation reads:—

> Then was the Germane Raven in disguise
> That Romane Eagle seene to cleave asunder,
> And towards heaven freshly to arise.

A failure to understand the syntax of his original leads to another queer translation of a passage in Sonnet XI, alluding to the disappearance of the Goths after they had destroyed Rome. The French runs:—

> Ce peuple adonc, nouveau fils de la Terre,
> Dardant par tout les fouldres de la guerre,
> Ces braves murs accabla sous sa main,
> Puis se perdit dans le sein de sa mere.

For this we find in the English version:—

> Then gan that nation, th'earths new giant brood,
> To dart abroad the thunder bolts of warre,
> And, beating downe these walls with furious mood
> Into her mothers bosome, all did marre.

A further comparison of Spenser's sonnets with their French originals will reveal similar mistranslations elsewhere; e. g. in Sonnets XVII, XXII, and XXVIII.

Together with the *Visions of Bellay,* the *Ruines of Rome* deserves our attention because of the evidence it offers of Spenser's poetic sympathy for a prominent member of the *Pléiade.* In another connection it has been pointed out that the English poet also came under the influence of Du Bellay's *Deffence et Illustration,* which was accepted as the authoritative manifesto of the new movement in French poetry. However, Du Bellay was more personal than partisan and, in spite of his *Deffence,* not the most representative member of the group to which he belonged. It was his rich vein of romantic sentiment that must have attracted the youthful Spenser. However early and imperfect the translations, they show a significant tendency in the development of the poet's taste, which was catholic enough to relish poets so strikingly dissimilar as Du Bellay and Marot.

REFERENCES

Koeppel, E. *Ueber die Echtheit der Edmund Spenser Zuge-schriebenen "Visions of Petrarch" und "Visions of Bellay."* Englische Studien, XV (1891), 74 ff.

CHAPTER X

MUIOPOTMOS

IN a letter of exceptional ardour, Spenser has dedicated his *Muiopotmos* or *The Fate of the Butterflie* to Lady Carey, whom as Charillis [1] in *Colin Clouts Come Home Again* he had called

> the paragone
> Of peerless price, and ornament of praise,
> Admyr'd of all, yet envied of none,
> Through the myld temperance of her goodly raies,

Further on, in language touched with Platonism, he addresses her as

> the pride and primrose of the rest,
> Made by the Maker selfe to be admired,
> And like a goodly beacon high addrest,
> That is with sparks of heavenlie beautie fired.

Taking together the rhetoric of the letter and of the passage just quoted, we may conclude that Spenser's relations with Elizabeth Carey were closer than with either

---

[1] An alternative identification is with Phyllis, "the eldest of the three." As a matter of fact Lady Carey was the eldest of the three sisters; but, on the other hand, Charillis is a transparent anagram for Elizabeth (Elisa) Carey.

of the other two daughters of Sir John Spenser whom he has honored in his verse. It should be noted, too, that Elizabeth like her sisters was in the way of literary associations. Her husband was the Lord Chamberlain, whose company of players, once the company of his brother-in-law Lord Strange, included no less a person than William Shakespeare. This situation makes more than likely an acquaintance between the two greatest poets of the century.

In the volume of *Complaints* the *Muiopotmos* shares with the *Teares of the Muses* and *Mother Hubberds Tale* the distinction of a separate title page. This bears the date 1590, whereas the other title pages, including that for the volume as a whole, are dated 1591. We may conclude, then, that *Muiopotmos* was published before the other *Complaints*. There is reason to suppose, further, that it was united with *Visions of the Worlds Vanitie, Visions of Bellay,* and *Visions of Petrarch* to make a single booklet. It is not only that this group of four poems, like the other sections of the volume, fills a multiple of four pages, but it is definitely unified by repeated dedications to Lady Carey. First of all her name appears on the title-page, and, then, to her is addressed the ardent letter of dedication. Again, she is addressed in the concluding lines of the first sonnet of *Visions of the Worlds Vanitie* and finally in the last sonnet of the volume. The circumstance that this final sonnet appears without number and by itself on the last printed page of the Quarto edition seems to mean that it is in effect not the concluding sonnet of *Visions of Petrarch* but the Envoy of the whole book or more probably of the *Muiopotmos* booklet.

Whatever the time and circumstances of its publication,

Muiopotmos has lent itself to a variety of interpretations. There are those, like Palgrave, who have found in the poem only the delicate play of the poet's fancy. They infer from its lightness of touch that it has no deeper meaning than what appears on its surface. Since, however, Spenser's other epyllion, *Virgils Gnat,* is certainly allegorical, and since in the concluding words of his letter to Lady Carey he begs her to make of all things "a milde construction," it seems likely that, however delicate the threads of his fancy, he has woven in *Muiopotmos* a fabric of personal or political allegory.

Recognizing the probability that the poem has some ulterior meaning, Lowell and others have identified Clarion, the butterfly, with the poet himself, calling attention to the propriety of the symbol for a genius so ethereal, so much at home as Spenser's in the wide regions of the air. If one agrees with Dr. Long that the lady of the *Amoretti* is Elizabeth Carey, one might be tempted to accept his identification of her with Aragnoll. This would certainly have required of her "a milde construction"; but we should not forget that the poet of the *Amoretti* and sonneteers generally were in the habit of calling their ladies hard names. An alternative and more chivalrous reading of the riddle of *Muiopotmos* shifts the rôles as assigned above, making Spenser the spider and his mistress the butterfly. This latter interpretation receives some support from Sonnet LXXI, the theme of which is stated in the opening lines:—

> I joy to see how, in your drawen work,
> Your selfe unto the bee ye doe compare,
> And me unto the spyder, that doth lurke
> In close awayt to catch her unaware.

Where the personal allegory of *Muiopotmos* has been abandoned, a political interpretation has sometimes been attempted. The conjecture has been ventured that its theme is the relations between Leicester and Burghley,—that Leicester is the butterfly caught in the toils of the spider, Burghley. More plausibly it has been argued that the poem treats in allegory the well-known feud between Essex and Raleigh, of which Spenser would certainly have heard during Sir Walter's visit to Ireland. The opening stanzas of the poem may be cited in support of this view, unless these are to be interpreted merely as illustrations of its mock-heroic style. The strife between the two was, indeed, "a deadly dolorous debate betwixt two mightie ones of great estate." According to this theory, Clairon represents Raleigh and may take his name from the house of Clare with which some supposed that Raleigh was connected. The gay gardens in which the butterfly makes his home are then the court, and Clarion's brilliant wings and elaborate armor represent the sumptuous tastes of the mighty lord. Aragnoll, on the other hand, is Essex, symbolizing fittingly in the eyes of Raleigh's friends the envy of the Essex party that was focussed upon the Queen's favorite and that sought to destroy him.

Still another theory is that *Muiopotmos* deals with the Sidney-Oxford feud of 1579. This famous quarrel, which came to a head when Oxford publicly insulted Sir Philip on the tennis courts, may have been of large political significance. The two men belonged to hostile political factions. Oxford, the son-in-law of Burghley, was attached to the party favorable to France. On the other side, was the Leicester-Sidney group opposed to the Lord Chancellor in both his foreign and domestic policies. Sidney, it seems, was caught in the web of intrigue. If so, we may suppose that the weaver of the web was Burghley, and that therefore Aragnoll should be identified with the Lord Chancellor rather than with his son-in-law.

All of this ingenious speculation has its legitimate interest; but it would seem that we are as far as ever from solving the puzzle of the *Muiopotmos*. From the probably insoluble problem of its personal or political allegory, we may turn to the more vital question of its art. Upon the recurring themes of *Complaints*—the vicissitudes of fortune or the vanity of human wishes—we have here a charming variation. Opposed, on the one hand, to the overwrought rhetoric of the *Ruines of Time* and the *Teares of the Muses,* and, on the other hand, to the middle style of *Mother Hubberds Tale* and *Colin Clouts Come Home Againe, Muiopotmos,* like *Virgils Gnat,* shows a *délicatesse* and refinement of delineation which marks the genius of Spenser as, in this case, significantly Alexandrian. Accepting without question the *Culex* as Virgil's and producing in *Muiopotmos* an original work in the same kind, Spenser must have been conscious of extending his discipleship to the master. In the descriptions of *Muiopotmos* Spenser has advanced far beyond the art of the emblem books, represented by the *Visions.* The fine etching and delicate brush-work of *Muiopotmos* remind us of *Culex;* but here the play of fancy is freer, the touch at once lighter and surer, and we mark a fineness and richness of texture to which the other poem can lay no claim. Here and there, as in certain passages of the *Faerie Queene,* the *Muiopotmos* seems to take wing and "raine in th' aire from earth to highest skie" :—

The woods, the rivers, and the medowes green,
With his aire-cutting wings he measured wide,
Ne did he leave the mountaines bare unseene,
Nor the ranke grassie fennes delights untride.

For the pictures fashioned by Arachne and Pallas Spenser drew upon Ovid. To the description of Minerva's design in the *Metamorphoses* he has added the detail of the butterfly in order to account for the enmity between Clarion and Aragnoll. Then, he originated the pretty myth of Clarion, taking some suggestion perhaps from the Cupid-Psyche legend. The way in which he expanded his source may be illustrated by the following parallels. Describing the Rape of Europa, Ovid wrote:—

Mæonis elusam designat imagine tauri
Europen: verum taurum, freta vera putares.
Ipsa videbatur terras spectare relictas,
Et comites clarare suas, tactumque vereri
Assilientis aquae; timidasque reducere plantas.

These five lines Spenser has amplified into two stanzas and in a third added, according to the conventional pattern of mediæval tapestries,

a faire border wrought of sundrie flowres,
Enwoven with an yvie winding trayle.

Enlarging upon the sketch of Ovid he has stressed the timidity of Europa looking upon "a wilde wilderness of waters deepe," and has added the figures of Love and his brother Sport,

light fluttering
Upon the waves, as each had been a dove.

. . . .
. . . .

And manie Nymphes about them flocking round,
And manie Tritons, which their hornes did sound.

REFERENCES

Draper, J. W. *Spenserian Biography; a Note on the Vagaries of Scholarship.* The Colonnade. N. Y., 1922.

Emerson, O. F. *Spenser, Lady Carey, and the Complaints Volume.* Publications of the Modern Language Association, XXXII (1917), 306 ff.

Grierson, H. J. C. *Spenser's "Muiopotmos."* Modern Language Review, XVII (1922), 409 ff.

Hurlbert, Viola B. *A New Interpretation of Spenser's "Muiopotmos."* Studies in Philology, XXV, 128 ff.

Long, P. W. *Spenesr's "Muiopotmos."* Modern Language Review, IX (1914), 457 ff.

Lyons, Jessie M. *Spenser's Muiopotmos as an Allegory.* Publications of the Modern Language Association, XXXI (1916), 90 ff.

CHAPTER XI

VISIONS OF THE WORLDS VANITIE

IN several cases Spenser added to a translation from foreign literature an original work of a similar kind. For example, he has left us besides his version of Du Bellay's *Antiquitez* his own *Ruines of Time,* and to match his translation of the Virgilian *Culex* he produced his *Muiopotmos.* Similarly, along with his *Visions of Bellay* and *Visions of Petrarch* goes the original *Visions of the Worlds Vanitie.*

The date of composition of Spenser's *Visions* cannot be definitely determined. The fact that they are cast in the Spenserian sonnet form in preference to the looser Elizabethan form of the other *Visions* has suggested to some commentators a relatively late date. We should not forget, however, that Spenser had already used the linked quatrains in the dedicatory sonnet to *Virgils Gnat,* which was certainly written before Leicester's death in 1588. Rhetorically there is certainly nothing in *Visions of the Worlds Vanitie* to suggest late composition.

The theme of the *Visions* is the power of the weak to injure and, in the case of one sonnet (XI), to serve the mighty. For example, the little gadfly makes the big bull miserable, the sword-fish vexes the Leviathan, and the worm brings the lofty cedar to decay. Conversely, the goose saved the Roman empire, as a gnat in the *Culex* saved a man from a serpent. As in the translated *Visions,* the art here is obviously that of the emblem-books with their set, moralized descriptions answering to the simple lines of the accompanying wood-cuts. The comparison in the case of this series is particularly pertinent in view of the obvious indebtedness of two sonnets, those describing the Scarabee and the Remora, to the well-known emblem-book of Alciati. Perhaps the chief interest of the naïvely imaged didacticism of the *Visions* is to be found in their relation to the richer moralized art of the *Faerie Queene.*

REFERENCES

Green, Henry. *Shakespeare and the Emblem Writers.* London, 1870.

CHAPTER XII

THE VISIONS OF BELLAY AND THE VISIONS OF PETRARCH FORMERLY TRANSLATED

A T the close of *Complaints* come translations by Spenser
from Du Bellay's *Songe* and from Marot's translation of Petrarch's sixth canzone in twelve-line stanzas in
Morte di Madonna Laura. The first work was published
by Du Bellay with the *Antiquitez de Rome,* also, as we
have seen, translated by Spenser, the volume bearing the
title, *Le premier livre des Antiquitez de Rome contenant
une générale description de sa grandeur, et comme une dé-
ploration de sa ruine. . . . Plus un Songe ou Vision sur le
mesme subject.* Du Bellay's *Songe,* like his *Antiquitez,*
was a series of Italian sonnets, and Marot's rendering of
Petrarch, from which Spenser translated, preserved the
twelve-line stanzas of the Italian original.

Now it seems highly probable that these poems as published in *Complaints* give us a revision of an earlier
draft. In the case of the *Visions of Petrarch,* its title
as printed certainly points to this conclusion; since "formerly translated" is most easily interpreted as translated
before by the author himself. Furthermore, we find English translations of almost all these *Visions* in a book published in London in 1569. The full title of this work is:
*A Theatre, wherein be represented as wel the miseries
and calamities that follow the voluptuous worldlings as*

also the greate joyes and plesures which the faithful do enjoy. An argument both profitable and delectable to all that sincerely love the Word of God. Devised by S. John vander Noodt. This title at once invites comparison with that of Spenser's volume.

Apart from the German version of 1572, which need not here concern us, the *Theatre* was published in three successive editions, the first two during the year 1568 in Flemish and French respectively. The third, which appeared the year following and of which the title has just been given, was in English. The book, or perhaps more exactly speaking the pamphlet, consisted in the first edition chiefly of translations into Flemish of Du Bellay's *Songe* and Petrarch's sixth canzone. To these van der Noot added four sonnets of his own composition inspired by the *Book of Revelations* and dealing with the approaching ruin of the Great Babylon. As in the case of the *Shepheardes Calender,* the poem is furnished with woodcuts and a commentary of about a hundred pages, which explains the visions and denounces the Roman Church. Closely following this Flemish edition of the *Theatre,* appeared one in French dedicated to Roger Martens, Lord Mayor of London, and prefaced with a very flattering letter addressed to Queen Elizabeth. In this edition we find Du Bellay's text of the *Songe* and Marot's version of Petrarch which he called *Epigrammes.* Then in the next year followed the English edition, in which most critics think that Spenser had a hand. It was published by Henry Bynneman, who in 1580 was to be the publisher also of the Spenser-Harvey correspondence. One Théodore Roest was professedly the translator; and he declared that his translation was from the Flemish text. So far as the

Visions or *Epigrammes* of Petrarch are concerned, investigation has shown that they are based upon the French text of Marot. It is not unlikely, however, that the translator or some one supervising the translation consulted occasionally the Flemish and the original Italian versions.

It should be remarked at this point that the maker of the *Theatre for Worldlings,* Jonker Jan van der Noot, was a poet of note. Besides the book with which we are here concerned he wrote a poetic miscellany entitled *Bocage,* which he dedicated to the Marquis of Northampton; the Marchioness of Northampton, it should here be recalled, is probably the Mansilia of Spenser's *Colin Clout.* A more ambitious work of van der Noot's is the *Olympiade,* which, as an allegory of the moral life, is not without its interest for students of the *Faerie Queene.* Born in 1539 or 1540 at Brecht near Antwerp into a family of much distinction, van der Noot took refuge in England, when about twenty-seven years old, from Spanish persecution in the Netherlands. His Protestant zeal was the inspiration of the *Theatre,* as was Spenser's of the *Shepheardes Calender.* The pride, which in the *Visions* comes before destruction, is turned to the account of anti-Catholic propaganda in the commentary; for to his and Spenser's Protestant thinking there was no pride like that of Rome.

There is now a rather general disposition to credit the youthful Spenser with the English translations of the *Visions* in the third edition of the *Theatre for Worldlings.* The versions published in *Complaints* would then be revisions of these early drafts. Professor Koeppel, indeed, after comparing the two sets of translations, arrived at a contrary opinion. He argued that the translations in the earlier publication showed a more exact knowledge of French than those later published; and that, therefore, they could not be accepted as Spenser's first draft. In answer to this criticism it is urged that the literalness of the early versions and the freedom of the later have been over-stressed; but, conceding the point of difference, we may contend with Professor Dodge that the work of the youthful translator would have been "supervised to secure accuracy." It is certain that the two renderings have more similarities than would be absolutely insured by a common original. Professor Friedland, who after a careful consideration of the whole matter was convinced of Spenser's authorship of the *Theatre* versions, notes the likeness between other translations by Spenser—his renderings of Du Bellay's *Antiquitez de Rome* and of four Du Bellay sonnets omitted by van der Noot but included in *Complaints*—and those which he is thought to have done for van der Noot's volume. We find in each case the same inversions, transpositions, expansions, and shortenings of phrase. However, as Professor Friedland sensibly observes, "it is as certain as it is natural that Spenser's later work in translation should show signs of a more elastic conception of the translator's art, should abound not in inaccuracies or perversions of sense, but in liberties demanded in great part by the stern exigencies of metrical form." It is, indeed, important to remember, as affecting the translations, the metrical differences between the earlier and the later renderings. In the case of the six *Epigrams* of the *Theatre,* Spenser, except in visions one and three, preserves the twelve-line stanza of his original; in the exceptional cases by adding a couplet he achieves two Elizabethan sonnets. This early version preserves, too, the original Envoy, consisting of two couplets. In what we regard as the later versions for *Complaints,* all of the visions are regular Elizabethan sonnets and a Spenserian sonnet takes the place of the Envoy. In the case of the *Visions of Bellay* the unrhymed quatorzains of the *Theatre* were all transformed into Elizabethan sonnets and there were added translations of four sonnets of Du Bellay (Nos. 6, 8, 13, 14) not represented in the original publication.

The literary form illustrated in the *Visions of Bellay* and the *Visions of Petrarch* is compounded of those didactic and descriptive elements that reappear in varied combinations throughout the whole compass of Spenser's poetry. The modest art of the *Visions* has, however, its special character. It is the art of the emblem books, in which from Alciati on the moralizing poet of the Renaissance enlisted, as in the *Theatre for Worldlings* and the *Shepheardes Calender,* the services of the engraver in wood. These picture books of the moralists enjoyed a great popularity. Of Alciati's *Emblems* alone 150 editions appeared between 1531 and 1621. The set descriptions of such books, of a piece with their conventional moralizing on the vicissitudes of fortune and the fall of the mighty, are well represented in Spenser's translations and in his original *Visions of the Worlds Vanitie.* The traditional themes of course lent themselves to the melancholy mood as well as to the moralizing tone, as for example in the *Ruines of Rome* or where Spenser following Petrarch laments the passing of such visions of beauty as the woodland spring to which Muses and nymphs resorted to attune their voices to the water's fall (*Visions of Petrarch,* IV). Here is obviously a care for beauty as well as a regard for moral truth. The note of melancholy becomes dominant in the final sonnet which Spenser substituted for the original Envoy. This poem, following upon the Visions, shows how easy was the transition for a man like Spenser from moralism to romantic melancholy.

REFERENCES

Fletcher, J. B. *Spenser and the Theatre of Worldlings.* Modern Language Notes, XIII (1898), 409 ff.

Fletcher, J. B. *Spenser's Earliest Translations.* Journal of English and Germanic Philology, XIII (1914), 305 ff.

Friedland, L. S. *Spenser's Earliest Translations.* Journal of English and Germanic Philology, XII (1913), 449–470.

Galland, René. *Un Poète Errant de la Renaissance, Jean Van der Noot et l'Angleterre.* Revue de Littérature Comparée, II (1922), 337 ff.

Koeppel, E. *Ueber die Echtheit der Edmund Spenser Zugeschriebenen "Visions of Petrarch" und "Visions of Bellay."* Englische Studien, XV (1891), 53 ff.

Koeppel, E. *Ueber die Echtheit der Edmund Spenser Zugeschriebenen "Visions of Petrarch" und "Visions of Bellay."* Englische Studien, XXVII (1900), 100 ff.

Pienaar, W. J. B. *Edmund Spenser and Janker van der Noot,* English Studies (Amsterdam), VIII (1926), 33–44; 67–76.

CHAPTER XIII

THE FAERIE QUEENE

IT is in a letter from Spenser to Harvey dated April,
1580, that we first learn of the *Faerie Queene*. The
sentence in question reads as follows: "Nowe, my *Dreames*
and *Dying Pellicane* being fully finished (as I partelye
signified in my last letters) and presentlye to be imprinted,
I wil in hande forthwith with my *Faery Queene,* whyche
I praye you hartily send with al expedition, and your
frendly letters, and long expected judgement withal,
whyche let not be shorte, but in all pointes such as you
ordinarilye use and I extraordinarily desire." With reference to this passage Harvey in his letter of reply wrote :—
"In good faith, I had once again nigh forgotten your
Faerie Queene: howbeit, by good chaunce, I have nowe
sent hir home at the laste, neither in better nor worse
case than I founde hir. And must you of necessitie have
my judgement of hir in deede? To be plaine, I am voyde
of al judgement, if your *Nine Comœdies* . . . come not
neerer Ariostoes comœdies, eyther for the finenesse of
plausible elocution, or the rareness of poetical invention,
than that *Elvish Queene* doth to his *Orlando Furioso,*
which, notwithstanding, you wil needes seeme to emulate,
and hope to overgo, as you flatly professed your self in
one of your last letters. . . . If so be the Faerye Queene
be fairer in your eye than the Nine Muses, and Hobgoblin

runne away with the garland from Apollo, marke what I saye: and yet I will not say that I thought, but there an end for this once, and fare you well, till God or some good aungell putte you in a better minde."

From the above it is clear that the great work, of which the first instalment was not to appear until ten years later, was already under way in the spring of 1580, and that while it was still in its initial stages it elicited from the classicist Harvey, engaged at the moment in reviving classical meters, a kind of opinion which was to be echoed in much subsequent criticism, and in which, indeed, there centered a critical war in sixteenth-century Italy. A critic of classical tastes like Minturno felt in much the same way about Ariosto's *Orlando Furioso* as Gabriel Harvey did about Spenser's *Faerie Queene*. It was a Renaissance battle of the books.

Over against Harvey's criticism of the *Faerie Queene* should be set first of all Spenser's plan as explained by himself. The first explanation of the kind we find in a book written by Lodowick Bryskett entitled *A Discourse of Civill Life*. This work, not published until 1606 but written before 1589, and ostensibly reporting the conversation of a party of military men and civilians including Spenser at Bryskett's cottage in Ireland, is largely based upon Giraldi Cinthio's *Tre Dialoghi*. The passage of particular interest to students of Spenser is that, already quoted, in which the poet, after having declined to speak on moral philosophy, offered as his reason that he had already "undertaken a work tending to the same effect, which is in heroical verse, under the title of a *Faerie Queene,* to represent all the moral virtues, assigning to every virtue a knight to be the patron and defender of the same: in whose

actions and feats of armes and chivalry the operations of
that virtue whereof he is the protector are to be expressed,
and the vices and unruly appetites that oppose themselves
against the same to be beaten down and overcome. Which
work," he concludes, "I have already well entered into."
A quotation from Book II, Canto IV in Abraham
Fraunce's *Arcadian Rhetorike,* issued in 1588, offers further proof that the *Faerie Queene* before publication was
in circulation among the poet's friends.

The sketch of Spenser's plan which is found in Bryskett's *Discourse* was elaborated in *A Letter of the Authors
addressed to Sir Walter Raleigh,* "expounding his whole
intention in the course of this worke." Bearing the date
January, 1589 (new style, 1590), this letter was evidently
written while the first three Books of the *Faerie Queene*
were going through the press. Accordingly, it first appears
with the Commendatory Verses and the Dedicatory Sonnets at the close of the volume of 1590. The famous letter
may be properly regarded as Spenser's defence of the
romanzi against the conventional classical attack implicit
in Harvey's comment and elaborated in Trissino's criticism
of Ariosto's *Orlando Furioso.* The lines of his defence
are in part similar to those laid down by such apologists
of romance as Giraldi Cinthio, who in 1549 wrote his
Discorso intorno al comparre dei Romanzi. With Spenser's declared "general end of all the book," namely, "to
fashion a gentleman or noble person in vertuous and gentle
discipline," we may compare Cinthio's position that the
purpose of the *romanzi* is to teach "good morals and honest living." Of the three types of heroic poem distinguished by Cinthio,—the poem imitating one action of one
man, that is, the epic as described by Aristotle; that imitat-

ing many actions of many men, such as the romances of Boiardo and Ariosto; and that dealing with many actions of one man, or a biographical poem like the *Theseid*—the *Faerie Queene,* taken as a whole, belongs to the second class, but in its several books it illustrates class three. For its episodic character still further authority might have been found in Scaliger and Trissino, both of whom maintained that such a collection of stories as we have in the Decameron might constitute a complete epic. Spenser stresses the biographical interest of the *Faerie Queene* when in the letter to Raleigh he compares his poem with the *Cyropædia* of Xenophon. With the biographical form Cinthio was in special sympathy as we may see in his *Ercole,* published in 1557.

With respect to his subject, the unity of his action, and the characters of his story, Spenser found further support in the critical doctrine of his time. For example, the proper subject of an heroic poem, Tasso maintained, was one neither too ancient nor too modern; and he had particularly recommended the times of Charlemagne and Arthur as offering subjects most suitable for heroic poetry; they were neither too near at hand to be familiar nor so far away as to be absolutely alien in manners and customs. Further, the advantage of a Christian subject for Christian readers is that it preserves the element of the miraculous without losing the effect of verisimilitude. In the matter of the persons of the story, Spenser evidently has in mind Aristotle's prescription, echoed by Tasso, to the effect that the epic hero should illustrate a type of virtue, as Æneas, piety, and Ulysses, prudence; for he plans to make twelve knights the patrons respectively of twelve virtues. As to the action, the critical question was that of its unity. Although in this connection the wording of the letter to Raleigh is not explicit, it seems probable that Spenser, following Aristotle's requirement, planned to limit the action of the *Faerie Queene* to a single year, so that with the return of the annual feast of the Queen the twelve several adventures of the twelve days would have been achieved, and the stage thus cleared for the politic virtues, whose fortunes he planned tentatively to make the theme of the second half of his poem. Regarding the several books as biographical—answering to the type of story that recounts many actions of one man—Spenser, following the prescription of Horace, plunges *in medias res,* a procedure which he also follows and indeed explicitly justifies for the work as a whole.

Aristotle's view of the characters in an heroic poem and the doctrine of Horace that all poetry should be both useful and pleasant opened the way for the type of allegorical epic that we have in the *Faerie Queene.* "To some, I know," writes Spenser in the letter to Raleigh, "this methode will seeme displeasaunt, which had rather have good discipline delivered plainly in way of precepts, or sermoned at large, as they use, then thus clowdily enwrapped in allegoricall devises." And yet there were definite reasons in critical theory for his dark conceits. According to Sir John Harrington, in his Preface to the Translation of the *Orlando Furioso,* published in 1591, "men of greatest learning and highest wit in the auncient times did of purpose conceale these deepe mysteries of learning and, as it were, cover them with the vaile of fables and verse"; these so covered their thought "that they might not be rashly abused by prophane wits in whom science is corrupted, like good wine in a bad vessel"; but "a principall cause of all, is to be able with one kinde of meate and one dish (as I may so call it) to feed divers tastes. For the weaker capacities will feede themselves with the pleasantnes of the historie and sweetnes of the verse, some that have stronger stomaches will as it were take a further taste of the Morall sence, a third sort, more high conceited than they, will digest the Allegorie: so as indeed it hath been thought by men of verie good judgement, such manner of Poeticall writing was an excellent way to preserve all kinde of learning from that corruption which now it is come to since they left that mysticall writing of verse."

The narrative art of the *Faerie Queene,* thus finding some support in the theory of the heroic epic, quite clearly imitates no single model. Whatever impressions Spenser may create by mentioning in his letter to Raleigh the famous classical and Italian epics, his art is prevailingly that of neither Homer, Virgil, nor Ariosto. Varying from book to book it seems to result from a complex of influences. It is reminiscent of the biographical romances of chivalry, reminding one particularly of the narrative patterns of the *pèlèrinage* and the quest. While Books III and IV are in the manner of the episodic *romanzi* as illustrated by Ariosto, Book VI in part is like the Arcadian romance as illustrated by Sidney. In view of the moralizing stanzas which introduce many cantos of the *Faerie Queene,* one can but think, too, of the *sententia* and *exemplum* of the mediæval rhetoric. Indeed, from one point of view the *Faerie Queene* may be regarded as an exemplum-book of chivalry, within the loose framework of which the poet permitted himself a variety of narrative forms.

The support which Spenser had found in the theory of the classical and Italian epic for his conceptions of plot and character in the *Faerie Queene,* he discovers in Aristotle's *Nicomachean Ethics* for its underlying ethical philosophy. "I labour," he writes, "to pourtraict in Arthure, before he was king, the image of a brave knight, perfected in the twelve private morall vertues, as Aristotle hath devised, the which is the purpose of these first twelve bookes." Further on in the letter he declares: "in the person of Prince Arthure I sette forth magnificence in particular, which vertue, for that (according to Aristotle and the rest) it is the perfection of all the rest, and conteineth in it them all, therefore in the whole course I mention the deedes of Arthure applyable to that vertue which I write of in that booke. But of the xii. other vertues I make xii. other knights the patrones, for the more variety of the history."

The difficulty raised by Mr. Jusserand with respect to the number of Aristotle's virtues as given by Spenser need not disturb us if we are careful to note that Spenser recognizes, not twelve as Mr. Jusserand states, but thirteen Aristotelian virtues. Having mentioned magnificence, set forth in the person of Arthur, he adds, "but of the xii. *other vertues,* I make xii. other knights the patrones, for the more variety of the history." In Aristotle a total of thirteen has been arrived at by adding justice to the twelve virtues enumerated in Book II, chapter VIII; and, again, by omitting from that list "the mean concerning ambition," as not sufficiently distinguished from high-mindedness, and adding continence or ἐγκράτεια described in Book II.

A more important question than that of twelve or thirteen virtues in Aristotle is one of the correspondence in particular between the six virtues actually celebrated by Spenser and similar ones to be found in the *Nicomachean Ethics*. Reserving for later chapters a fuller consideration of the virtues of the *Faerie Queene,* we may here admit a few brief explanations. [At the outstart Holiness obviously presents a difficulty. This may be met, in accordance with the suggestion of Miss Winstanley, by considering it a Christian version of Aristotle's Manliness, this taken, however, not in Aristotle's restricted sense of courage in war but in the more inclusive Platonic sense of moral courage, the foundation of all the other virtues; or we may regard Holiness, with Dr. DeMoss, as a Christian version of the Aristotelian Highmindedness. As compared with the other books, Book II is most patently Aristotelian, giving in the second Canto an allegorical version of Aristotle's central doctrine of the Golden Mean. Its titular virtue, Temperance, corresponds to both σωφροσύνη and ἐγκράτεια in Aristotle—or, as we might say, Temperance and Continence. For Book III, the Book of Chastity, Spenser seems to make a distinction between the two, his Chastity corresponding to σωφροσύνη or temperance. [However, here as elsewhere, Spenser's Aristotelianism has its Platonic leanings. As Miss Winstanley observes, Spenser "improves upon the somewhat cold theme of the Aristotelian ethics by drawing on the inspiration of Plato; his Chastity is really Plato's ideal and noble love—the love born of the Uranian Aphrodite." Accordingly, Britomart, unlike Sir Guyon, is never tempted, and her virtue, as compared with that of the hero of Book II, is positive and constructive. The virtue of the Fourth Book, Friendship, in both Aristotle and Spenser is treated broadly enough to include both love and what is commonly denominated friendship. Next, Justice, in Spenser as in Aristotle, includes the subject of equity. Finally, Courtesy, though it exactly corresponds to nothing in Aristotle, may be related to the kindred Aristotelian virtues of Truthfulness and Gentleness. In general, it would seem that Spenser, while greatly indebted to Aristotle for general ideas and particular details, has used this source of his ethical philosophy with considerable independence, now freely combining Aristotle with Plato and again with Christianity.

In more than one way Spenser has assisted us in the interpretation of his ethical allegory. Very often he has given his characters such transparent names as Fradubio, Malecasta, and Furor; elsewhere, as with Care, Occasion, and Despair, it is not necessary even to translate the names, as is true also of the House of Holiness and the House of Pride. The reader is often enlightened, too, by the verse arguments prefixed to the several cantos and, again, by their opening stanzas, as in I. vii., st. 1. The special significance of Arthur in the ethical allegory should here be stressed. Since, says the letter to Raleigh, the virtue "magnificence," represented by Arthur, "is the perfection of all the rest and conteineth in it them all, therefore in the whole course I mention the deedes of Arthure applyable to that vertue which I write of in that booke." If Spenser has, indeed, carried out this idea, the ethical significance of Arthur will vary from book to book.

Turning from its ethical to its political allegory, students of the *Faerie Queene* are confronted by a bewildering variety of interpretations. The divergences are due in some measure to a lack of agreement upon the limits, chronological and geographical, within which the allegory may be said to apply. For example, early commentators sought the historical meaning of the first book in the early annals of the Christian Church, a contributor to *Notes and Queries* going so far as to suggest that the Red Cross Knight's adventures in Error's Den had reference to the rise of the Pelagian heresy in the fourth century. Similarly wild shots are taken in Keightley's commentary on the same book. For example, he identified the Lion with the Counts of Toulouse, and Sansloy with the papal adherents who under De Montfort and others overcame them. In the satyrs he detected the Waldenses, who lived in the woods and valleys of Switzerland, in Satyrane the Huguenots, and in Arthur British loyalty as illustrated by the House of Tudor.

Although more recent commentators have been disinclined to give the allegory of the *Faerie Queene* so wide a scope chronologically, they have sometimes been disposed, while keeping it within the sixteenth century, to make it more or less extensively European. In the case of Book V it is, of course, clear that we are dealing broadly with international affairs, and elsewhere there are more or less obvious allusions to continental conditions with which England was concerned. However, in explaining a book so professedly English as the "Legend of St. George," we may well hesitate to go so far afield as Professor Buck does in interpreting Sansloy's treatment of Una as the Duke of Alva's oppression of the Netherlands, in identifying the satyrs with the Beggars of the Sea, who defied the forces of Alva, and Satyrane with the Prince of Orange.

It is unlikely that all of the identifications in Spenser's

political allegory are personal. Granted that the Red Cross Knight carries a suggestion of Henry the Eighth and Una a suggestion of Elizabeth, they are first of all the English Church and the truth with which it seeks to be allied. In Book V the giant with the scales is by common agreement communism, and Orgoglio in Book I may be equated with the power of Rome, or more plausibly the might of Spain embodied in Philip II. Keightley was of the opinion that Arthur represents British loyalty and Upton thought that Sansfoy, Sansjoy, and Sansloy stood for different aspects of the Moslem power allied with the Catholic cause. The Blatant Beast has been thought by some commentators to symbolize intolerant Puritanism. Less convincing than such equations are the attempts to make the characters of the *Faerie Queene* correspond to different nations; as, for example, when the Lion is equated with the Netherlands (Howard), Sansloy with France (Buck), and the Squire of the Red Cross Knight's dream with Germany (Padelford).

Turning to Italy, as we have seen, for his theory of the romantic epic, it was from this quarter, also, that Spenser derived much material and many suggestions for the plot of the *Faerie Queene*. The passage already quoted from Harvey's letter and an allusion to the Italian poem in the letter to Raleigh direct us at once to a comparison with the *Orlando Furioso*. Harvey, it will be remembered, had remarked that Spenser's *Nine Comedies* came nearer to Ariosto's *Comedies* than the *Faerie Queene* did to his *Orlando Furioso,* "which, notwithstanding, you will needes seeme to emulate, and hope to overgo;" and, again, in the letter to Raleigh, comparing the Orlando of Ariosto with the Æneas of Virgil, Spenser had said that in each case the poet had united in his hero "a good governour and a virtuous man." From these quotations it becomes first of all clear that Spenser was sufficiently ambitious to match his genius with that of the greatest humanist poet of sixteenth-century Italy; and, in the second place, that in common with such critics of Ariosto as Fornari and Toscanella, Spenser was interested in what he supposed to be the underlying moral intention of the poem. In thus regarding the high seriousness of Ariosto, Spenser was, further, in agreement with Sir John Harrington, the English translator of the *Orlando Furioso.*

Ludovico Ariosto (1474–1533), who died about a score of years before Spenser was born, dedicated his genius to the honor of the Este, the ruling house of Ferrara. In so doing he was continuing the work of Matteo Maria Boiardo (1434–1494), "The Flower of Chivalry," who, as the author of *Orlando Innamorato,* was Ariosto's predecessor in the romantic epic. Quite similarly, Spenser, in the *Faerie Queene,* honors Elizabeth in particular and the House of Tudor in general; and just as the real hero and heroine of the *Orlando Furioso* are Ruggiero and Bradamante, the founders of the House of Este, so the chief interest in the *Faerie Queene* centers in Arthegall and Britomart, the ancestors of Elizabeth, rather than in Arthur and Gloriana. Such being the case, it is only natural that in the Arthegall-Britomart story Ariosto should be placed most heavily under contribution. Indeed, as Professor Dodge has remarked, "every point of the story has its counterpart in the *Furioso;* the correspondence from beginning to end is complete."

A detailed study in subsequent chapters of Spenser's debt to Ariosto will prove instructive of the divergent tastes and talents of the two poets. Here we need only touch upon this divergence in general terms. In the first place, it is manifest that what he borrowed from the *Orlando* Spenser has in a real sense made his own; so that every likeness to his original seems to illustrate a more significant difference. In almost every case it is clear that the English poet is concerned to maintain his prevailingly serious or spiritual tone, so that what is comic or obliquely ironic in Ariosto is grave and direct in Spenser. The rare instances in which the English poet carries over something of the comic spirit of his original, reveal a procedure which Professor Dodge has aptly described as "toning down." This, as will appear in the proper place, is well illustrated by a comparison of the Marfisa-Zerbino joust (O.F. XX, 106–129) with the duel between Blandamour and Braggadocchio. Here, whereas Ariosto develops to the full the comic possibilities of the situation, Spenser by leaving it unrealized characteristically preserves a balance of seriousness.

Though Spenser's art is thus in a sense more simple, it is not for that reason more passionate. The English poet seems rather to tone down the Italian's passion as well as his comedy. For example, as we shall see later, in a comparison of Bradamante with Britomart, Ariosto makes a woman's love-longing and jealousy much more accentual and real than Spenser does. And surely, too, where Ariosto's situation is thoroughly felt and clearly visualized, Spenser's will be vaguely conceived, much less circumstantial, and by no means so sharply etched.

A good oppotrunity of testing the differences between the Italian and the English poem is offered by Ariosto's device, not infrequently adopted by Spenser, of beginning a canto with certain general reflections which state or suggest its theme,—a kind of *sententia* followed by an *exemplum*. Compare, for example, the ironic tone of the following stanzas of Ariosto with the seriousness of the corresponding passage in Spenser:—

I

Ladies, and all of you that ladies prize,
Afford not, for the love of heaven, an ear
To this, the landlord's tale, replete with lies,
In shame and scorn of womankind; though ne'er
Was praise or fame conveyed in that which flies
From such caitiff's tongue: and still we hear
The sottish rabble all things rashly brand,
And question most what least they understand.

II

Omit this canto, and—the tale untold—
My story will as clear and perfect be;
I tell it, since by Turpin it is told,
And not in malice or in rivalry:
Besides, that never did my tongue withhold
Your praises, how you are beloved by me
To you I by a thousand proofs have shown,
Vouching I am, and can but be, your own.

(Canto XXVIII)

The corresponding passage of Spenser with which this passage should be compared consists of the first two stanzas of Book III, Canto IX of the *Faerie Queene*.

Although Spenser has borrowed more from Ariosto than from Tasso (1544–1595) it is to the latter's genius that his own is more nearly akin. The unfortunate author of *Rinaldo* and *Gerusalemme Liberata* was mentioned, it will be recalled, along with Ariosto in the letter to Raleigh. Speaking of epic characters, Spenser had there said that "the characters united by Ariosto in Orlando, Tasso dissevered againe, and formed both parts in two persons, namely that part which they in philosophy call *Ethice,* or vertues of a private man, coloured in his *Rinaldo;* the other named *Politice* in his *Goffredo.*" However, it is not in his treatment of the persons of his story that we particularly observe Tasso's influence upon Spenser. This is noticeable rather in his descriptive art and the prevailing tone of his poetry. "The skill and imagination of Tasso," wrote Henry Hallam in his *Literature of Europe,* "make him equal to descriptions of war; but his heart was formed for that sort of pensive voluptuousness which most distinguishes his poetry, and which is very unlike the coarser sensuality of Ariosto." As is equally true of Spenser's treatment of the Bower of Bliss, "Tasso," remarked Hallam, "lingers around the gardens of Armida as though he had been himself her thrall."

In a further passage that should interest students of Spenser's descriptive art, Hallam compares Tasso suggestively to the Bolognese painters :— "It is not easy," he writes, "to find a counterpart among painters for Ariosto. . . . But with Tasso the case is different; and though it would be an affected expression to call him the founder of the Bolognese school, it is evident that he had a great influence on its chief painters, who came but a little after him. . . . No one, I think, can consider their works without perceiving both the analogy of the place each holds in his respective art, and the traces of a feeling, caught directly from Tasso as their prototype and model. We recognize his spirit in the sylvan shades and voluptuous forms of Albano and Domenichino; in the pure beauty that radiates from the ideal heads of Guido; in the skilful composition, exact design, and noble expression of the Caracci." But for "the enchanting grace and diffused harmony of Tasso, we must look back to Correggio as his representative." Certainly, it is among these painters rather than, as has sometimes been suggested, in the work of Rubens, that we find a correspondence in the realm of art for Spenser's descriptive poetry.

For the framework of the *Faerie Queene,* Spenser could have derived nothing either from Ariosto or Tasso. In mediæval romance, on the other hand, he would have found suggestions for his plan. Morgan le Fay, it will be recalled, was a sister of Arthur; and many romantic stories, such as *Lanval* and *Ogier the Dane,* deal with communication between the fairy world and the land of mortals. The most famous of all fairy romances is *Huon of Bordeaux,* the plot of which, as we shall see, has been compared with that of the first book of the *Faerie Queene.* Among the characters in this romance is Oberon, the king of the fairy world. One might recall, further, the episode of the Gawain legend which tells of Arthur in Fairy Land receiving Renouart and pointing out to him Roland, Iwain, and Gawain. However, it seems most likely that the immediate suggestion for Spenser's scheme came to him not from the romances but from royal entertainments at Kenilworth and Woodstock. The complimentary show at Woodstock is particularly interesting in this connection because that pageant represents the feast of the Fairy Queen preceded by a knightly tournament. From this similar situation Spenser might be supposed to have elaborated the plan of his great pageant-like poem dedicated to Elizabeth.

No consideration of the *Faerie Queene* would be complete without some account of its metrical form, the so-called Spenserian stanza. This stanza is not, as commentators used to affirm, a variation of the Italian *ottava rima,* as employed by Ariosto and Tasso. The Italian measure running *ab ab ab cc,* indeed, concludes with a couplet on the third rhyme, but its rhyme arrangement varies after the middle of the stanza and it does not conclude with an Alexandrine. A more simple hypothesis, now generally accepted, derives the famous strophe from an old French eight-line ballad stanza rhyming *ababbcbc.* This, frequently employed in Middle English, Spenser would have known in Chaucer's *Monk's Tale.* The idea of varying it with a concluding couplet on the c-rhyme might have come to him from the *ottava rima,* the rhyme royal, or the common six-line stanza that he had used in the *Calender.* He might conceivably, too, have received a hint for his concluding Alexandrine from Sir Thomas More's varied rhyme-royal stanzas on the death of Elizabeth of York or from Ferrer's rhyme-royal with concluding Alexandrine in the *Princely Pleasures of Kenilworth.* If it seems too simple to say that it occurred independently to Spenser to add an Alexandrine to the octave of the *Monk's Tale,* we might accept Professor Skeat's explanation that "the Spenserian stanza resulted from a judicious combination of metres employed by the most obvious models, viz. Chaucer and Surrey." From Chaucer came the octave and from Surrey the idea of combining the Alexandrine with lines of different length.

Whatever might be the genesis of the Spenserian stanza, opinions have varied with respect to its propriety in the case of a long narrative poem like the *Faerie Queene*. Here eighteenth-century judgments have been echoed by many subsequent critics. Warton's objections in his famous *Observations on the Faerie Queene* may be regarded as typical. In his opinion an excessive recurrence of the second and third rhymes led the poet to dilate what he had to express, however unimportant, with trifling and tedious circumlocutions. When matter failed him at the end of a stanza he found it necessary "to run into a ridiculous redundancy and repetition of words," or under the necessity of "filling out his complement of rhymes to introduce a puerile or impertinent idea." On the other hand, he argued that in some cases the limits of the stanza were responsible for omissions. With the opinion of Warton, Upton, the editor of an early edition of Spenser, agrees. "Many a bad spelling," he writes, "many a lame thought and expression is he forced to introduce, merely for the sake of a jingling termination." To this view may be added the opinion of Dr. Johnson, who roundly denounced the Spenserian stanza as "at once difficult and unpleasing, tiresome to the ear by its uniformity and to the attention by its length."

To these pronouncements, which in substance are still often repeated, may be opposed more favorable and sympathetic criticism. In the Spenserian stanza, Lowell found "soothingness, indeed, but no slumberous monotony; for Spenser was no mere metrist, but a great composer. By the variety of his pauses—now at the close of the first or second foot, now of the third, and again of the fourth —he gives spirit and energy to a measure whose tendency it certainly is to become langourous." Professor Mackail's judgment, though not so favourable, recognizes some of the potentialities of the stanza which Spenser was able to realize. Though as a rule "faulty for narrative because it lacks speed," and though the thought and even the imagery at times "become exhausted before the end of the stanza is reached," it numbers among its striking effects a swelling rhythm up to the very end, as in II, xii, 71; a slow ebbing off, as in IV, ii, 34; or a sliding forward "with equable rhythms till near the end, and then, in the eighth and ninth lines, a rising into a great crescendo and storm of sound," as in II, viii, 37. But perhaps Professor Mackail's most interesting impression is that "normally and habitually the ninth line is felt coming through the whole stanza which implies it and converges upon it."

Criticism has, however, considered the stanza not simply by itself but in its sequence. When the story, some say, should be making rapid progress from stanza to stanza, it is arrested at regular intervals by the recurrent Alexandrines. Such an opinion we find expressed by John Hughes, the editor of the 1715 edition of Spenser. "Every stanza," he wrote, "made as it were a distinct paragraph, grows tiresome by continual repetition and frequently breaks the sense, when it ought to be carried on without interruption." Upon other critics the break between the stanzas has seemed to be less sharply marked. Lowell, for example, felt that one stanza was "forever longing and feeling forward after that which is to follow. Wave follows wave with equable gainings and recessions, the one sliding back in fluent music to be mingled with and carried forward by the next." Similarly, to Professor Saintsbury's thinking, each Alexandrine is "a great stroke by a mighty swimmer: it furthers the progress for the next as well as in itself. And it is greatly in this that the *untiring* character of the *Faerie Queene* consists."

Professor Tucker Brooke, having raised the question why "reasonably sympathetic readers actually feel so seldom any serious inconsecutiveness or choppiness in the poem's flow," answers it in part by calling attention to devices by which Spenser "solders together his stanzas and minimizes the jar." Sometimes as in II, i, 20–21 or V, x, 31–32, he carries over the c-rhyme of one stanza to the a- or b-rhyme of the next; again, as in I, v, 8–9, he employs recurrent lines or, as in V, iv, 17–18, the Alexandrines in successive stanzas are identical. Elsewhere he begins a stanza with a relative or some close-binding conjunction or, as in II, v, 26–27, he will carry over important words from the Alexandrine into the first line of the next stanza. Again, for example in I, v, 10–11, the last word or words of the Alexandrine recur not at the beginning but at the end of the next line; or, as in II, x, 3–4, words from the beginning of the Alexandrine are carried over usually with a turn of thought into the next line. What Professor Brooke calls "the last and most common as well as the most effective type of repetition," consists not simply in repeating, but in echoing, applying, elaborating, and playing upon the concluding words of the Alexandrine throughout the opening verse of the next stanza." Making "consciously increasing use of the artifice through Book III," Spenser "gradually gave it up as he acquired the uncanny naturalness both of narrative and versification which is so remarkable in the fifth and sixth books."

REFERENCES

Baskervill, C. R. *The Genesis of Spenser's Queen of Faerie.* Modern Philology, XVIII (1920), 48 ff.

Bayne, Ronald. *Masque and Pastoral.* Cambridge History of English Literature, VI, ch. xiii.

Blanchard, H. H. *Spenser and Boiardo.* Publications of the Modern Language Association, XL (1925), 828–851.

Blanchard, H. H. *Imitations from Tasso in the "Faerie Queene."* Studies in Philology, XXII (1925), 198 ff.

Bond, R. W. Ariosto. Quarterly Review, ccviii (1908), 139–143.

Bradner, Leicester. *Forerunners of the Spenserian Stanza.* Review of English Studies, IV, 207–208.

Brooke, Tucker. *Stanza Connection in the Fairy Queen.* Modern Language Notes, XXXVII (1922), 223 ff.

Buck, P. M. Jr. *On the Political Allegory in "The Faerie Queene."* University of Nebraska Studies, XI, Lincoln, 1911.

Buyssons, E. *Calvinism in "Faerie Queene" of Spenser.* Revue belge de philologie et d'histoire, V (1926), 1 ff.

Coe, Ada H. *Spenser and Ovid.* Classical Weekly, XXI, 91–92.

Crane, Ronald S. *The Vogue of Guy of Warwick from the close of the Middle Ages to the Romantic Revival.* Publications of the Modern Language Association, XXX (1915), 125 ff.

Cunliffe, J. W. *The Queenes Majesties Entertainment at Woodstocke.* Publications of the Modern Language Association, XXVI (1911), 92 ff.

DeMoss, W. F. *Spenser's Twelve Moral Virtues "according to Aristotle."* Modern Philology, XVI (1918), 23–28, 245–270.

Dixon, W. M. *Epic and Heroic Poetry.* London, 1912. Chapter viii: "The Romantic Epic: Spenser."

Dodge, R. E. N. *Spenser's Imitations from Ariosto.* Publications of the Modern Language Association, XII (1897), 151 ff.

Dodge, R. E. N. *Spenser's Imitations from Ariosto.* Addenda. Publications of the Modern Language Association, XXXV (1920), 91–92.

Donady, Jules. *Spenser et la Reine des Fées.* La Mer et les Poètes Anglais. Paris, 1912, 66 ff.

Draper, John W. *The Narrative Technique of the "Faerie Queene."* Publications of the Modern Language Association, XXXIX (1924), 310 ff.

Fletcher, J. B. *Huon of Burdeux and the "Faerie Queene."* Journal of Germanic Philology, II (1898), 203 ff.

Gilbert, A. H. *Spenser's Imitations from Ariosto: Supplementary.* Publications of the Modern Language Association, XXXIV (1919), 225 ff.

Gray, M. M. *The Influence of Spenser's Irish Experiences on The Faerie Queene.* The Review of English Studies, VI (1930), 413 ff.

Greene, H. E. *The Allegory as employed by Spenser, Bunyan, and Swift.* Publications of the Modern Language Association, IV (1889), 145 ff.

Hughes, Merritt Y. *Virgilian Allegory and The Faerie Queene.* Publications of the Modern Language Association, XLIV (1929), 696 ff.

Hulbert, Viola B. *Spenser's Twelve Moral Virtues "according to Aristotle and the rest."* Univ. of Chicago, Abstracts of Theses, Humanistic Series, V, 479–485.

Jones, H. S. V. *The "Faerie Queene" and the Medieval Aristotelian Tradition.* Journal of English and Germanic Philology, XXV (1926), 283 ff.

Jusserand, J. J. *"Twelve Private Morall Vertues as Aristotle hath devised."* Modern Philology, III (1906), 373 ff.

Ker, W. P. *Epic and Romance*. London, 1897.

Koeppel, E. *Edmund Spenser's Verhältniss zu Tasso*. Anglia, XI (1889), 341 ff.

Lemmi, C. W. *The Influence of Trissino on the Faerie Queene*. Philological Quarterly, VII, 220 ff.

Lemmi, C. W. *The Symbolism of the Classical Episodes in The Faerie Queene*. Philological Quarterly, VIII, 270 ff.

Mackail, J. W. *The Springs of Helicon*. London, 1909; 85 ff.

MacArthur, J. B. *The Influence of Huon of Burdeux upon the Faerie Queene*. Journal of Germanic Philology, IV (1902), 215 ff.

Millican, Charles Bowie. *Spenser and The Arthurian Legend*. Review of English Studies, VI, No. 22 (1930), 167 ff.

McMurphy, Susannah Jane. *Spenser's Use of Ariosto for Allegory*. University of Washington, 1924.

Maynadier, H. *The Arthur of the English Poets*. Boston, 1907. Chapter XV: Spenser.

Notcutt, H. Clement. *"The Faerie Queene" and its Critics*. Essays and Studies by Members of the English Association, XII (1926), 63 ff.

Padelford, F. M. *The Muse of the Faerie Queene*. Studies in Philology, XXVI (1930), 111–12.

Pope, Emma F. *The Critical Background of the Spenserian Stanza*. Modern Philology, XXIV (1926), 31 ff.

Pope, Emma F. *Renaissance Criticism and the Diction of the "Faerie Queene."* Publications of the Modern Language Association, XLI (1926), 575 ff.

Reyher, Paul. *Les Masques Anglais*. Paris, 1909; 142–146.

Spingarn, J. E. *Literary Criticism in the Renaissance*. N. Y., 1912. Chapter IV: The Theory of Epic Poetry.

Stovall, Floyd. *Feminine Rimes in the "Faerie Queene."* Journal of English and Germanic Philology, XXVI (1927), 91 ff.

Walther, Marie. *Malory's Einfluss auf Spenser's Faerie Queene,* Eisleben, n. d.

The monster encountered by the Red Cross Knight and Una in the Wandering Wood is, for Ruskin, "Error in her universal form, the first enemy of Reverence and Holiness; and more especially Error as founded on learning; for when Holiness strangles her,

> Her vomit *full of bookes and papers was,*
> With loathly frogs and toades, which eyes did lacke.

Having vanquished this first open and palpable form of Error, as Reverence and Religion must always vanquish it, the knight encounters hypocrisy, or Archimagus." Unequal to the machinations of this new enemy, Holiness is separated from Truth, and then, first of all, quite naturally meets Infidelity and Falsehood. Just as he triumphed over obvious Error, so, even though separated from Truth, he can now overcome clear Infidelity. On the contrary, being vulnerable to the wiles of the devil, he can be outwitted by Duessa as he had previously been by Archimago. Turning now to Una's story, Ruskin thought that in introducing the lion Spenser wished to show "how Truth, separated from Godliness, does indeed put an end to the abuses of Superstition (Kirkrapine) but does so violently and desperately,"—not a wholly satisfactory explanation as we shall see later. Further on in the story, when Una mistakes Archimago for her lord, we are reminded that "Hypocrisy not unfrequently appears to defend the Truth"; and when Sansloy takes Truth captive, he is represented as typical of those "who," in the words of St. Paul, "hold the truth in unrighteousness,"—"that is to say, generally, of men who, knowing what is true, make the truth give way to their own purposes, or use it only to forward them." The deliverance of Una by the satyrs shows that "Nature, in the end, must work out the deliverance of the truth, although, where it has been captive to Lawlessness, that deliverance can only be obtained through Savageness, and a return to barbarism." Satyrane, in turn, typifies "the early steps of renewed civilization and its rough and hardy character 'nousled up in life and maners wilde,'" while his conflict with Sansloy shows "how the early organisation of a hardy nation must be wrought out through much discouragement and Lawlessness." Turning again to the story of the Red Cross Knight, we see how "the man who has vanquished Infidelity may next be assailed by the Pride of Life and exposed to distress of mind and loss of his accustomed rejoicing before God (Sansjoy)." Then, in due course, he is "exposed to drowsiness and feebleness of watch; as, after Peter's boast, came Peter's sleeping, from weakness of the flesh, and then, last of all, Peter's fall." Rescued from Orgoglio by the Grace of God and from Despair by Truth, and having undergone the discipline of the House of Holiness and been vouchsafed a vision of the New Jerusalem, the Red Cross Knight "goes forth to the final victory over Satan, the old serpent."

From the previous paragraph it will be clear that Spenser's convictions about the relations of virtues and vices has in a sense directed the movement of his plot. They have as clearly, in the second place, something to do with his delineation and analysis of character. Certainly, in the cases of the hero and heroine of the first book the poet's sense of such relations has so penetrated and informed his characterization that the Red Cross Knight and Una pass out of the sphere of a merely algebraic allegory into that of a humanized fiction that carries its lesson of universal truth. The Red Cross Knight is, of course, not simply Holiness, but, like Everyman and Bunyan's hero, a universalized type of the Christian man advancing through sin and repentance to a realization of his difficult ideal; and Una, while illustrating the poet's talent for translating into an exact and appealing symbolism the authority and beauty of abstract truth, answers well to that type of faithful and resourceful womanhood which Shakespeare as well as Spenser was fond of portraying. In the following paragraphs it will be seen that the poet's ethical allegory is as closely woven with his characterization as it is with his plot.

Nowhere does the contrast between the Red Cross Knight's easy credulity and Una's steadfast faith, come out more clearly than in their conversations with Arthur in Cantos VII, VIII, and IX. In these passages one is interested more in the essential womanhood of Una than in her symbolic meaning. With dignified reserve, she hesitates at first to explain her sorrow, and, unlike the over-confident Red Cross Knight, she is even afraid that through the weakness of the flesh she, the ever faithful, will lose her faith. She would seem to live by Wordsworth's counsel, "to fear oneself and love all human kind." When, at length, in compliance with Arthur's repeated requests she tells her story, we can but contrast her charitable construction of the Red Cross Knight's evident fault with that knight's harsh and hasty judgment of her seeming misconduct in the hermitage of Archimago. Having attributed to the magician all the blame for his error, she finds her satisfaction in passionately affirming her devotion:—

> Be judge, ye heavens, that all things right esteeme,
> How I him lov'd and love with all my might!

She has no thought of reproach when she sees her knight again, now liberated from the dungeon of Orgoglio, but runs to meet him with "hasty joy" and declares it the fault of his evil star that he has been "berobbed of himself." Making the best of their situation, she looks to the future with a fine bravery and a new hope:—

> But welcome now, my lord, in wele or woe,
> Whose presence I have lackt too long a day;
> And fye on Fortune, mine avowed foe,
> Whose wrathful wreakes them selves doe now alay
> And for these wronges shall treble penaunce pay
> Of treble good: good growes of evils priefe.

Yet, for all her brave hope and all her "wondrous faith, exceeding earthly race," Una is altogether human in her implied comparison of her own case with Arthur's:—

> O happy Queen of Faeries, that hast fownd,
> Mongst many, one that with his prowesse may
> Defend thine honour, and thy foes confownd!
> True loves are often sown, but seldom grow on grownd.

If we center in Una our interest in the action and characters of Book I, we may properly think of "The Legend of Holiness" as a Legend of Faith; for, gathered about Una, herself perfect faith or the true object of faith, its various characters may be related to this dominant idea. For example, in her duplicity Duessa is the false object of faith or its very contradiction. Similarly, Archimago is counterfeit faith or hypocrisy; Sansfoy is infidelity; Corceca is blind faith; and Lucifera and Orgoglio are different forms of that mistaken, introverted faith which we call pride.

The Red Cross Knight himself is a man who lives in a

sense by faith,—faith in himself and others; but since he lacks the critical faculty, since he has had no experience of the world, his excellent intentions, his armor of a Christian man, cannot protect him from fatal mistakes of judgment. The prudence that sometimes came to his aid is only a dwarf,

> That lasie seemd, in being ever last,
> Or wearied with bearing of her bag
> Of needments at his backe.

Clearly, the Red Cross Knight is imprudent. Deficient in prudence, which St. Thomas Aquinas defines as the *ratio recta agibilium,* the Knight of Faith easily degenerates into a Knight of Credulity. In spite of Fradubio's warnings, he exhibits, in his relations with Archimago and Duessa, Corceca's blindness of heart, and in his relations with Una, Sansfoy's infidelity. That is, with respect to the faith which he professes, the Red Cross Knight is guilty of both the sin of excess and the sin of deficiency. "Although," in the words of a well-known peripatetic treatise on ethics, "he had an irrational impulse to the right, right action had not resulted because reason had not supervened and given its vote the right way."

It is to be noted that the type of believing man illustrated in the Red Cross Knight is chiefly exposed to the assaults of ghostly enemies. His world of hope and fear is the world of the unseen. In the armor of God he is in no great danger from obvious evil as symbolized by the monster in the Wood of Error, nor from mere worldly pride as represented by Lucifera. In the one case, his natural courage insures his victory; in the other, prudence shows a way of escape. But his peril is real in the presence of Despair and the spiritual pride for which Orgoglio stands. Again, the Red Cross

Knight, lacking judgment, shows the defects of his qualities. Just as his faith became credulity, so his hope has sunk into despair and his self-confidence has changed to pride; for the uncritical, self-confident optimist was all along the potential pessimist and egoist.

Imprudence, it would appear, is the root of all evil; for, once he has neglected prudence, the Red Cross Knight proceeds to violate the other cardinal virtues, which it is the office of prudence to foster. For example, he is intemperate in his anger with Una and in his dalliance with Duessa; he has lacked fortitude in Aquinas's sense of *firmitas mentis* in his encounter with Despair; and his conduct has run counter to justice, a virtue which like prudence penetrates the others, in his condemnation of Una. It need hardly be said that the traditional Catholic ethic here illustrated is in complete harmony with the Catholic discipline of the House of Holiness.

The character of the Red Cross Knight that has deteriorated in the manner described, his folly defeating his good intentions, can be reconstructed only by starting with a quality diametrically opposed to that from which he had at first proceeded. It is accordingly Humility who admits the once too confident knight to the House of Holiness; and, once admitted, he learns that his faith which had at first been a matter of impulse must now be a ground of discipline. In a word he must now be schooled in the faith.

Starting once more with Una, we may further enlarge our understanding of the ethical allegory of Book I, if we think of her as truth, the object of faith, rather than as faith itself. The adventures of Una during her separation from the Red Cross Knight will help us to understand the poet's comprehension of his theme. Here evidently truth is not transcendent, the remote reward of a painful quest; rather, she is an intimate and, at the same time, a very active agency of helpfulness and healing that, like Christ himself, walks in all humility among men. By her enemies as well as by her friends shall we know her. Particularly opposed to her are Sansloy, Corceca, and Kirkrapine, and to her aid come the lion, the satyrs, and Satyrane. If we observe that the forces opposed to her are specifically those of lawlessness, we may infer that for Spenser truth was to be conceived under the attribute of law. In this respect he was in full accord with Richard Hooker, the eminent apologist of the Anglican Establishment. Of the many forms of law described in the first book of the *Ecclesiastical Polity,* Spenser would seem to have in mind particularly the law of nature; and if we consider the climactic progress from the lion by way of the satyrs to Satyrane, we may conclude that for Spenser simple nature, as well as nature developed by training and experience, was friendly to truth. This position would be fully in accord with Renaissance educational doctrine as represented, for instance, by Ascham. Further, it is in accord with Christian humanism, which traditionally, for example in St. Thomas Aquinas and Melanchthon, invoked the Law of Nature to reconcile Aristotelian ethics with the doctrines of the Bible, that Spenser should place on the side of truth not only the law of God in the person of Arthur but the law of nature as symbolized by the lion.

If now we may go a step further and identify Una with that exalted virtue which was often described as the science of things both human and divine, we may perhaps describe Book I as Spenser's Book of Wisdom, as well as his Book of Faith and Truth. Una then bears to the transcendent Sapience of the *Fourth Hymn* a relation similar to that which the man-Christ bears to the God-Christ. Spenser has thus translated into feminine symbolism a familiar theological idea. Passages from the Wisdom literature of the Bible and the *Apocrypha,* adduced by Professor Osgood to interpret the Sapience of the *Fourth Hymn,* apply as well to Una. When the Red Cross Knight becomes proud, he is separated from Una, and before he can be restored, he must learn humility; for, as Solomon said (*Proverbs* 11, 2), "With the lowly is Wisdom." Then, to describe her ministrations while in company with her knight, what better than *Proverbs* 8, 30: "Then was I (Wisdom) with him as a nourisher." Again, in the *Book of Wisdom* 8, 3 and 4, we read a good description of Una's relations with both Arthur and the satyrs: "In that she is conversant with God, it commendeth her nobilitie; yea the Lord of all things loveth her. For she is the school-mistress of all knowledge of God." Further, we might understand better Spenser's studied contrast between Una and Duessa in the light of the seventh chapter of *Proverbs,* in which Wisdom is contrasted with "the strange woman which flattereth with her words"; and when at the close of the story Una is unveiled, we might imagine the Red Cross Knight exclaiming with the Psalmist (*Psalm* 50): "The unseen and secret things of thy Wisdom, thou hast manifested to me."

If at this point we pause to ask where we can find Holiness among the virtues which Aristotle has "devised," our answer must be that it is not and could not be in the *Nicomachean Ethics.* It is perhaps sufficient to say that without reference to Aristotle Spenser celebrated Holiness as a necessary virtue of the Christian gentleman. However, as approximately comparable virtues, critics have instanced Aristotle's Highmindedness and Manliness. "So far as possible," thinks Dr. DeMoss, "Spenser has made him [the Red Cross Knight] conform to Aristotle's conception of Highmindedness." Like the Aristotelian type, he not only thinks he is worthy of great things but in the long run is worthy of them and, deriving from a distinguished line, he is in quest of the highest earthly honor. However, even if we accept this unlikely view, we should not overlook the fact that the blending of the Christian with the Aristotelian ideal has brought about a very considerable modification of the Greek virtue. The highminded man of Aristotle was scarcely humble, and yet, as we have seen, the lesson of humility was fundamental for the Red Cross Knight. Then, he certainly received at the hands of others more favors than would have been acceptable to one who is described by Aristotle as more fond of conferring favors than of receiving them.

Miss Winstanley has suggested the alternative comparison of holiness with manliness or courage (ἀνδρεία), taken, however, "in the Platonic rather than the Aristotelian sense of the term." In the *Protagoras* Plato describes this quality, to him corresponding with what we call "moral courage," as fundamental in the moral life. Without it the other virtues fail. So in Spenser, as Miss Winstanley points out, "Holiness really is the moral courage which is the true foundation of all the other virtues and is essential to them all"; and, since the holiness in the first book of the *Faerie Queene* is "essentially that of the church militant, we may notice that the warlike associations of ἀνδρεία are not missing."

Whatever may be the closest approximation in Aristotle to the Christian virtue of the first book, Spenser describes Holiness in Aristotelian terms. That is, like his other virtues, it is conceived as a golden mean. The corresponding vice of deficiency is represented by Sansfoy and the vice of excess by Corceca and Abessa, who symbolize Superstition. Again, to take a suggestion from Dr. DeMoss, Holiness should be a cheerful faith which lies between the "joyaunce" of Lucifera and the joylessness of Sansjoy. "He [The Red Cross Knight] is least fortified," says Dr. DeMoss, "on the side of Joylessness; we are told upon our first introduction to him that 'of his cheere [he] did seeme too solemne sad.' Accordingly, the battle which ensues with Sansjoy is one of the hardest of his career"; and the critic might have cited in this connection the later experience of the hero in the Cave of Despair. If we think of highmindedness as implied in Holiness, it may be further noted that the Red Cross Knight's over-estimation of his worth in the beginning of the story is his sin of excess and his underestimation in the Cave of Despair his sin of deficiency; or thinking of Manliness as the Aristotelian virtue most nearly corresponding to Holiness, we may say that the hero's vices in these situations are Foolhardiness and Cowardice.

In passing from the ethical to the political allegory we may, following Mr. Whitney, use at the outstart the clue that Spenser has given us in naming the Red Cross Knight, St. George (Canto X, stanza 61) :—

> For thou, emongst those saints, whom thou doest see,
> Shalt be a saint, and thine owne nations frend
> And patrone: thou *Saint George* shalt called bee,
> *Saint George* of mery *England,* the signe of victoree.

Since St. George is the patron saint of England, the poet's intention, we may suppose, is to figure in the adventures

of the Red Cross Knight the fortunes of the English Church
during the reign of the Tudors. The storm which drives
the knight and his lady into the Wood of Error may then
be interpreted as the tempest of the Reformation, which
resulted in general bewilderment and confusion. The effect
upon Henry the Eighth was, at first, to confirm him in the
older faith. In recognition of the service rendered by the
pamphlet in which he answered Luther's "Babylonian
Captivity of the Church of God," he was honored with the
title *Fidei Defensor*. So, in the allegory, Una and her
knight, after the latter has killed the monster in the Wood
of Error, seek shelter in the hermitage of Archimago. Here
it is shown that the true faith, which for all good Anglicans
took a middle course, was more endangered by the deceit
of the Roman Church than by the errors of controversial
Protestantism, with its large sectarian brood. More particularly, it may be supposed that Archimago, unless we
vaguely associate him with papal influence, should be identified with Stephen Gardiner, Bishop of Winchester, who
passed the Six Articles Bill, and, as the friend of Catherine
of Aragon and Mary, worked with energy for a Catholic
restoration. The Red Cross Knight's championship of
Duessa may, then, point definitely to Henry's open defense
of the Mother Church, and the defeated Sansfoy we should
perhaps equate with the arrogant Wolsey whom Henry
disgraced. During the period of increasing Catholic influence, the true faith takes refuge among the lowly, just as
Una is protected by the satyrs; the lion, perhaps, standing
for Cromwell, who was regarded by Elizabethans as a
Protestant martyr. Like the Red Cross Knight fleeing from
Lucifera, the Church of England, having come under the
influence of pride, escaped for the short reign of Edward

VI, only to be oppressed by the Bloody Mary as St. George was by Orgoglio. In Cantos VII and VIII, the giant Orgoglio may thus be identified with the papal power in England, and Prince Arthur with the English national spirit. With Professor Padelford we may, then, agree that the House of Holiness represents "the spiritual training which the national church enjoyed after the chains of Roman Catholicism were broken." In the final fight with the Dragon, there seems to be symbolized the long struggle between Elizabeth and the Catholics who accepted the Queen of Scots as their leader; and in the letter of Duessa there is, no doubt, suggested the claim of Mary to the throne of England.

In the above explanation of the first book of the *Faerie Queene,* additions and alterations may be made, as will appear from the following list of suggested identifications:—Una, Queen Elizabeth (Buck) or Anne Boleyn (Winstanley); Duessa—Mary Tudor as well as Mary Queen of Scots (Winstanley); Archimago—Cardinal Pole (?) (Buck); Sansfoy—France (Buck), Sir Thomas More (Winstanley), Wolsey (Padelford); Lucifera—Mary Tudor (Winstanley); Sansloy—Duke of Alva (Buck), Edward Courtney (Winstanley), Gardiner (Padelford); Satyrs—"Beggars of the Sea" (Buck), Common People of England (Winstanley and others); Lion—"Common English People" (Buck), Henry VIII (Winstanley); Satyrane—Prince of Orange (Buck), Sir John Perrot (Upton and Winstanley), Cranmer (Padelford); Sansjoy—Philip II (Buck), Reginald Pole (Winstanley and Padelford); Orgoglio—Francis, Duke of Guise (Buck).

Although in stating his subject in the introductory stanzas of the *Faerie Queene,* Spenser echoes Ariosto's

> Le donne, i cavalier, l'arme, gli amori,
> Le cortesie, l'audaci imprese io canto,

we find in his first book relatively little indebtedness to the *Orlando Furioso*. The most familiar parallel is that between Archimago and the magician in the guise of a hermit, who is encountered by Angelica when fleeing from Rinaldo (*Orlando Furioso,* Canto II, stanzas 12ff.). Suggestive of the magic of Spenser's hermit is stanza 15 :—

> This [the magician's book] opened, quick and mighty marvel
> wrought,
> For not a leaf is finished by the sage,
> Before a spirit, by his bidding brought,
> Waits his command in likeness of a page.

However, the stories develop quite differently in the two poets. Almost as well known as this parallel, is that between the Fradubio episode and the story of Astolfo's transformation into the myrtle by the witch Alcina (OF. VI, st. 23 ff.), which is heard by Rogero just after his hippogriph has alighted upon the beautiful island. Further, the English poet's account of Satyrane's bringing-up follows in many details Ariosto's story of Ruggiero's education as recounted by Melissa, disguised as Atlante (OF. VII, 57). Addressing the youth who, under the spell of Alcina, has lost his manhood, Melissa says :—

> Is this the fruit at last
> Which pays my tedious pain and labour past?

57

> The marrow of the lion and the bear
> Didst thou for this thine earthly banquet make,

And, trained by me, by cliff or cavern-lair,
Strangle with infant hands the crested snake,
Their claws from tiger and from panther tear,
And tusks from living boar in tangled brake,
That, bred in such a school, in thee should I
Alcina's Atys or Adonis spy?

Then Arthur's diamond shield is like Atlante's (OF. II,
55–56); and we may compare Arthur's horn (VIII, st. 3
and 4) to Astolfo's (OF. XV, 15), of which Ariosto says
that its mere sound put brave men to flight; the brightness
of the shield corresponds to the description in OF. XXII,
85. Finally, the description of Duessa is like that of the
witch Alcina (OF. VII, 72–73), who, though apparently
beautiful, was actually the ugliest old hag in the world:—

Pale, lean, and wrinkled was the face, and white,
And thinly clothed with hair Alcina's head;
Her stature reached not to six palms in height,
And every tooth was gone; for she had led
A longer life than ever mortal wight,
Than Hecuba or she in Cuma bred;
But thus by practice, to our age unknown,
Appeared with youth and beauty not her own.

More significant than these parallels with Ariosto are the
similarities which have at various times been pointed out
between the first book of the *Faerie Queene* and certain
romantic stories of the Middle Ages. In matters of detail
parallels will readily present themselves. For example, the
incident of Una and the Lion may derive from a passage in
Sabra and the Seven Champions in which the heroine is
protected by two lions, and details of the Red Cross Knight's
final conflict with the dragon seem to echo the account of a

similar incident in *Sir Bevis of Southampton*. For the general idea of the Fairy Court one has been reminded of the legend of Arthur in Fairyland receiving Renouart and pointing out to him Roland, Iwain, and Gawain. In this connection, too, one thinks of *Huon of Bordeaux,* the best known fairy romance in England, particularly as Spenser makes mention of it in Book II. Professor Fletcher has here not only noted a number of parallels in detail but has drawn attention to a general similarity in plot,—a similarity perhaps too general to have very great significance. In each case we have a knight essaying a difficult quest, "fortified by his own purity of purpose, sustained from above, and clad in more than iron invulnerability. As a result of opposing his own judgment to that of his supernatural helper, he falls into misfortune, but is each time saved from the consequences of his own folly by the diligence of a faithful human love, or by the intercession and atonement of a more than human pity; until at last he is forced to see that the final victory is to be won through his own effort indeed, but not by his own strength alone."

More often mentioned than Huon as a source of Book I is the story of Gareth and Linet. If one turns to Book vii of Sir Thomas Malory's *Morte Darthur,* one will note that the story there told has several points in common with the tale of the Red Cross Knight and Una. In each case the hero first appears as an uncouth knight demanding the quest of a damsel who is little pleased with his offer. Nevertheless, he sets forth as her champion, attended by a dwarf. These parallels are interesting, but we should note that the stories bear little similarity to each other after this introduction. The more striking parallel, as Professor Broadus pointed out some time ago, is that between Book I and

Libeaus Desconus, which, to judge from the version in the *Percy Folio MS.,* was printed in England as early as the sixteenth century. A brief outline of *Libeaus Desconus* will reveal its points of likeness with Spenser's story:—

Ginglein, the illegitimate son of Sir Gawain, has been brought up in ignorance of knightly usages. Arthur, while demurring on account of his youth, nevertheless grants his request that he be made a knight. The king, moreover, promises him the first adventure that presents itself. There arrives a damsel attended by a dwarf. When she demands that she be granted a knight to liberate her mistress confined in her own castle by an enchantress, Libeaus offers himself. Though the maiden objects to so young and uncouth a champion, he insists upon accompanying her. Soon they encounter a knight who declares that his *amie* is fairer than the hero's, and in the ensuing fight Libeaus kills his opponent. In a later encounter with a giant, the protector and keeper of the beautiful sorceress of the *Ile d'Or,* the hero falls backward into a stream which revives him. Proud of his victory, Libeaus now enters the castle and falls a victim to the enchantress. After he has lingered here twelve months, his fair guide restores him to a sense of duty, and having in due course reached the goal of his quest he overcomes two magicians and transforms the lady of the enchanted castle from a serpent to a beautiful woman.

Since the Red Cross Knight is identified by Spenser with St. George, the patron saint of England, one might expect to find some correspondence between the legend of this saint and Spenser's story. Details common to the two stories do indeed exist. If one compares with the *Faerie Queene* Mantuan's version of the legend, supposedly translated by

Barclay, he will note as common to the two stories, the presence of the watchman; the command of the prince after the struggle to open the brazen gates; the presence of the royal family, the nobility, and the populace; the obeisance made to the conqueror and the suggestion that he was divinely sent; the gifts of ivory and gold made by the king; and the reception to the princess with the final festivities. Furthermore, in each dragon fight, we may note, though these details are of less significance, the half-walking, half-flying approach of the dragon and other more or less conventional details.[1]

Whatever were Spenser's sources in mediæval romance for the story of the first book of the *Faerie Queene,* his nearest prototypes in allegory will be found in the work of Stephen Hawes. This poet's *Example of Virtue* and *Passetyme of Pleasure* are like Spenser's poem tales of moral instruction couched in the terms of the romances of chivalry, the former dealing with the quest for moral purity and the latter with the search for worldly glory. Though the details of these allegories are so conventional that Spenser must have met with them elsewhere, it is difficult to imagine him unaware of the correspondences between Hawes's work and his own. Both Youth in the *Example* and Grand-

---

[1] Mr. Whitney Wells has made an interesting study of Spenser's sources for his dragon of sin in Canto XII. The combat "is a composite glare of romance high-lights; where one or two sufficed the romance original, Spenser took all." With the description of the dragon the case is different. Here, "in only one or two minor details has he followed the romances." From the *Vision of Tundale,* which seems also to have influenced the descriptions of the Cave of Mammon in Canto vii, and of the Well of Life, Spenser derived many details from descriptions of Satan, devils, and monstrous beasts. The dragon, Mr. Wells concludes, is "a true beast from the mediæval Hell, compact of the beasts from the hell of Tundale."

amour in the *Passetyme* fortify themselves like the Red
Cross Knight by donning the armor of God as described
by St. Paul, and they go forth to achieve adventures similar to those of St. George. Youth conducted by Discretion
will remind us of The Red Cross Knight attended by the
Dwarf, and his temptation by Sensuality mounted on a
goat and Pride riding an elephant will suggest the experiences of Spenser's knight in the House of Lucifera. Note,
too, that Humility, who serves as a warden of the Castle in
the *Example,* acts as Porter of the House of Holiness in
the *Faerie Queene.* Nor can we miss the correspondence of
the final victory in both poems over a dragon with three
heads, and the subsequent marriage of the hero. Finally,
we may compare Grandamour's search for La Bel Pucell,
after he has heard a description of her beauty, with Arthur's
quest of Gloriana after he has seen her in a dream.

REFERENCES

Kitchin, G. W. Ed. *Faery Queene,* Book I. Oxford, 1905. For
the new edition an excellent glossary was prepared by the
Rev. A. L. Mayhew.

Winstanley, Lilian. Ed. *Faerie Queene.* Book I. Cambridge,
1920.

———

Broadus, E. K. *The Red Cross Knight and Lybeaus Desconus.*
Modern Language Notes, XVIII (1903), 202–204. Compare Atkins, *Cambridge History of English Literature,* I,
295.

Carpenter, F. I. *Spenser's Cave of Despair.* Modern Language Notes, XII (1897), 257 ff.

Cook, A. S. *The House of Sleep: A Study in Comparative Literature.* Modern Language Notes, V (1890), 9–12.

Dodge, R. E. N. *The Well of Life and the Tree of Life*. Modern Philology, VI (1909), 191–196.

Greenlaw, Edwin. *Una and her Lamb*. Modern Language Notes, XLII (1927), 515 ff.

Heffner, Ray. *Spenser's Allegory in Book I of the Faerie Queene*. Studies in Philology, XXVII (1930), pp. 142–61.

Lowes, J. L. *Spenser and the Mirour de l'Omme*. Publications of the Modern Language Association, XXIX (1914), 388–452.

Padelford, F. M. *The Political and Ecclesiastical Allegory of the First Book of the Faerie Queene*. Boston, 1911. See the review by R. E. N. Dodge, Journal of English and Germanic Philology, XII (1913), 490–496.

Padelford, F. M. *The Spiritual Allegory of the "Faerie Queene," Book One*. Journal of English and Germanic Philology, XXII (1923), 1–17.

Padelford, F. M., and O'Connor, Matthew. *Spenser's Use of the St. George Legend*. Studies in Philology, XXIII (1926), 142–156.

Ruskin, John. *Stones of Venice,* Vol. II, ch. viii and Vol. III, Appendix, 2.

Tuve, Rosemond. *The Red Crosse Knight and Mediœval Demon Stories*. Publications of the Modern Language Association, XLIV (1929), 706 ff.

Wells, Whitney. *Spenser's Dragon*. Modern Language Notes, XLI (1926), 143 ff.

Whitney, J. E. *The Continued Allegory in the First Book of the Faery Queene*. Transactions of the American Philological Association, XIX (1888), 40–69.

CHAPTER XV

THE FAERIE QUEENE, BOOK II

IN passing from Book I to Book II of the *Faerie Queene* Spenser maintained his hold on allegory. His ethical ideas are still patent in such names as Furor, Pyrochles, Braggadocchio, Medina, Alma, Mammon, the Idle Lake, and the Bower of Bliss; and his underlying ethical philosophy is clearly outlined in Canto II. Similarly, he who runs may read the ethical meaning of the sequent episodes, dealing with such themes as the angry passions, avarice, worldly ambition, idle mirth, and lasciviousness.

The similarity here noted between the two books is extended from the poet's general conception of his story to certain circumstances and details of his narrative. In each case the hero is attended by a guide, and the action moves to a climax in the eighth canto, where King Arthur appears to rescue the knight. In Book II the Cave of Mammon occupies a position similar to that of the Castle of Orgoglio in Book I, and the House of Alma presents a general parallel to the House of Holiness. Then, after the complication has been duly resolved, the action in each book passes on to the final test and resolution of the last canto. Moreover, the two books are linked by carrying over from the first to the second the characters of the Red Cross Knight, Archimago, Duessa, and Sansloy.

Over against these similarities in the two books we may

set certain differences. Although the ethical allegory is equally prominent in Book II, its political allegory is less insisted upon. As contrasted with the bifurcated plot of Book I, made necessary by the separation and reunion story, the linear action of the second book moves straight to its term ; and its interest, instead of being divided between two chief characters, is centered upon one.

From the letter to Raleigh it appears that Spenser at some time had in mind a version of the story in which the Palmer was to present himself at the court of Gloriana with Amavia's baby in his arms. By introducing Ruddymane in the midst of Canto I, Spenser has emphasized the motivation of the story and, as Dean Kitchin remarked, "put the action in its course." Again in Canto V the objective is brought more vividly before us in the account of Atin's journey to the Bower of Bliss in quest of Cymochles. Almost constantly throughout the story the hero is kept in view. Only in the Braggadocchio episode of Canto III do we lose sight of him for a moment, and this is doubtless in answer to the demands of the political allegory. The final canto not only presents the conclusion of the story but, in the sea voyage of Sir Guyon, offers a kind of recapitulation of the allegory.

The simplicity which marks the plotting of Book II may be noted also in the relation of its hero to his story. Whereas in the first book we had a chemical action of plot upon character, bringing about first its disintegration and then achieving its restoration, the legend of Sir Guyon serves mainly to illustrate or demonstrate his virtue. The difference is that between a Christian and an Odyssean pilgrimage. Sir Guyon, following his level course, knows neither the humiliation nor the ecstasy of the Red Cross

Knight. In the case of the former our theme is reasoned morality; with the latter, it is the religious life, ranging from rapture to despair.

It is, however, not merely on the score of its narrative art that the "Legend of Sir Guyon" merits careful study. In the range of its symbolism it is significant of Spenser's catholicity of taste. First of all, we may note the mediæval schematism of the House of Medina and the House of Alma, the latter more meticulously diagrammed than any other structure of allegory in the *Faerie Queene*. However bizarre may be such passages to modern taste, they certainly interested a generation that took pleasure in the conceits of the sonneteers and the patterned prose of Euphuism; but, in contrast to these other modes of artifice, Spenser's is here not largely rhetorical. As a poet careful of every idiom of morality, he has chosen, for one thing, to illustrate the rigid forms in which the moral sense of the Christian world had traditionally found expression.

To the modern reader the appeal of the House of Medina and the House of Alma will come not so much from the architecture of the allegory as from those gracious presences—such as, Medina, Alma, Prays-desire, and Shame-fastness—who are reminiscent of the symbolic refinements of the *Romance of the Rose*. Here the pictorial art is that of fresco in its simple lines and abstract beauty. It may carry too some suggestions of sculpture, as is notably true in the statuesque charm of Belphoebe. If we compare such representations of the virtues with the poet's customary symbols of vice, we may infer an important distinction between Spenser's sense of good and evil. In contrast to his nice economy of delineation in the former cases is his lavish use of detail in the latter,— as though we were to set side by side a Fra Angelico and a Teniers.

That which particularly impresses one in Spenser's description of Maleger and, indeed, of the whole rout of vices besieging the House of Alma is what Professor Dodge describes as "allegorical intensity." The poet communicates a sense of the terror and hatefulness of evil in bringing before us the captain of the wicked crew, riding a fierce tiger as swift as the wind and looking "like a ghost whose grave-clothes were unbound."

Very different from the examples of Spenser's descriptive art so far noted are the episodes of the Idle Lake, the Bower of Bliss, and the Garden of Proserpine. In all of these cases, we should remember, Spenser is heavily in debt to other poets. His description of the Idle Lake, as we shall see, he derives largely from Tasso's *Jerusalem Delivered,* for details of the Bower of Bliss and the journey there he turned both to the *Jerusalem Delivered* and the *Odyssey,* and for the Garden of Proserpine he follows rather closely a passage in Claudian's *Rape of Proserpine.* Under the guidance of these authors Spenser passes from the level of schematic allegory to the plane of a highly artistic symbolism. The details of his description are not here ticketed with a moral sense. Made graphic and suggestive in themselves, they blend in each case to create the atmosphere of a place perceptibly different from that of any other which we have visited in the poet's land of faëry. In the first two cases we have preserved that "pensive voluptuousness" which Hallam detected in the poetry of Tasso; and in the last a vivid Dantesque quality which will recall Duessa's visit to the underworld in Book I. We may say that in all these cases the poet's moral sense, instead of determining and directing his technique, is rather attendant upon his accomplished art.

The second book of the *Faerie Queene* offers as comprehensive a treatment of morality from Aristotle's point of view as Book I presents from the point of view of Christian ethic. That there is no necessary conflict between the two systems is clearly the implication of the arrested duel between the Red Cross Knight and Sir Guyon. Though agencies of evil may try to antagonize reason and religion, these are, properly understood, friendly one to the other. It is this idea, rather than the mere carrying over of characters, that serves to link closely the first two books of the *Faerie Queene*.

To understand the ethical allegory of the "Legend of Sir Guyon," one must give some attention to certain ideas fundamental to Aristotle's ethical system. In general, Aristotle classifies his virtues as intellectual and moral, or virtues respectively of the rational and the irrational parts of the soul. If we bar that which is purely vegetative and which has therefore nothing to do with virtue, the irrational in man is concupiscent. If this concupiscent part of the soul is obedient to reason, it may produce the virtues of liberality and temperance. To the rational part of the soul belong the virtues of wisdom and prudence. The necessary connection between these two sets of virtues is suggested in Aristotle's definition of temperance ($\sigma\omega\phi\rho\sigma\sigma\acute{\nu}\nu\eta$) as the preservative of prudence. Aristotle still further clarifies his distinction when he says that intellectual virtue is inculcated and developed by teaching; whereas moral virtue is formed by habit.

Now these fundamental distinctions Spenser incorporates

in his allegory. In the main, the Palmer represents the intellectual; Sir Guyon, the moral virtues. However, the free technique of Spenser's allegory permits us to think of his hero not so much as an embodiment of the moral virtues, but as a human being attaining to moral stature by instruction and through habit. In his relation to Sir Guyon the office of the Palmer is not so much to command as to instruct and persuade. He not only in emergencies checks the evil impulses of Sir Guyon, but on occasion he turns to moral advantage the episodes of the story. His function may be compared roughly to that of the Chorus in a Greek play; or we might think of him as using different episodes somewhat as the mediæval preacher used *exempla*. For instance, taking the case of Amavia as an awful example, he lays down the principle of the golden mean and shows, like Aristotle, its application to pleasures and pains. Again in Canto IV he employs two stanzas to point the moral of the Furor-Phedon episode. Sir Guyon, thus learning the lessons of the Palmer as well as those of experience, becomes a knight both of prudence and temperance. Indeed he believes so much in the value of instruction that he sometimes practises it himself. In Canto V, stanzas fifteen and sixteen, he preaches to Pyrochles in words that the Palmer himself might have employed.

In the next place, in order to understand Spenser's allegory we should remember, besides Aristotle's two chief classes of virtues, his observation that virtue, in general, is concerned with both pleasures and pains. He remarks that the pleasure or pain which follows upon action is the test of a person's moral state. Accordingly, the true education "produces pleasure and pain in presence of the right objects."

Using the criteria of pleasure and pain Aristotle discriminates the virtues of continence and temperance. "If the existence of strong and base desires is essential to continence," he writes, "the temperate man will not be continent, nor the continent man temperate; for it is inconsistent with the character of the temperate man to have extravagant or wrong desires. Yet it must be so with the continent man; for if his desires were good, the moral state which prevents his following them would be wrong, and therefore continence would not in all cases be virtuous. If on the other hand they were feeble and not wrong, it would be no great credit, and if they were wrong and feeble, it would be no great triumph to overcome them."

To this point of difference Aristotle adds that of the two virtues continence has the wider scope, since "there may be incontinence in all things, whereas intemperance applies only to the sensual emotions." In the sphere of continence there are both pleasures and pains, and of things which produce pleasure we may distinguish those which are necessary, such as nutrition and sexual love, from those which are not necessary but desirable in themselves, such as victory, honor, and wealth." If we speak of incontinence with reference to necessary things we use the term absolutely; if we apply it to things only desirable, we employ it relatively.

To this Aristotle adds that "a person is incontinent in respect of angry passions in the same sense as in respect of honour or gain"; so, a person "mastered by his angry passions ought to be called incontinent in respect of anger, but not incontinent in the absolute sense." And he adds: "incontinence of angry passions is not so disgraceful as the incontinence of the desires. For it is as if the passion heard reason more or less, but misheard it, like hasty servants who run out before they have heard all that is said to them, and so mistake their orders, or like dogs who bark at a person, if only he makes a noise, without waiting to see if he is a friend. In the same way the temper from its natural heat and impetuosity hears something, but does not hear the voice of command, when it rushes to revenge."

More narrow in its scope than continence, is the virtue which Aristotle calls steadfastness; for, whereas steadfastness appears only in our resistance to pain, continence implies as well our victory over pleasure. "The opposite of the incontinent character," says the *Nicomachean Ethics,* "is the continent, and of the effeminate the steadfast; for steadfastness consists in holding out against pain, and continence in overcoming pleasure, and it is one thing to hold out, and another to overcome, as it is one thing to escape being beaten and another to win a victory. . . . If a person gives in where people generally resist and are capable of resisting, he deserves to be called effeminate and luxurious; for luxury is a form of effeminacy. . . . If a person is fond of amusing himself, he is regarded as licentious, but he is really effeminate; for amusement, being a relaxation, is a recreation, and a person who is fond of amusing himself is one who carries his recreation to excess."

These distinctions, like that already noted between prudence and temperance, are clearly reflected in the "Legend of Sir Guyon." Evidently our hero stands Aristotle's test of the true moral state by taking pleasure in his virtues. Entering the Cave of Mammon he

> evermore himselfe with comfort feedes
> Of his own vertues and praise-worthie deedes

In the second place, though occasionally temperate, he is more often continent. Ordinarily he has to contend against extravagant or base desires. Having come to the large and spacious plain in which the Bower of Bliss was situated,

> Much wondered Guyon at the fayre aspect
> Of that sweet place, yet suffred no delight
> To sincke into his sence, nor mind affect,
> But passed forth, and lookt still forward right.

However, when he sees the bathing girls, he slacked his pace,

> Them to behold, and in his sparkling face
> The secrete signes of kindled lust appear;

so that the Palmer

> much rebukt those wanderings eyes of his.

Since continence, unlike temperance, is not limited to sensual pleasures, this virtue is further illustrated in those episodes dealing with the angry passions and with wealth and worldly ambition. In these cases we have to do, as Aristotle has said, not with absolute but with relative continence. In his duel with Pyrochles, Guyon had to temper his passion "with advizement slow." But it is perhaps to Pyrochles himself that Aristotle's description of the angry man most fittingly applies; for he heard reason more or

less but misheard it, and his temper heard something but
it did not hear the voice of command when it rushed to revenge. At any rate, Pyrochles thinks he has reason and
justice on his side:—

> "Dreadlesse," said he, "that shall I soone declare:
> It was complaind that thou hadst done great tort
> Unto an aged woman, poore and bare,
> And thralled her in chaines with strong effort,
> Voide of all succour and needfull comfort:
> That ill beseemes thee, such as I thee see,
> To worke such shame. Therefore I thee exhort
> To chaunge thy will, and set Occasion free,
> And to her captive sonne yield his first libertee."

In the Cave of Mammon episode Spenser treats together
the other cases of relative incontinence; that is, incontinence relative to wealth and honor. Here, however, we observe a difference. In the Cave of Mammon Sir Guyon has
none of the base and extravagant desires which are a mark
of incontinence; he is not tempted by wealth or worldly
ambition, though his tour of inspection is attended by much
discomfort and annoyance. The theme of the episode then
seems to be not so much continence in resisting the allure-
ments of pleasure as steadfastness in enduring pain. To
Mammon's promise of the "worldes blis" and the "grace to
be happy," Sir Guyon replies that he prefers the life of
arms and brave achievements. Earlier in stanza 10 he had
declared that only weak men are bewitched by "the beauteous baite and pleasing charmes" of Mammon. Note that the
knight at the end is exhausted not by the force of tempta-

tion or the urge of unruly passions but by the mere strain of his "hardy enterprize." [1]

Illustrations of the vice opposed to steadfastness, which Aristotle calls effeminacy, are found in the characters of Amavia and Phædria. Amavia, the lover of life, unequal to the burden of her sorrow, seeks through self-destruction an escape from her misfortunes. To Guyon, who has tried to heal her self-inflicted wound, she cries:—

> Leave, ah! leave of, whatever wight thou bee,
> To lett a weary wretch from her dew rest,
> And trouble dying soules tranquilitee.

Aristotle's comment upon suicide is directly applicable. "It is effeminacy," he says, "to fly from troubles, nor does the suicide face death because it is noble, but because it is a refuge from evil." Guyon, comparing Amavia's death with her husband's, makes clear Aristotle's point:—

> The strong through pleasure soonest falles, the weake through smart.

[1] The significance in the ethical allegory of Arthur's rescue of Sir Guyon will be found in that part of the Aristotelian highmindedness which applies to the virtue of temperance. It stands to reason that Aristotle's type of personal perfection will illustrate preëminently the fundamental principle of the golden mean. The highminded man shows moderation, for example, in such matters as self-assertion, haste, and admiration. Accordingly, he is ideally the gentleman that Guyon seeks to become through the exercise of due restraint in all the relations of life. Further, it should be noted that since the highminded man prefers nobleness to profit, he is on that count particularly qualified to restore the hero of the second book from the effect of his journey through the Cave of Mammon.

From his tragic treatment of the theme of steadfastness in the Amavia story Spenser passes to a lighter version in the episode of Phædria and the Idle Lake. Amavia sought in death an end of her sorrow; Phædria in idle mirth forgets the cares and petty annoyances of life. The very terms of the Phædria Canto—the Idle Lake and the Floating Island—reveal its subject. Phædria's guests, transported to her island in the rudderless boat, become slothful and effeminate, not grossly sensual as the victims of the Bower of Bliss. It is to be noted that she leaves on the bank not only the Palmer or Prudence but Atin or Strife. Phædria is clearly one of those persons whom Aristotle calls effeminate because they are "fond of amusing themselves." He distinguishes them from those properly called licentious, just as we distinguish Phædria from Acrasia. And "luxury," he adds, "is a form of effeminacy." Phædria's philosophy of life is seductively voiced in her song to the slumbering Cymochles (VI, 15 ff.). Consider, she says, the lilies that neither toil nor spin :—

> Why then doest thou, O man, that of them all
> Art lord, and eke of Nature soveraine,
> Wilfully make thy self a wretched thrall,
> And waste thy joyous howres in needelesse paine,
> Seeking for daunger and adventures vaine?
> What bootes it al to have, and nothing use?
> Who shall him rew, that swimming in the maine
> Will die for thrist, and water doth refuse?
> Refuse such fruitlesse toile, and present pleasures chuse.

The philosophy of life here lyrically expressed receives its dramatic application when Cymochles and Guyon come to blows. After Phædria has failed to restore "lovely peace and gentle amity" between the combatants—

> She no lesse glad, then he desirous, was
> Of his departure thence.

If Phædria is "effeminate," Guyon is steadfast :—

> Her dalliaunce he despisd, and follies did forsake.

Though Phædria did all

> that might his constant hart
> Withdraw from thought of warlike enterprize,

he was prudent, and

> wary of her will,
> And ever held his hand upon his hart:

so that at length she knows that he is

> A foe of folly and immodest toy,
> Still solemne sad, or still disdainfull coy,
> Delighting all in armes and cruell warre.

On still another plane of feeling, lack of steadfastness or effeminacy is suggested by Sir Guyon's "causeless ruth" for Pyrochles (V, 24) and by his impulse to go to the aid of

> A seemely maiden, sitting by the shore,
> That with great sorrow and sad agony
> Seemed some great misfortune to deplore,
> And lowd to them for succour called evermore.

So far we have followed Spenser's illustrations in Book II of the *Faerie Queene* of Aristotle's distinction between intellectual and moral virtues, and his narrative treatment

of virtue as related by the Greek philosopher to pleasure
and pain. We now pass on to Aristotle's principle of the
golden mean, and then to Spenser's illustration of it.

Virtue, says Aristotle, in Book II, Chapter 5, of the
Nicomachean Ethics, is a moral state, and such a moral state
as makes a man good and able to perform his proper function well. More particularly, the philosopher describes the
character of this virtue as a mean between excess and deficiency. This mean may be either the absolute mean, which
"is equally distinct from both extremes," and which is "one
and the same thing for everybody"; or it may be the mean
relative to the individual. "Everybody who understands
his business," says Aristotle, "avoids alike excess and deficiency; he seeks and chooses the mean, not the absolute
mean, but the mean considered relatively to ourselves." In
aiming at the mean, "virtue is like the good artist, but it
is more accurate and better than any art." The principle
of the mean, Aristotle goes on to explain, applies to moral
virtue, "as it is moral virtue which is concerned with emotions and actions, and it is these which admit of excess and
deficiency and the mean. Thus it is possible to go too far,
or not to go far enough, in respect of fear, courage, desire,
anger, pity, and pleasure and pain generally, and the excess
and deficiency are alike wrong; but to experience these
emotions at the right times and on the right occasions and
towards the right persons and for the right causes and in
the right manner, is the mean or the supreme good, which
is characteristic of virtue. Similarly there may be excess,
deficiency, or the mean in regard to actions. But virtue is
concerned with emotions and actions, and here excess is an
error and deficiency a fault, whereas the mean is successful and laudable, and success and merit are both character-

istics of virtue." That Aristotle admits a qualitative as well as a quantitative distinction to his explanation of the mean and the extremes, becomes clear from what he says in Chapter VI by way of further explanation of his observation that the mean is also the supreme good. "It is a general rule," he says, "that an excess or deficiency does not admit of a mean state, nor a mean state of an excess or deficiency."

It is in Canto II of the second book that we find Spenser's allegorical version of the doctrine outlined in the previous paragraph. Ruddymane, the child of Amavia, is received at the House of Medina, by the second of three sisters—

> The children of one syre by mothers three.

Medina's eldest sister is named Elissa from the Greek ἐλάσσων meaning too little, while the youngest bears the name Perissa from the Greek περισσή, which means too much. That is Elissa stands for the vice of deficiency, Perissa for that of excess, and Medina for the golden mean. To Elissa and Perissa Spenser assigns suitable lovers; to the former Huddibras, and to the latter Sansloy, who had already appeared in the first book. Of Huddibras he says that "sterne melancholy did his courage pas," and Sansloy he describes as

> The most unruly and the boldest boy,
> That ever warlike weapons menaged,
> And to all lawlesse lust encouraged
> Through strong opinion of his matchlesse might.

In illustration of Aristotle's observations that "the extremes are opposed both to the mean and to each other," and that "while there is this mutual opposition between the extremes and the mean, there is greater opposition between the two extremes than between either and the mean," Spenser represents Huddibras and Sansloy as in daily war with each other and as both, though less violently, hostile to Medina and Sir Guyon.

> The eldest did against the youngest goe,
> And both against the middest meant to worken woe.

When, further, Spenser writes of Medina's sisters:—

One thought her cheare too little, th'other thought too much,

we seem to have an echo of the following passage from the eighth chapter of Aristotle's second book: "For as the equal if compared with the less is greater, but if compared with the greater is less, so the mean states, whether in the emotions or in actions, if compared with the deficiencies, are excessive, but if compared with the excesses are deficient. . . . The temperate man appears licentious as compared with the insensible but insensible as compared with the licentious." In general, Medina's treatment of her sisters and their suitors well illustrates the relation between the mean and the extremes:—

> That forward paire she ever would asswage,
> When they would strive dew reason to exceed;
> But that same froward twaine would accorage,
> And of her plenty adde unto their need:
> So kept she them in order, and herselfe in heed.

If Sir Guyon were to be other than a negative character, a kind of knight of the Everlasting No, it was necessary

that Spenser should endow him with the positive qualities
of courage and sympathy. To understand the relation of
courage to temperance, it was not necessary for the poet to
turn to Plato; for Aristotle had declared (III, x) that "the
courageous man in his emotions and actions has a sense of
fitness and obeys the law of reason," which is as much as
to say that the courageous man is necessarily temperate.
Courage may be defined as "a mean state in regard to sentiments of fear and confidence." In his endurance of pain
the courageous man will show the virtue of steadfastness,
which has been already described. "It is the endurance of
painful things," says Aristotle, "that entitles people to be
called courageous" (III, xii); and the courageous man, he
has said too, is one who both "faces and fears the right
things for the right motive and in the right way and at the
right time, and whose confidence is similarly right." Among
the things to be feared is ignominy; for "to fear ignominy
is to be virtuous and modest, and not to fear it is to be
shameless" (III, ix). As courage, then, is a form of temperance, modesty is a form of courage.

To understand the elements of fear and confidence that
enter into the courage of the temperate man, one should
contrast the character of Sir Guyon with that of Pyrochles.
The latter illustrates not so much Aristotle's fool-hardiness
($\theta\rho\acute{\alpha}\sigma\sigma\varsigma$)—see, III, x—as his $\theta\acute{\upsilon}\mu\sigma\varsigma$, described in III, xi, 3.
It is clear that we cannot say of Pyrochles that he "affects a
courage that he does not possess," and that he "refuses to
face real terrors." He is rather like "people who under the
influence of passion turn like wild beasts upon those who
have wounded them." As passion "is preëminently eager to
encounter perils," Pyrochles in the poet's allegory is represented as seeking out Occasion; and, like the wild beasts

mentioned by Aristotle, he is "goaded by pain and passion to rush upon peril without any foresight of the dangers which he incurs." "To be goaded by pain or passion into facing perils," Aristotle concludes, "is not to be courageous."

In the second place, just as Pyrochles, unlike Guyon, does not face "the right things for the right motive and in the right way and at the right time," so his brother Cymochles in similar ways does not fear the right things. For an understanding of his character and of Sir Guyon's we should contrast their behavior in the Phædria canto. Just as in the Bower of Bliss Cymochles forgets his pain in "creeping slomber" (II, vi, 30), so with Phædria, far from "despising her dalliaunce" and "forsaking her follies," he loses in her company all memory of his former purpose:—

> Her light behaviour and loose dalliaunce
> Gave wondrous great contentment to the knight,
> That of his way he had no sovenaunce,
> Nor care of vow'd revenge and cruell fight,
> But to weake wench did yield his martiall might:
> So easie was, to quench his flamed minde
> With one sweete drop of sensuall delight;
> So easie is, t'appease the stormy winde
> Of malice in the calme of pleasaunt womankind.

Cymochles is shameless here because he does not fear ignominy.

As Pyrochles represents one kind of false courage, so Braggadocchio stands for another. Between them comes Sir Guyon, embodying "the mean state in regard to sentiments of fear and confidence." Now in Braggadocchio, it has been noted, are merged two of Ariosto's characters, types of the coward and the *miles gloriosus* respectively; similarly, Braggadocchio seems to blend Aristotle's cowardice and foolhardiness with the emphasis, of course, upon the former quality. Like Aristotle's foolhardy man, Braggadocchio is an impostor; he "affects a courage that he does not possess"; he imitates the courageous man "so far as he *safely* can." On the other hand, like Aristotle's coward, he "fears the wrong things and fears them in the wrong way," as all will admit who remember his flight to the bushes at the mere sound of Belphœbe's approach.

Similar to Braggadocchio is Sir Huddibras, the lover of Medina's eldest sister. He, too, seems to combine rashness and lack of manly spirit. He was

> not so good of deedes as great of name,
> Which he by many rash adventures wan.

He "reason with foole-hardize over ran." When the poet adds that in the case of Huddibras, "sterne melancholy did his courage pas," he introduces still another mark of cowardice. "The coward," says Aristotle, "is a despondent sort of person;" whereas "it is natural to a confident person to be sanguine."

As an example of the mean between the cowardly and the passionate spirit, Guyon's steadfastness in enduring pains and his continence in resisting pleasure have been already sufficiently noted. To these we must add other traits of the man truly brave. Among these, as noted above, must be counted modesty. Spenser did not overlook this in his obviously careful study of Aristotle. The damsel whom Sir Guyon "entertains" in the house of Alma is named Shamefastness. When the knight marvels at her, Alma says,

> Why wonder yee,
> Faire sir, at that which ye so much embrace?
> She is the fountaine of your modestee;
> You shamefast are, but Shamefastnes it selfe is shee.

In explaining the mean, Aristotle had remarked, it will be remembered, that virtue is concerned with both emotions and actions; and in Book II, Chapter iv, he had explained that the virtues are moral states, rather than emotions or faculties; but he had already called moral states those in respect of which we are well or ill disposed towards the emotions. Among these emotions he lists pity, and he had remarked in a passage already quoted that "it is possible to go too far, or not to go far enough in respect of pity and other emotions." Toward this emotion of pity we might say that Sir Guyon was well-disposed when in taking away Amavia's child (II, ii, 1)

> ruth empersed deepe
> In that knightes hart, and wordes with bitter teares did steepe.

On the other hand, he was ill-disposed in his impulse to rescue Pyrochles (V, 24), and in his desire to go to the assistance of the "seemly maiden sitting by the shore" in XII, 28.

The better to understand the more liberal view of courage which relates it to the prudence, the steadfastness, the temperance or continence of Sir Guyon, we may turn to a book that helped to form the educational idealism of the Renaissance. Along with Plato and Aristotle its author contributed to the ethical thought of Sir Thomas Elyot's *Governour* which, as a book of education, may be placed

in the line of descent of the *Faerie Queene*. In Chapter
20 of the first book of the *Offices* Cicero had written: "Now
all true courage and greatness of mind is more especially
seen in these two things: the first is a generous contempt
or disregard of all outward goods, proceeding from an
opinion that it is unworthy of a man to admire, or wish
for, or endeavour after anything, unless it be that which is
honest and becoming; to make himself subject to any one's
will; to be a slave to his own irregular passions, or any way
dependent on the caprices of fortune." [2] In this "temper
of mind" Cicero finds "the groundwork and foundation of
all true greatness." It is made up of two parts: "the first is
an opinion that nothing is truly and really good, but only
what is honest; the second, a freedom from all sort of passion or disturbance of mind"—what Spenser calls "the
goodly peace of stayed mind," which particularly in Medina
he contrasts with the false and insecure peace of Phædria
that depends upon outward conditions. "The truly courageous man," Cicero continues, "can both bear up valiantly
against fear and resist desire." It would not be consistent
that "he who could never be conquered by pain, should
suffer himself to be captivated by pleasure." If one at-
tains to the calm and undisturbed mind, Cicero concludes,
"the whole life becomes graceful and uniform."

While the Knight of Temperance has no place in a de-

[2] Compare the words of Guyon to Arthur (ix, 8):—

> "Fortune, the foe of famous chevisaunce,
>   Seldome," said Guyon, "yields to vertue aide,
>   But in her way throwes mischiefe and mischaunce,
>   Whereby her course is stopt and passage staid.
>   But you, faire sir, be not herewith dismaid,
>   But constant keepe the way in which ye stand."

veloped love story, it will be remembered that he replies to
Mammon's offer of his daughter with the words,

> yet is my trouth yplight,
> And love avowd to other lady late.

His logical lady, if one might so express himself, is Medina.
In elaborating the schematism of the second canto Spenser
seems to have linked with the masculine virtue of courage
(Guyon) the feminine virtue of gentleness (Medina), and
then to have pivoted upon these means the associated and
corresponding vices of deficiency and excess. Thus, in the
person of Perissa, Passionateness is connected with Fool-
hardiness (Sansloy); just as Impassivity (Elissa) is
courted by Cowardice in the person of Huddibras.[3] The
contentious knights Medina seeks to pacify by commending "lovely concord, and most sacred peace." Over against
her moderation and active gentleness is set, on the one hand,
the sulkiness of Elissa; she would neither eat, nor speak,
nor show solace to her paramour. Perissa, on the other hand,
was "quite contrary to her sisters kynd":—

> No measure in her mood, no rule of right,
> But poured out in pleasure and delight;
> In wine and meats she flowd above the banck,
> And in excesse exceeded her owne might;
> In sumptuous tire she joyd her selfe to pranck,
> But of her love to lavish (little have she thanck.)

As Cicero has helped us to understand the virtue of
courage, broadly conceived, we may properly turn to him

---

[3] It seems difficult to avoid at this point a confusion due to
Spenser's uniting of two types in Huddibras as in Braggadocchio
—the coward and the *miles gloriosus*. As noted above, Huddibras
"overran reason with fool-hardize."

now for an account of temperance. Under this virtue, he says in Chapter 27 of the first book of the *Offices,* "we comprehended bashfulness, temperance, modesty, government of the passions, and the observing a just order as to time and place in our words and actions; from all which arises a certain engaging kind of beauty and gracefulness which serves to set off and adorn our lives," what he describes later on as "a certain sweet air of gentility and good manners." Although he grants the relation of decorum to the other virtues, 'the nature of decency is more peculiarly seen in temperance." It is decorum, he maintains, which "gives a sort of lustre and grace to our lives." Decorum shows itself in "actions free from precipitancy and rashness on the one hand, from all carelessness and negligence on the other"; in a becoming speech and discourse; in such small matters as "the moving of our eyes," or "the merry or sorrowful air of our countenances," "our laughter, freedom, or reservedness in discourse"; and "the raising or falling the tone of your voice."

That Spenser, in carrying out the educational purpose of the *Faerie Queene,* which he had announced in his letter to Raleigh, considered the relation of courtesy to temperance is seen in many passages of Book II. Guyon's temperance has not made of him a somber or a sour Puritan; on the contrary, it has borne the fruit of gentleness and consideration, of careful and accomplished manners:—

> His carriage was full comely and upright
> His countenance demure and temperate.

He is tactful:—

> So can he turne his earnest unto game,
> Through goodly handling and wise temperaunce.

As we have noted, he is duly sympathetic (II, i). In the House of Medina his courtesy, like that of Medina herself, is set in contrast to the boorishness of Elissa, Perissa, and their suitors. In leaving Ruddymane with Medina he conjures her,

> In vertuous lore to traine his tender youth,
> And all that gentle noriture ensueth.

His skill in horsemanship is particularly commemorated and contrasted with Braggadocchio's ineptitude:—

> In brave poursuitt of honorable deed,
> There is I know not what great difference
> Betweene the vulgar and the noble seed,
> Which unto things of valorous pretence
> Seems to be borne by native influence;
> As feates of armes, and love to entertaine;
> But chiefly skill to ride seemes a science
> Proper to gentle blood: some others faine
> To menage steeds, as did this vaunter; but in vaine.

One may compare what Sir Thomas Elyot wrote in the *Governour,* Book I, Chapter XVIII: "But the most honorable exercise, in myne opinion, and that beneath the estate of every noble persone, is to ryde suerly and clene on a great horse and a roughe."

Even while disapproving Phædria, Guyon does not forget to be a gentleman:—

> But he was wise, and wary of her will,
> And ever held his hand upon his hart:
> Ye would not seeme so rude, and thewed ill,
> As to despise so curteous seeming part,
> That gentle lady did to him impart;

and so, departing, he

> to that damsell thankes gave for reward.

In beginning the House of Alma canto the poet contrasts the physical dignity of the temperate with what is "fowle and indecent" in the intemperate. The passage merits quotation as illustrating a familiar aspect of Renaissance education:—

> Of all Gods workes, which doe this world adorne,
> There is no one more faire and excellent,
> Then is mans body both for powre and forme,
> Whiles it is kept in sober government;
> But none then it more fowle and indecent,
> Distempred through misrule and passions bace:
> It growes a monster, and incontinent
> Doth loose his dignity and native grace.
> Behold who list, both one and other in this place.

Again Guyon's modesty (IX, 43) contributes with his sympathy, his horsemanship, his excellent body, his courteous manners, to fill out the ideal of the gentleman which he represents.

Medina, like Guyon, illustrates the relation of temperance to good taste and courtesy. She reminds us of Sir Thomas Elyot's description of Temperance as "a sad and discrete matrone and reverend governesse." She is

> A sober sad, and comely courteous dame;
> Who, rich arayd, and yet in modest guize,
> In goodly garments, that her well became,
> Fayre marching forth in honorable wize,
> Him at the threshold mett, and well did enterprize.

The bad manners of the intemperate, as compared with the good breeding of the temperate, appears in the pointed contrast between Medina and Phædria. Guyon is conducted by Medina

> into a goodly bowre,
> And comely courted with meet modestie,
> Ne in her speach, ne in her haviour,
> Was lightnesse seene, or looser vanitie
> But gratious womanhood, and gravitie,
> Above the reason of her youthly yeares.

Phædria, on the other hand, drowned all her words with vain laughter—

> And wanted grace in utt'ring of the same.

Clearly, proper speech as well as comely deportment enters into the educational ideal of the gentleman and gentlewoman. A contrast similar to that noted above is drawn by the poet in Canto VIII between Arthur on the one hand and Pyrochles and Cymochles on the other.

The "vertuous and gentle discipline" to which Spenser gave special attention in the second book is further illustrated in the character of Belphœbe. Here a statement of the educational ideal involves such criticism of the frivolity of courts as we meet with again in *Mother Hubberds Tale* and *Colin Clouts Come Home Againe*. We are reminded, particularly, of the Renaissance ideal of education for women. Asked why she roams the woods instead of remaining at court, Belphœbe in response reveals succinctly her educational position:—

> "Who so in pompe of prowd estate," quoth she,
> "Does swim, and bathes him selfe in courtly blis,

Does waste his dayes in darke obscuritee,
And in oblivion ever buried is:
Where ease abounds, yt's eath to doe amis:
But who his limbs with labours, and his mynd
Behaves with cares, cannot so easy mis.
Abroad in armes, at home in studious kynd,
Who seekes with painful toile, shall Honor soonest fynd.

In woods, in waves, in warres she wonts to dwell,
And wilbe found with perill and with paine;
Ne can the man that moulds in ydle cell,
Unto the happy mansion attaine:
Before her gate High God did sweate ordaine,
And wakeful watches ever to abide:
But easy is the way, and passage plaine
To Pleasures pallace; it may soone be spide,
And day and night her dores to all stand open wide.

The House of Alma in Book II occupies a structural position similar to that given to the House of Holiness in Book I. In each we have a summary treatment of the ethical subject. After an explanation in Canto IX of the plan of the House with some account of its occupants, Spenser describes in Canto XI the attack upon the dwelling place of Temperance by twelve troops led by their Captain Maleger. Seven of these troops are the seven deadly sins and the five others are the temptations that assail the five senses. Their Captain's name, derived from the adjectives *malus* and *aeger,* implies "worn out with evil desires, terrible to others, and miserable in himself." It is appropriate that he should be followed by the hags, Impotence and Impatience. All of this has been suggestively related by Miss Winstanley to Aristotle's three species of moral character that are to be avoided: viz., vice (κακία), incontinence (ἀκρασία), and brutality (θηριότης). Of these, the first and third would seem to be united in Maleger, while the hags represent Incontinence which, as Aristotle says, sometimes appears as weakness and sometimes as impetuosity. "The opposites of vice and incontinence are clear," says Aristotle. "We call the one virtue, and the other continence. As the opposite of brutality it will be most appropriate to name the virtue which is above us, i. e., what may be called heroic or divine virtue. . . . If then it is true, as is often said, that apotheosis is the reward of preëminent human virtue, it is clear that the moral state which is opposite to the brutal, will be some such state of preëminent virtue." Now in the "Legend of Sir Guyon" the man of preëminent virtue, whom Aristotle also calls the "divine man," is obviously Arthur, the effect of whose heavenly splendour is heightened by setting him over against the apparition of all that is bestial and of the earth earthy. Of Maleger the poet writes :—

> As pale and wan as ashes was his looke,
> His body leane and meagre as a rake,
> And skin all withered like a dryed rooke,
> Thereto as cold and drery as a snake,
> That seemd to tremble evermore and quake:
> All in a canvas thin he was bedight,
> And girded with a belt of twisted brake:
> Upon his head he wore an helmet light,
> Made of a dead mans skull, that seemd a ghastly sight.

So obscure is the political allegory of the second book of the *Faerie Queene*, that no interpretation of it is likely to inspire confidence. Professor Buck offered many years ago the following explanation :— Guyon is Thomas Radcliffe, Earl of Sussex, a favorite of the Queen, whose character in its main lines seems to agree with that of Spenser's Knight of Temperance. The temporary enlistment of Guyon in the cause of Duessa might be explained as an allusion to Sussex' loyalty to Catholicism during the reign of Mary. Then, just as Guyon transferred his devotion to the Red Cross Knight, so Sussex promptly became a Protestant upon the accession of Elizabeth. Acrasia is Mary, Queen of Scots, and the Palmer, not quite so clearly, John Knox. It is suggested that Amavia, also, might stand for the Queen of Scots. Mortdant would, then, be the murdered Darnley and Ruddymane would be identified with James VI of Scotland and I of England. Passing over Canto II, in which no political allegory is detected, we may recognize in Braggadocchio and Trompart respectively Alençon, the French suitor of the Queen, and Simier, his secretary. Archimago's offer to steal Arthur's sword for Braggadocchio seems to glance at the effort of the Catholics to undermine the influence of Leicester, who was, of course, hostile to the French match. Since Belphœbe, according to Spenser's own account, is Elizabeth, Trompart's praise of her and his master alludes to the manner in which Simier pressed the suit of Alençon. The episode of Furor in Canto IV points to Sussex' deputyship in Ireland, Furor fighting like the Irish chieftains Shan O'Neill and Sorley Boy Mac Donnell, against whom Sussex had to contend. Like Furor, the two Irish chieftains, though once subdued, broke into rebellion again in 1569. Omitting Professor Buck's very doubtful identification of Phedon with Edward de Vere, Earl of Oxford, it should be remarked that he rejects Upton's guess that Pyrochles and Cymochles stood for Sorley Boy and Shan O'Neill and

identifies them with the most prominent of the northern
rebels, that is, the Earls of Northumberland and Westmoreland. This fits the allegory very well at two points. It is
not only that we have in Cymochles' amour with Acrasia an
allusion to Westmoreland's love for the Queen of Scots
but in Guyon's hostility to the brothers and in the aid
rendered him by Arthur, we may detect an allusion to Sussex' campaign against the Northern earls, his temporary
check, and the timely aid rendered by Lord Hunsdon or the
Earl of Warwick, Leicester's brother. This would involve
a temporary substitution in the allegory of one of these
lords for the other. At this point Professor Buck perti-
nently quotes the following lines from the dedicatory sonnet addressed to Hunsdon :—

> When that tumultuous rage and fearful deene
> Of Northerne rebels ye did pacify,
> And their disloiall powre defaced clene,
> The record of enduring memory.
> Live, Lord, forever in this lasting verse,
> That all posteritie thy honor may reherse.

If the foregoing interpretation is approved, then the
curious incident of the beheading of Pyrochles points to
the execution of Northumberland. Further, the flight of
Archimago may then be explained as an allusion to the
withdrawal of the Catholics from active conspiracy after
the suppression of the Northern Rebellion. It is suggested
that Arthur's duel with Maleger in Canto XI symbolizes
Leicester's almost fatal struggle with those impetuous passions that led to his successive marriages with Amy Robsart
and the Countess of Essex, and that almost brought about
his political downfall. In the service rendered by the Squire

to Arthur we may detect an allusion to Sidney's defense of his uncle in print; or if Timias is Raleigh, the passage alludes to some unknown aid that Leicester received from Raleigh during these times. Finally, we are to interpret the capture of Acrasia as the imprisonment of Mary. Verdant, who is taken with Acrasia, is perhaps Thomas Howard, Duke of Norfolk. As Guyon despatches Verdant to the Fairy Queen, so Sussex pleaded with Elizabeth for the life of Norfolk.

Spenser's borrowings from the *Orlando Furioso* in the second book of the *Faerie Queene,* though not extensive, are significant of the use to which he put his chief Italian source. The derivation of the character of Braggadocchio illustrates in an interesting manner the English poet's free handling of borrowed material. As Professor Dodge pointed out long ago, Spenser has here combined two characters of Ariosto,—Mandricardo, the braggart, and Martano, the coward; and with details drawn from the adventures of both of these knights he has skilfully constructed the story of the braggart-coward Braggadocchio. Neither Mandricardo nor Braggadocchio will use a sword in battle until he can get one that has belonged to the best of knights; the former will be satisfied only with Orlando's Durindana and the latter aspires to the possession of Arthur's Morddure. In subsequent chapters we shall see that parallels in Ariosto to the Braggadocchio story extend to the tournament of Satyrane (IV, iv and v) and to the tournament in celebration of Florimel's wedding.

As in Braggadocchio we have an interesting case of Spenser's skilful use of Ariosto in the creation of character, so in the story of Phedon in Canto IV we find an illustration of his deft adaptation of his source to the requirements of allegory. The corresponding passage in the *Orlando* tells the story of Ariodante (O.F. IV, 57 to VI, 16). The conclusion of Ariosto's story Spenser has notably changed in order to make it an *exemplum* of violent wrath. Ariosto's beguiled lover Ariodante, instead of wreaking vengeance upon the authors of his misfortune, tries to destroy himself at first with his sword and then by leaping into the sea. Having failed in these attempts, he appears in a trial by combat as a champion of his lady, Guevara, even though he believes in her guilt. The situation is made the more dramatic by the fact that it is his own brother with whom he has to fight.

As another example of Spenser's allegorical adaptation of his source, may be cited the parallel between Arthur's fight with the monsters besieging the Castle of Alma in Canto XI and Ruggiero's encounter with similar creatures near the abode of the witch Alcina. Of these creatures Ariosto says that one never beheld any of more hideous mien or more monstrous shape. Some had the heads of cats and others of apes. One had the hoof of a goat. They rode a variety of mounts:—some rode an eagle, others a centaur, still others a goat. Of their leader, to be compared with Maleger, Ariosto gives the following description:—

63

The captain of this crew, which blocked the road,
Appeared, with monstrous paunch and bloated face;
Who a slow tortoise for a horse bestrode,
That passing sluggishly with him did pace:
Down looked, some here, some there, sustained the load,
For he was drunk, and kept him in his place;
Some wipe his brows and chin from sweat which ran,
And others with their vests his visage fan.

Further parallels between the second book of the *Faerie Queene* and the *Orlando Furioso* may be here summarily indicated. A suggestion for the theft of Guyon's horse may have been derived from any one of several episodes in the *Orlando;* note, for example, the stealing by a youthful rustic of Astolpho's horse Rabican in Canto XXII of Ariosto's poem, and the theft of the same horse by Rodomont in Canto XXIII, 33 ff. Compare Archimago's promise to steal Arthur's sword for Braggadocchio with Mandricardo's appropriation of Orlando's sword in O.F. VII, 11–16. Arthur's recovery of his sword in Canto IX, 2, is like Orlando's in O.F. XLI, XLII. The genealogical passage in Canto X, as well as that in Canto III of the third book, should be associated with the third canto of the *Furioso,* and Ariosto's exordium with Spenser's first four stanzas in the tenth canto. In this connection may be quoted Professor Dodge's comment: "Here, as in several other imitations, Spenser directly translates the first few lines, and then drifts into an entirely original rendering of the theme suggested."

Now that we have computed Spenser's debt to Ariosto in the second book of the *Faerie Queene,* we shall have to note that Tasso's influence is here the more significant. This appears in two of Spenser's most beautifully descriptive passages: the episode of the Idle Lake (Canto VI) and that of the Bower of Bliss (Canto XII). In each case he levies contributions from passages in the *Jerusalem Delivered* describing the abode of the enchantress Armida, who brought under her spell so many of the Christian knights vowed to recover the Holy Sepulchre. Details will be found in Cantos X, XIV, XV, and XVI of the Italian epic. With the lake and island of Phædria, who was a servant of

Acrasia, we may compare Tasso's Dead Sea, in which
nothing would sink, with its castle in the midst (Canto X,
61 ff.) :—

> This is the pool in which whate'er is thrown
> Will never sink, but on the surface float;
> Men, iron, marble, brass, and solid stone,
> All that has weight, is buoyed up as a boat:
> A castle crowns the flood, and o'er its moat
> A narrow bridge gives access to the pile,
> Thither we went; within sweet mysteries smote
> Our senses,—Nature wore her brightest smile;
> Gay shone the summer sea, and laughed the enchanted isle.

Among the myrtles and lilacs a silver fountain played, and
the rustling leaves brought slumber to tired eyes. Bees were
humming, doves cooing, and one heard the voice of the
nightingale. Rich viands covered the ivory tables that stood
"on the smooth turf near the melodious wave"; and a hundred charming nymphs crowned with roses waited on the
guests. Of Armida herself Tasso writes :—

> With radiant smiles and fond engaging speech
> She brewed enchantments fatal to our fame;
> Whilst at the feast, from Love's full goblet, each
> Quaffed off a long forgetfulness to shame.

With magic wand and book she transforms the warriors
into fish :—

> Fast as she read, I felt a secret change
> Invest at once volition, sense, and thought;
> I longed the watery element to range,
> Leaped from my seat, and flounced in amorous sport
> Through the smooth wave—so wonderfully wrought

Her spell! my legs combined; my arms began
To incorporate; my tall form grew spare and short;
O'er all my skin bright scales of silver ran;
And the mute fish possessed the late majestic man.

Corresponding to the sea voyage of Sir Guyon and the Palmer to Acrasia's Bower of Bliss is the passage of Ubaldo and Carlo to Armida's island (G.L. XV). We should remark, however, that Spenser alters the authentic geography of Tasso by substituting details from the journey of Ulysses. The English and Italian poems have in common the magic rod that serves to drive away evil spirits and in both we find the doors pictorially decorated. The closeness with which the English poet has followed his source in descriptions of the enchanted land may be illustrated by the following parallels. Spenser's details of description in Canto XII, stanza 58 are painted flowers, trees upshooting high, the dales for shade, the hills for breathing space, the trembling groves, the crystal running by. With these details may be compared Tasso's still waters, moving crystal, various flowers and plants, diverse herbs, little hills open to the sky, shady valleys, groves and caves. Though these lists are not identical, they have most of their items in common. And just as Spenser adds:—

And, that which all faire workes doth most aggrace,
The art, which all that wrought, appeared in no place.

So Tasso (Canto XVI, 9):—

and what increased their play
Of pleasure at the prospect, was to find
Nowhere the happy Art that had the whole designed.

There is a similar parallel between stanza 59 in Spenser and the tenth stanza of Canto XVI in Tasso. In Spenser we read:—

> One would have thought, (so cunningly the rude
> And scorned partes were mingled with the fine)
> That nature had for wantonesse ensude
> Art, and that Art at nature did repine.

Similarly Tasso writes:—

> So natural seemed each ornament and site,
> So well was neatness mingled with neglect,
> As though boon Nature for her own delight
> Her mocker mocked, till fancy's self was checked.

Another close correspondence between the *Faerie Queene* and the *Jerusalem Delivered* is found in Spenser's beautiful lyric, "Ah! see the Virgin Rose," when compared with the following song in Tasso (Canto XVI, 14 ff.), sung by a bird instead of by the human voice as in Spenser:—

"Ah see," thus she sang, "the rose spread to the morning Her red virgin leaves, the coy pride of all plants!

14

Yet half open, half shut midst the moss she was born in,
The less shews her beauty, the more she enchants;
Lo, soon after, her sweet naked bosom more cheaply
She shews! lo, soon after she sickens and fades,
Nor seems the same flower late desired so deeply
By thousands of lovers, and thousands of maids!

15

So fleets with the day's passing footsteps of fleetness
The flower and the verdure of life's smiling scene:

Nor, though April returns with its sunshine and sweetness,
Again will it ever look blooming or green;
Then gather the rose in its fresh morning beauty,
The rose of a day too soon dimmed from above;
Whilst, beloved, we may love, let—to love, be our duty,
Now, now, whilst 'tis youth, pluck the roses of love!"

To his borrowings from the chief poets of the later Italian Renaissance Spenser added a debt in his second book to three great classical poets,—Homer, Virgil, and Claudian. From the *Odyssey* he derives details of Guyon's journey to the Bower of Bliss; for example, the Gulf of Greediness, corresponding to Homer's Charybdis; the Rock of Vile Reproach, similar to Homer's Wandering Rocks and also to the rock in which Scylla lives; and the mermaids, who will remind every reader of Homer's sirens. Guyon's capture of Acrasia in a net is borrowed from Homer's account of the trapping of Venus by Hephæstus (*Odyssey* VIII, 276 ff.). To Virgil Spenser's debt is less considerable. The death of Amavia seems to owe something to the death of Dido in the fourth book of the Æneid, the apparition of Belphœbe suggests that of Venus to Æneas in the first book, and Guyon's visit to the Cave of Mammon has points in common with that of Virgil to the lower world in the sixth book. For the Garden of Proserpine Spenser found several details in Claudian's *Rape of Proserpine,* and for the account of Tantalus in that passage he turns once more to the *Odyssey* (xi, 582 ff.).

REFERENCES

Kitchin, G. W. Ed. *Book II of the Faery Queene.* Oxford, 1910.

Winstanley, Lilian. *The Faerie Queene,* Book II. Cambridge, 1914.

Buck, P. M., Jr. *On the Political Allegory in "The Faerie Queene."* Lincoln (Nebraska University Studies, XI), 1911, 159–192.

Greenlaw, Edwin. *Two Notes on Spenser's Classical Sources.* Modern Language Notes, XLI (1926), 323–326.

Harper, Carrie A. *The Sources of the British Chronicle History in Spenser's Faerie Queene.* Bryn Mawr, 1910.

Padelford, F. M. *The Virtue of Temperance in the Faerie Queene.* Studies in Philology, XVIII (1921), 344 ff.

Powell, C. L. *The Castle of the Body.* Studies in Philology, XVI (1919), 197 ff.

Robin, P. A. *Spenser's House of Alma.* Modern Language Review, VI (1911), 169–173.

Whitney, Lois. *Spenser's Use of the Literature of Travel in the Faerie Queene.* Modern Philology, XIX (1921), 143–162.

CHAPTER XVI

THE FAERIE QUEENE, BOOK III

B OOK THREE of the *Faerie Queene,* it will be seen, is more loosely constructed than the first two books. Its chief character is kept less clearly in view and its episodes are less closely linked. The narrative, in a word, is much more episodic. If Spenser had here followed the plan of the earlier books, Britomart would have early appeared as the champion of Amoret; instead of that she is introduced as the heroine of the romantic quest of Arthegal, and the rescue of Amoret comes in at the end as though in response to a belated recollection of the original plan. No doubt the difficulty of plotting the story was inseparable from its theme. Unlike the Red Cross Knight, Britomart is constant, and unlike Sir Guyon, she is not exposed to temptation. Accordingly, Arthur, having no chance to rescue Britomart, becomes himself romantic in this book of love. Leaving the pursuit of the "wicked foster" to Timias, he chases unavailingly the fleet Florimell, wishing that she might be his Fairy Queen or that his Fairy Queen might resemble her. Furthermore, whereas the second book relates its hero directly to a variety of themes—the angry passions, avarice, worldly ambition, and sensuality—the third book is wholly concerned with love.

The danger of monotony to which his romantic idealism

here exposed him, Spenser avoids by having the heroine share the principal interest of the reader with a number of other characters. The most important of these is Florimell, since she, like Britomart, is in quest of her beloved. However, the facts that Marinell has renounced love and that Florimell lacks Britomart's powers of self-defence, lend to her story both suspense and variety. It therefore properly claims our interest after Britomart drops out of sight in the fourth canto until she reappears in Canto IX. One may note, too, as an interesting detail of structure that the two stories are linked by the encounter between Britomart and Marinell. The attempt here illustrated to promote unity through parallelism and contrast, Spenser again employs in setting the twin birth of Belphœbe and Amoret over against that of Argante and Ollyphant. In this case the contrast is particularly pointed. The "whole creation" of the first two showed them

> pure and unspotted from all loathly crime.

On the other hand, Argante and Ollyphant come to monstrous birth as the fruit of incest. In this case of compared and contrasted themes, as in the other, we see that even though Britomart is not constantly before us in the story, she serves to link its episodes as well as to embody its central idea. As she connected with the Florimell story through the defeat of Marinell, here her rôle is to rescue Amoret and to drive off Ollyphant from the boy that he is pursuing. Finally, the Malbecco episode, which otherwise might stand apart, is employed to bring Britomart once more into the story. Although then Britomart's rôle is unlike that of the heroes of the earlier books, she gives a kind of unity to the third book by connecting in one way or another with its various episodes.

Corresponding to the relative freedom of its structure and responsive to a relaxation of the more rigid demands of allegory, the third book of the *Faerie Queene* exhibits a rich and diversified art. Sumptuously decorative in passages that take their design and color from the art of tapestry and the masque, this book of womanhood is memorable for a vein of sentiment notably feminine. Britomart, her armor laid aside, and in need of comfort from her nurse, is a fearful, love-lorn girl; and Belphœbe, the huntress and devotee of Diana, is all tender solicitude when she comes upon the wounded Timias in the forest. A similarly plaintive or pathetic note is the key of the passage which describes the sea-nymphs' care for the wounded Marinell. In at least two cases the poet enlists nature to prompt a mood and deepen our emotional interest in character. In Britomart's soliloquy by the sea and in Arthur's apostrophe to the night Spenser has advanced beyond the conventional pathetic fallacy or mythological treatment of nature to a realizing sense of its closer bearing upon human experience. In the process, the tempo of his descriptive or narrative style achieves a lyric *élan* that still further heightens the poetic appeal of the book. As a foil to the refinements and the depths of his romantic sentiment, the poet quite characteristically makes us aware in the Malbecco and the Argante-Ollyphant episodes of what is most sordid and vicious. From the height of Platonic love we descend here to the depths of degradation.

From the point of view of Spenser's descriptive art the most noteworthy passages in the third book are found in the eleventh and twelfth cantos. In the former, reminiscent of the pictured walls of mediæval story, no one is likely to forget the coming of Jove to Leda as she slept in her bed of daffodils:

> Shee slept, yet twixt her eielids closely spyde
> How towards her he rusht, and smiled at his pryde;

nor the shepherds calling to Ganymede to take firmer hold of the eagle (st. 34) ; nor the seahorse of Neptune (st. 41). More brilliant, however, than the tapestry poem in Canto XI is the Masque of Cupid in Canto XII. For his treatment of the *Chateau Merveil* theme the poet might have received suggestions from many sources. Most significant are the parallels that have been pointed out by Professor Greenlaw in the English Wagner book or *Second Report* (1594), the *Amadis of Gaul,* the legend of the Holy Grail, and the *Arthur of Little Britain.* Upon whatever source Spenser has drawn, he has succeeded in transforming his borrowed material with a sumptuous and ceremonial rhetoric; so that the interest of masque and romance seems now and then to give way to the deeper significance of ritual.

Chastity, the subject of the third book, is obviously not understood by Spenser in an ascetic sense—as a virtue of the cloister. Comparing it with the virtue of the second book, we are reminded of Aristotle's distinction between virtue as a habit and virtue as a state. Britomart's pleasures are those which one feels "not in the process of acquiring certain powers but in the exercise of the powers when acquired." Her pleasure is "in the consummation and complete realization of her nature." The distinction between temperance and continence, which was made in the chapter on the second book, may here be recalled. "It is inconsistent with the character of the temperate man to have extravagant and wrong desires," says Aristotle. In view of this observation we may say that Britomart's chastity is not only a state but it is also the state of temperance.

As compared with the relatively negative virtue of Sir Guyon, the chastity of Britomart appears not only positive but passionate. Her spirit declares itself not only in her love for Arthegall but in her righteous indignation, as shown, for example, at the castle of Malecasta. For an explanation of this aspect of her character one should turn to the account of temperance which Plato gives in the fourth book of his *Republic*. There passion or spirit is distinguished from desire. "Anger," says Socrates, "differs from the desires and is sometimes at war with them"; and, further, "in the conflict of the soul, spirit is arrayed on the side of the rational principle." Evidently Britomart is temperate or chaste not only because her desires are under the control of her reason but also because her reason is in league with what Plato calls passion or spirit. She is stronger than Sir Guyon in their conflict in the first canto of the third book not only because her temperance is self-assured and self-contained, needing no palmer to point the way, but because it is more positive and passionate. Unlike the impulses of Sir Guyon, her feelings are always on the side of the rational principle.

Britomart's chastity, considered as a form of temperance, may be related not only to these Aristotelian and Platonic ideas but also to the Christian version of this Greek virtue. For example, Melanchthon, commenting upon the apostolic use of ethical terms, wrote of temperance: "In apostolic writings temperance in food and drink is called sobriety; but the Latins properly call it modesty (*pudicitia*), S. Paul sometimes αγνεία, sometimes *sanctificatio*. Σωφοσύνη

(Sophrosune) he uses more broadly and it generally means modesty, that is, moderation in one's whole bearing, discourse, gait, and pleasures of every kind, according to Cicero; it is what the Germans call *zuchtig*." Having quoted first Timothy, ii, 15 to the effect that Eve shall be saved by faith, love, and sanctification with sobriety, Melanchthon goes on to say that temperance as here understood embraces such necessary virtues as faith, the fountain of true prayer; love, which involves the honorable discharge of one's duties toward one's husband, children, and other relations; then, sanctification, which implies modesty, chastity, and conjugal faith. The virtues temperance, sobriety, and modesty, all pertain, he adds, to the sixth commandment. Such an account of temperance shows the relation of this virtue to Britomart's love for Arthegall, to her championship of the Red Cross Knight, and to the prevailing dignity and courtesy of her manners. With the Red Cross Knight, Spenser says, she had made "a friendly league of love perpetual."

Remembering that chastity is a kind of temperance and that temperance is fundamental to personal or private morality, we may regard it as significant that Spenser should have symbolized in Britomart's love for Arthegall the affinity of this virtue for justice, the fundamental virtue of social relations. Here again he forges a link in the golden chain of the virtues. If, further, we regard chastity as an ideal form of love, the romantic symbolism declares that the closest of personal ties is related to broad political and social obligations, an idea which like so many others the poet derived from Aristotle. Having declared in the fourth chapter of the fifth book that "justice is not a part of virtue but the whole of virtue," Aristotle went on to say in the first chapter of the eighth book that "friendship or love is the bond which holds states together, and that legislators set more store by it than by justice; for concord is apparently akin to friendship, and it is concord that they especially seek to promote, and discord, as being hostility to the state, that they especially try to expel. If people are friends, there is no need of justice between them; but people may be just and yet need friendship." Further, in the eleventh chapter of the same book, Aristotle wrote: "It appears, as has been said at the outstart, that friendship and justice have the same occasions and the same sphere; for every association seems to involve justice of some kind and friendship as well." Though in these passages Aristotle speaks more often of friendship than of love, he makes as a matter of fact no clear distinction between the two; so that what is said of one relation may be regarded as true of the other. Furthermore, the third and fourth books of the *Faerie Queene,* considered as a continuous narrative, offer a blended treatment of the two themes. Britomart's friendships and antipathies figure as prominently as her love in the third book, and the fourth book is as much a book of love as a book of friendship. We need have no hesitation then, in applying to Spenser's ethical allegory Aristotle's distinctions noted above.

With the Aristotelian idea of the relation between friendship or love and justice, Spenser combines the Platonic idea that love is divine. This is set forth partly in his symbolism and partly in his rhetoric. Merlin's mirror, for example, obviously relates itself to the figure of speech so frequently employed by Platonizing poets. It will be remembered that in the October eclogue Piers, commending the poet's love for Rosalind, had said:—

Such immortall mirrhor as he doth admire
Would rayse ones mynd above the starry skie.

Likewise, in the *Hymne in Honour of Love,* the poet had
written :—

Such is the powre of that sweet passion,
That it all sordid basenesse doth expell,
And the refyned mynd doth newly fashion
Unto a fairer forme which now doth dwell
In his high thought, that would itself excell;
Which he beholding still with constant sight,
Admires the mirrour of so heavenly light.

Besides this detail of Platonic symbolism, one should note
the descriptions of love in the third book which run parallel
to passages in the *Hymne.* A good illustration is the first
stanza in Canto III :—

Most sacred fyre, that burnest mightily
In living brests, ykindled first above,
Emongst th' eternall spheres and lamping sky,
And thence pourd into men, which men call Love;
Not that same which doth base affections move
In brutish mindes, and filthy lusts inflame,
But that sweete fit that doth true beautie love,
And chooseth Vertue for his dearest dame,
Whence spring all noble deedes and never dying fame.

If one seeks to analyze further the ethical allegory of
the third book, it is seen to offer no such progressive sequence of moral ideas as was found in books one and two.
The poet has, indeed, still in mind the Aristotelian principle
of the golden mean. Malecasta, no doubt, represents a vice
of excess, and Marinell and Belphœbe a vice of deficiency

with respect to the ideal love illustrated by Britomart, whose victories over the other two prove the superiority of the golden mean. Nevertheless, Professor Dodge rightly remarks, "one cannot but see that, whatever else this allegory might do, it certainly does not, like that of the first two books, present a succession of distinct spiritual states considered in the abstract." He maintains that "the men and women of the third book should be regarded not as allegorical figures strictly speaking, but rather as certain general types engaged in actions which are typically moral." Showing in this regard a closer approximation to Ariosto than appeared in the legends of the Red Cross Knight and Sir Guyon, "the legend of Britomart has allegorical episodes but of general allegory only so much as one might read into almost any romance poem."

Having presented in Britomart and Malecasta examples of the chaste and the unchaste woman, Spenser further develops his theme by delineating types of womanhood in whose natures forces of good and evil come into conflict. Evidently Amoret runs the risks of strong passions. The symbolism of the House of Busirane can only mean that she needs to be rescued from these passions by the purity for which Britomart stands. In this we are concerned with an inner struggle. With Florimell the case is different. Just as her own love for Marinell is not reciprocated, so the passions she excites in all sorts of men she cannot or would not return.

Opposed to both Amoret and Florimell is Belphœbe. The adopted child of Diana, she is not, like Amoret, subject to lust, nor like Florimell is she weak and fearful; but she has unfortunately the defects of her qualities. With her self-reliance there goes a harsh and ungenerous disposition.

While we approve her repulse of Braggadocchio's advances, we deprecate her treatment of Timias. As with the advance of the story she grows in sympathy, her character like Amoret's achieves its balance. Her heart is softened at the sight of Timias's sufferings. "Thus," says Professor Padelford, "did Belphœbe learn that austere virtue is itself unlovely and wrong, and that chastity must be softened by mercy."

The political allegory of the third book may be regarded as even more conjectural than that of the earlier ones. In the third book Spenser had said that the Queen would be able there "in mirrours more than one herself to see." "Taking this literally," Professor Buck argues, "it seems reasonable to regard many of the heroines of this book as Elizabeth under her several characteristics." The forester pursuing Florimell he would identify with the Irish rebels, whom Raleigh (Timias) would destroy; Arthur (Leicester) and Guyon (Sussex) are in the meantime more interested in winning the favor of the Queen. The victory won by the Red Cross Knight over the champions of Malecasta is supposed to glance at the war waged by Sir John Norris against the Holy League in France. As Malecasta sought the favor of Britomart, so Catherine tried to win that of Elizabeth, for example by offering her sons in marriage. If Arthegall, according to the traditional interpretation, is Arthur, Lord Grey, Britomart's love for Arthegal should be interpreted to mean the Queen's devotion to Spenser's patron in Ireland. Taking exception to Upton's identification of Marinell with Lord Howard of Effingham, Professor Buck thinks that the original of the character is Sir Walter Raleigh. It is pointed out that his arms, like those of Marinell, showed squared scutcheons and that the conflict with Britomart in the poem might correspond with the episode mentioned in the beginning of *Colin Clouts Come Home Againe*. Further, Raleigh's temper, like that of Marinell, was brusque, and "the name Marinell is almost an anagram of Raleigh's as it was then pronounced." In Timias we have the love-lorn Raleigh contrasted with the more robust shepherd of the ocean. The witch, into whose hut Florimell goes, is Catherine, and her son the objectionable Alençon; the fisherman who attempts to violate Florimell is Lord Thomas Seymour, Lord High Admiral of England, whose courtship of Elizabeth, when she was a child of fourteen, is notorious. Proteus is Philip II, who, when Elizabeth at this time might have incurred suspicion of treason, came to her rescue. Assuming that the hyena that pursues Florimell is to be interpreted as the wrath of France, we may identify Satyrane with the Prince of Orange, who helped to check this wrath. The "false Florimell seems to be Elizabeth drawn into trifling courtships for political reasons"; Braggadocchio is "Alençon in another character," and Sir Ferraugh who takes off the false Florimell is the Archduke Charles of Austria, "who played hide and seek with Elizabeth and Alençon in the seventies to the utter disconcerting of all Englishmen." Paridell Professor Buck identifies with the Earl of Oxford, and Burghley's daughter with Malbecco's wife: Anne Cecil was deserted by Oxford as Malbecco's wife was deserted by Paridell. Perhaps in the final episode of the book we may see in Busirane Lord Burghley and in Scudamour Lord Essex, whose suit of Elizabeth the Lord Chancellor opposed.

To return to the heroine of the third book, it should be remarked that Britomart is not only the embodiment of a Christianized Greek virtue but also a type of epic character.

Her lineage may be derived from the famous Amazons of the Trojan epic, Camilla and Penthiselea, through Boiardo's and Ariosto's Marfisa and Bradamante. In the seventh book of the *Æneid* Camilla is described as coming from the race of the Volsci, leading a company of horsemen and troops resplendent in brazen arms,—a warlike woman, whose hands had never been accustomed to the distaff and wicker-basket of Minerva. Though a virgin, she had learned how to endure the hardships of war and to run swiftly before the winds. She could fly over the fields without injuring the grain and over the ocean without wetting her feet. Many would come out to watch her go by, her smooth shoulders adorned with purple, her hair bound with a golden clasp, bearing a quiver and the pastoral myrtle. Similarly Virgil describes Penthiselea in the first book of the *Æneid* as bringing to the aid of the Trojans a band of Amazons equipped with moon-shaped shields. She raged in the midst of thousands, and though a girl, she dared to contend with men.

In these classical Amazons may be recognized the remote ancestors of the Marfisa of Boiardo and Ariosto. As originally delineated by Boiardo, Marfisa exhibits along with great physical endurance a severity of temper that is unrelieved by any of the gentler emotions. A Saracen woman, she is in this regard set over against the Christian Bradamante. In illustration of her hardihood and resolution may be recalled her fulfilment of an oath not to divest herself of her armor until she had defeated three kings— Gradasso, Agricane, and Charlemagne. The coat-of-arms on her mighty shield made of bone and sinew was a crown, on the top of which was represented a green dragon spewing fire. So marvelous was this pictured fire that when blown upon by the wind it kindled into living flame, and in the midst of the battle the wonderful shield would flash forth terrible lightning. Marfisa's armor made by enchantment was such that in battle she could neither feel fear nor receive injury; and the horse on which she rode was the largest that nature had ever produced.

The portrait of the Saracen Marfisa as drawn by Boiardo is appreciably toned down by Ariosto. Nevertheless, though she still offers a contrast with Bradamante, the latter is first of all the virgin warrior and only in the second place a woman in love. "Bradamante," says Foffano, "is the virgin warrior of the Tuscan poets illuminated and as it were made gentle by love; but she is more pleasing under the first aspect than under that of the lover. Certainly there is lacking to the externals of her love story nothing that can make it interesting; separation from her youthful lover, opposition to their marriage on the part of others, the jealousy which assails her when she believes herself deceived, the fatal demand that she should take a husband who is pleasing to her parents; but we should like to see her more in love, more persistent in her purpose, in a word more of a woman."

Perhaps the most striking portrait of Bradamante offered by the *Orlando* is found in Canto XXXII. Having unhorsed the three kings, Bradamante has been admitted to the Tower of Tristram. Her unarming is described in the following stanzas:—

> As Bradamant unarms, and first her shield
> And after puts her polished casque away,
> A caul of shining gold, wherein concealed
> And clustering close her prisoned tresses lay,

She with the helmet doffs; and now revealed,
(While the long locks about her shoulders play)
A lovely damsel by that band is seen,
No fiercer in affray than fair of mien.

As when the stage's curtain is uprolled,
Mid thousand lamps, appears the mimic scene,
Adorned with arch and palace, pictures, gold,
And statues; or as limpid and serene
The sun his visage, glorious to behold,
Unveils, emerging from a cloudy screen;
So when the lady doffs her iron case,
All paradise seems opened in her face.

Already so well grown and widely spread
Were the bright tresses which the hermit shore,
These, gathered in a knot, behind her head,
Though shorter than their wont, the damsel wore;
And he that castle's master, plainly read,
(Who often had beheld her face before)
That this was Bradamant: and now he paid
Yet higher honors to the martial maid. (lxxix–lxxxi.)

Having so far considered Britomart as the embodiment
of a Christian idea of temperance, and as an epic type of
character, we may try further to understand her in the light
of a Renaissance ideal of education. Like the *Cortegiano*
of Castiglione the *Faerie Queene* is a book of the gentlewoman as well as of the gentleman; and temperance as much
in the third book as in the second is seen to be fundamental
to good breeding. Here and there it will be instructive to
supplement the description of Bradamante with details
drawn from the portrait of Belphœbe.

Some of the treatises dealing with the education of

women may be regarded in effect as answers to John Knox's celebrated broadside on the *Monstrous Regiment of Women*. Elyot's *Defence of Good Women* is in particular a defence of Queen Catherine; and it might be supposed that Spenser in naming Elizabeth Tanaquil had in mind one of the best known books of instruction for women produced during the Renaissance. In the third chapter of Vives's *Instruction of a Christian Woman,* which early in the century was translated into English by Richard Hyrde, the author praises Caia Tanaquil, an Etruscan born, as a very noble woman and a sad wife unto Tarquin Priscus. Besides the books by Vives and Elyot might be mentioned John Aylmer's *An Harborowe for Faithfull and Trewe Subjects* (Strasbourg, 1559), described by Foster Watson as a "doughty defence of a woman ruler"; Cornelius Agrippa's *De Nobilitate et Praecellentia Foeminei Sexus,* translated in 1542 by David Clapham under the title *The Excellency of Womankind;* and William Bercher's *The Nobylyte off Wymen.* Some of these books are obviously less concerned with doctrine than with praise. Their point of view is well indicated by the opening stanzas of Canto IV of the third book of the *Faerie Queene.*

The question whether women should have the same education as men was raised in the fifth book of Plato's *Republic;* and Plato asked in particular whether the art of war was one of those arts in which a woman can or cannot share. Castiglione, too, in the third book of the *Courtier* touches upon the same theme. In the dialogue of the *Courtier,* Lord Julian, who has been assigned the subject of women's education, is strictly excused from a consideration of such topics because "I fashion," he says, "a waiting gentlewoman of the Court, not a Queene." Nevertheless, he is willing to declare that "if you will consider the ancient histories (albeit men at all times have been very sparing in writing the praises of women) and them of later daies, ye shall finde that continually virtue hath reigned as well among women as men : and that such there have been also that have made war and obtained glorious victories, governed realmes with great wisdom and justice and done whatever men have done."

Elyot's *Defence,* which is one of the books written in praise of the great women of history, seeks to establish a similar contention. He takes as a model Zenobia of Palmyra. In view of Spenser's selection of temperance as the chief virtue of womanhood, it might be noted that Elyot has Zenobia declare that in a woman no virtue is equal to temperance. He goes on to say that Zenobia "always sat among her nobles and councillors and said her opinion ; she visited the whole realm and the marches, reëdified fortresses, and new made also sundry munitions."

This type of heroic woman, active in public life, was, in no uncomplimentary sense, called a virago in the Italy of the Renaissance. "The term," says Burckhardt, "implied nothing but praise." It was borne, for example, by Caterina Sforza. Burckhardt quotes a letter from Galateo to Bona Sforza offering the following advice :— "Act in such a manner that you will please wise men, that prudent and grave men will admire you, and despise the pursuits and opinions of vulgar people and little women." A good example of the virago seems to have been Ippolita Fioramonda, to whom the author of the *Cortegiano* wrote :— "Your ladyship has shown to all the world, in addition to her other qualities, to be a valiant lady in arms, and not only beautiful, but still bellicose." With Belphœbe in mind we might cite the case of Diana Saliceto Bentivoglio, described by a contemporary as follows :— "This lady was tall, rather thin than fat, and dark-skinned. She had black eyes, teeth white and regular, and a grave demeanour. She was swift in walking. She always wore beautiful veils. She had a ready and elevated mind and her conversation was always of the best. . . . She was not fond of music, singing, feasts, and dancing. Her pleasure after merry speech, full of propriety, was the forest,—to go fowling according to the season and to hunt. In this she was very intrepid not fearing the heat, the sun, the cold ; and accustomed herself readily to quiver and bow in hunting the boars and stags with the other nymphs like Diana, whose name she deserved to have."

In contrast with the virago is the type of woman which the system of Vives was calculated to produce. His *Instruction of a Christian Woman* stresses obedience and seclusion, training in medicine, needle-work, and cookery. In such characters as Medina and the gracious personalities of the House of Holiness we may perhaps recognize the influence of this type as well as that of the ideal waiting-woman, whom Castiglione undertook to fashion in the *Cortegiano*. In addition to the social graces, Castiglione would have his gentlewoman endowed with "staidness, nobleness of courage, temperance, strength of mind, wisdom, and the other virtues not so much to entertain (although notwithstanding they may serve thereto also) as to be virtuous : and these virtues to make her such a one, that she may deserve to be esteemed, and all her doings framed by them." (Everyman Edition, p. 195.)

Besides modeling the character of Britomart upon that of Bradamante, Spenser has borrowed from Ariosto many details and incidents for his legend of Chastity.

With Malecasta's love of Britomart may be compared that of Fiordispina for Bradamante in the twenty-fifth canto of the *Orlando Furioso*. The setting of the stories, to be sure, is different: in Ariosto the meeting takes place in the forest, in Spenser in the Castle of Delight. Nor in the *Orlando* is there any such sharp termination of the episode as we find in Spenser. Even after Bradamante has revealed her sex, which she does more in sorrow than in anger, Fiordispina cannot get the better of her love.

To form the story of the Castle of Delight this Fiordispina episode seems to have been combined by Spenser with the Ruggiero-Alcina story in the seventh canto of the *Orlando*. There Alcina goes to the chamber of Ruggiero just as Malecasta goes to the room of Britomart. Here as elsewhere we find the English poet altering and combining to suit his purpose.

A more striking parallel betwen the *Orlando* and the *Faerie Queene* is that presented by the visits of Bradamante and Britomart to the cave of Merlin. Each one is in quest of her lover: Bradamante of Ruggiero and Britomart of Arthegal. It should be noted, however, that the prophecies are differently managed in Spenser and Ariosto. In Ariosto Merlin is not present in the flesh to declare the prophecy of Bradamante's descendants. His voice comes as a voice from the dead, and there pass before the eyes of Bradamante the phantom shapes of those who shall succeed her. In both accounts Merlin prophesies not only the union of the lovers but the illustrious lineage which shall arise from their marriage. To Spenser's "shall spring out of the ancient Trojan blood" corresponds Ariosto's "l'antico sangue che venne da Troia"; to his "renowned kings and sacred emperors," Ariosto's "marchesi, duci, e imperatori"; and to his "brave captains and most mighty warriors" the "i capitani, i cavalier robusti" of the Italian poet.

It should be noted, further, that in Canto 28 of the *Orlando* King Rodomont and Jocundo out of mere curiosity make a quest similar to that upon which the Squire had been despatched in Spenser's seventh canto; and Britomart's adventure at the Castle of Malbecco corresponds to that of Bradamante at the Rocca di Tristano (O.F. XXXII).

The manner in which Spenser has treated his source in this last case is instructive of his method. In Ariosto the castle has a custom somewhat like that of Spenser's Castle of Delight. If a knight asking admission to this castle finds that others have already been admitted, he has to fight those who have anticipated him before his request will be granted. According to this custom it becomes necessary for Bradamante to overthrow three kings before she is given shelter. In Spenser's Malbecco story Britomart has a chance encounter with Paridell, who with other knights has taken shelter from a storm in a little shed. Again, the description of the unarming of Britomart follows closely Ariosto's account of the unarming of Bradamante; but Spenser has made several changes in the story of the jealous husband. In Ariosto that story is told Bradamante by the castellan after she has asked him about the origin of the customs of the castle. Moreover, Ariosto's Clodion is very different from Spenser's Malbecco. He is not an old man, and his punishment for his churlish refusal to entertain strangers is to spend a rainy night outside of his castle in jealous anxiety about his wife, who stays behind to entertain the stranger. In the morning the lady of the castle is returned unharmed to her lord. The story of Malbecco moving like a goat among the satyrs Spenser draws from quite a different place in Ariosto. This belongs to the story of the Orc in the seventeenth canto of the *Orlando,* and the disguise is there assumed by Norandino that he might gain access to his lady and also escape from the clutches of the monster. The whole situation is then quite different from that in the English poet. Finally, the prophecy which is attached to Paridell's tale of Troy is a weak version of Ariosto's prophetic paintings on the pictured walls of Tristan's castle. The idea of the pictured room seems to have been transferred to the House of Busirane. The independence here shown in handling sources is eminently characteristic of Spenser.

For the story of Florimell's flight Spenser used Ariosto's story of Angelica's pursuit by the hermit in the first canto of the *Orlando Furioso.* For the later narrative of Florimell he seems to have drawn on the legend of Britomart, who, as Warton, the historian of English poetry, long ago pointed out, was the daughter of Jupiter and Charme. The name among the Cretans was, indeed, only another name for Diana. Like Diana, again, Britomart was called Dictynna because she was a maker of nets for hunting. Antoninus Liberalis, who wrote in the second century after Christ, emphasizes the chastity of Britomartis. In his *Metamorphosis* he tells a story about her which is similar to Spenser's Florimell-fisherman episode. Like Florimell, Britomartis, fleeing from Minos, takes refuge in a fisherman's boat. When he attacks her, she jumps from the boat and escapes. If, as Koeppel has suggested, Spenser knew the 1568 Basel edition of Antoninus, we might conjecture that he pieced out Ariosto's story with the Britomartis legend. It may be further suggestive, as Koeppel also pointed out, that the love story of Proteus immediately follows the Hermit-Angelica story in the *Orlando.*

REFERENCES

Briggs, W. D. *Spenser's "Faerie Queene," III, ii, and Boccaccio's "Fiammetta."* Matzke Memorial Volume, Stanford University Publications, 1911.

Bruce, J. D. *Spenser's Faerie Queene, Book III, Canto vi, st. 11 ff., and Moschus' Idyl, Love the Runaway.* Modern Language Notes, XXVII (1912), 183–185.

Cook, A. S. *The Amazonian Type in Poetry.* Modern Language Notes, V (1890), 321–328.

Greenlaw, Edwin. *Spenser and Lucretius.* Studies in Philology, XVII (1920), 331 ff.

Greenlaw, Edwin. *Britomart at the House of Busirane.* Studies in Philology, XXVI (1929), 117 ff.

Koeppel, E. *Florimel and Britomart's Saga.* Archiv für das Studium der neueren Sprachen und Litteraturen. CVII (1901), 394 ff.

Padelford, F. M. *The Women in Spenser's Allegory of Love.* Journal of English and Germanic Philology, XVI (1917), 7 ff.

Padelford, F. M. *The Allegory of Chastity in the "Faerie Queene."* Studies in Philology, XXI (1924), 367 ff.

Tuell, Anne K. *Original End of Faerie Queene, III.* Modern Language Notes, XXXVI (1921), 309 ff.

CHAPTER XVII

THE FAERIE QUEENE, BOOK IV

TO many critics the fourth book of the *Faerie Queene* has appeared to be the most loosely organized of the entire poem; and, indeed, every reader's first impression must be one of much crowding of characters and confusion of episodes. We are frequently called upon to transfer our interest from one person of the story to another, and we seem to glimpse no clear objective among the quickly shifting scenes of the narrative. If we turn for guidance to the title of the book, we shall find mentioned there the heroes in no sense of the book as a whole, but only the chief characters of an interpolated episode. However, before condemning out of hand the structure of the "Legend of Friendship," we should be sure that we understand what Spenser is there trying to do.

Evidently the fourth book of the *Faerie Queene* departs even further than the third from the centralized biographical method of the first and the second. First of all it should be noted that in only a small portion of the narrative are we concerned with the titular heroes. This is no doubt due to the fact that the "Legend of Friendship" more than any preceding book is felt to be a sequel. As Upton says, the poet here "gives a solution of former distresses and plots." To be sure, as has already been pointed out, characters like Archimago, Duessa, the Red Cross Knight, and Sir Guyon were carried over from one to the other of the earlier books, but in each of the first two it may fairly be said that the plot was completed in the twelve cantos; whereas stories like those of Britomart and Arthegal, the false Florimell, Marinell, and the true Florimell, which were begun in the "Legend of Chastity," carry on through the "Legend of Friendship" into the "Book of Justice." Spenser's alteration of the Amoret-Scudamour story at the close of the third book is instructive of his changed method. With the publication in 1590 of the first three books that episode was closed with the union of the lovers. When in 1596 the second three books were added, the story was reopened by representing Scudamour and Glauce as abandoning their post before the House of Busirane in despair of seeing again either Amoret or Britomart. From what has been noted above it will then be clear that Spenser's task in the plotting of the fourth book was to keep in hand several threads of narrative interest which had been left at loose ends at the close of the third.

The continued stories in the fourth book are those of 1. the false Florimell; 2. Scudamour and Amoret; 3. Britomart and Arthegall; 4. Timias and Belphœbe; and 5. Marinell and Florimell. Before the opening of the fourth book these, we should observe, had been associated in one manner or another; the two Florimells had been opposed as the true and the false; Amoret and Belphœbe were both linked as twin sisters and contrasted as adopted children of Venus and Diana respectively; and Britomart is not only the lover of Arthegal but the friend and protector of Amoret. Furthermore, Spenser's return to the true Florimell story in the last two cantos of the fourth book is comparable to his treatment of the Amoret episode in the last two cantos of the third. The third, fourth, and fifth books are in this manner dovetailed, the stories with which the third and the fourth conclude being in each case developed in the sequel. To these continued stories are added two new episodes, which are here begun and ended,—those of Cambel-Triamond and Amyas-Placidas,—setting forth respectively a mystical and a romantic ideal of friendship.

To promote further the unity of his story Spenser extends the principle of contrast from his treatment of character to his handling of plot. The two main lines of narrative interest, that is, the stories of false Florimell and Amoret, are opposed as tales of false and true friendship. These two lines converge at the Tournament of Satyrane in Canto IV, at which the true knights and ladies of the Britomart-Amoret group contend with the false knights and ladies of the Blandamour-Florimell group, first in the tournament itself and then in the test of the girdle. So far a quite orderly progress is interrupted in the manner of the romantic epic only by the long parenthesis of the Cambel-Triamond episode. After the tournament the main interest shifts to the second of the contrasted stories, that of Amoret, which is developed principally through the next six cantos. Once more there is a focal point in the massing of good and evil characters during the assault upon Britomart in Canto IX, a situation which is just as far from the end of the story as the Tournament of Satyrane is from the beginning. Similarly in cantos approximately equidistant from the center of the book Spenser balances the interpolated episode of Cambel and Triamond against that of Amyas and Placidas.

At other points of his story it is evident that Spenser has employed this principle of comparison and contrast in order to hold together the elements of his diversified narrative. For example, Até, "the mother of debate and all dissention," is in studied contrast to Concord, "the mother of blessed Peace and Friendship trew," Até's dwelling being "hard by the gates of hell" (I, 20), whereas Concord's is a second Paradise (X, 23). One may contrast, too, the strife provoked by Até in II, 18 with the reconciliation brought about by Arthur in IX, 3; and a comparison may be drawn between the rôle of Cambina in the Cambel-Triamond story (II, III, IV), who creates friendship through her drink Nepenthe and her magic wand, with the services of Arthur,[1] who makes similar use of a precious liquor and a sword in the Aemylia-Amyas-Placidas plot (Canto VIII). To these examples it may not be fanciful to add the contrast between the strife-provoking girdle of the Florimel story (Canto V) and the reconciling ruby heart in the story of Belphœbe-Timias.

Friendship, one need hardly say, had received full attention from poets and philosophers long before Spenser celebrated it in the *Faerie Queene*. It had been defined and analyzed by Plato, Aristotle, Plutarch, and Cicero; Montaigne had treated it in a famous essay; and it was illustrated abundantly in such familiar stories as those of Orestes and Pylades, Damon and Pythias, and David and Jonathan. With the classical ideal is mingled in Spenser's poetry that of mediæval romance. Particularly was the English poet influenced by the romance of *Amis and Amiloun,* a story of

---

[1] As in Book III, Arthur, not needed for a major rescue, finds himself once more adrift, straying "through the wandring wood" and "seeking adventures, where he mote heare tell" (Canto VII, st. 42). His rescue of a youth from Corflambo in Canto VIII should be noted, but the "deedes of Arthur applyable" to friendship are obviously those of the peacemaker illustrated in Canto IX.

fratres jurati, in which Walter Pater was able to detect a mediæval anticipation of the spirit of the Renaissance. Further, while writing a book in which he particularly pays his respects to Chaucer, Spenser was not likely to overlook the Canterbury tale of the friendship of Palamon and Arcite, which in the sixteenth century was given dramatic form by both Edwards and Fletcher.

Though friendship in the *Faerie Queene* is accounted as one of the virtues which Aristotle "hath devised," Aristotle describes it as only "a kind of virtue" or as "something that goes along with virtue." It is, he says, a motive rather than a mode of conduct. Since it is not exactly a virtue, it cannot be used as an illustration of the golden mean, though we may so use the friendly manner which is a social quality avoiding overcomplaisance on the one hand and bluntness on the other. True friendship, going deeper than this, enters into all the fundamental associations of life. "It is indispensable to life," says Aristotle; "for nobody would choose to live without friends, although he were in possession of every other good." "There are some people," he adds, "who hold that to be a friend is the same thing as to be a good man." Since friendship includes the true love of man for woman (see the Prologue to Book IV), and indeed all the domestic relations, not to speak of the broader forms of social and political intercourse, it is not without good authority that Spenser illustrates friendship in the Arthegal-Britomart story and in that of the sons of Agapé. If in the former case friendship may be understood as in one aspect a political virtue, the narrative also serves well to introduce the political allegory of Book V.

According to Aristotle, there are friendships of pleasure, profit, and goodness; though, properly speaking, those which look merely to pleasure and utility are only semblances of the true association. For one thing, they are impermanent; whereas friendship based upon virtue is not only lasting but it insures the highest forms of both pleasure and profit. When Spenser wrote that "vertue is the band that bindeth harts most sure" (II, 29), he was echoing a commonplace of the philosophers from Aristotle to Cicero. Bad men, Aristotle had declared (VIII, viii, 5–6), can be friends only for the short time that they take pleasure in each other's wickedness. Writing of Blandamour and Paridell, Spenser declared:—

> Ne certes can that friendship long endure,
> How ever gay and goodly be the style,
> That doth ill cause or evill end enure.

If virtue is, thus, necessary to friendship, conversely, friendship is essential to the highest virtue. The classical moralists not only maintained that the association of friends is one into which enter all highly desirable things, such as, honesty, glory, tranquillity, and delight of mind, but they added that virtue cannot without this association attain to the highest good. Spenser's friendship is like his holiness and his Platonic love not simply a sphere of the virtuous life but an actual school of moral discipline. People, said Aristotle, cannot really be friends before each has shown the other that he is worthy of friendship and has won his confidence; as in the story of the *Faerie Queene* the Salvage Knight must prove himself worthy of Britomart.

To prove oneself worthy of one's friend was in a sense to become his equal. To be sure, Aristotle deals with the friendship of the unequal, though he admits that the disparity between two persons may be such that friendship is impossible. A father may, indeed, be a friend to his son, but to insure the equality of benefits necessary to friendship the former must receive "something greater in amount or more valuable in kind."

This inequality in friendship, which Spenser has particularly illustrated in the companionship of Britomart and Amoret, is regulated by the principle of distributive justice; each party to the friendship is rewarded in proportion to his merit. However, there is lacking a perfect communion because the rewards are of different kinds. In such relations as that of Britomart and Amoret the profit of the superior is honor; whereas that of the inferior is the help received. "In perfect friendships, the friends are really equal and each gets from the other a return of like and equal kind" (VIII, viii, 6). Spenser's Triamond is eligible for the friendship of Cambalo only after he has established his equality by annexing the souls of his brothers. This idea was formulated in a commonplace of the moralists, which, originating with Zeno, is echoed by Aristotle, Cicero, and Montaigne, but objected to by Bacon; namely, that a friend is an *alter ego,* or the replica of oneself. As an illustration of this ideal, Sir Thomas Elyot in the *Governour* cited the story of Orestes and Pylades, the famous friends whose story Euripides told both in the *Orestes* and the *Iphigenia in Tauris*. These friends so resembled each other that the King of Tauris wishing to kill Orestes could not distinguish him from his *alter ego*. The corresponding story in the *Faerie Queene* is that of Amyas and Placidas, which, as will appear, borrows several features from the mediæval romance of *Amis and Amiloun.*

An even more intimate or mystic relation is suggested in the episode of the sons of Agapé. Spenser says (II, 43) it was "as if but one soule in them all did dwell"; which might remind one of Aristotle's observation that "brothers are in a manner the same being though in different persons." Cicero in more general terms expressed a similar idea in the *De Amicitia* (xxi, 81): "It is natural," he says, "for a man to seek out another whose mind will so mingle with his own that instead of two we shall almost get one"; and elsewhere in the same treatise (xxv, 93) he had remarked that the strength of friendship is seen in its making one mind out of several. One might recall finally the wedding of the Thames and the Medway as symbolizing the more intimate union of spirits.

Only the friendship of the good, Aristotle observed, is secure against the assaults of calumny. An illustration of this and other themes may be noted in the story of Amoret; for, whereas the lives of Blandamour, Paridell, Até, Duessa, and the false Florimell are thoroughly and positively evil; and whereas Braggadocchio in Book IV as in Book II stands for a vice of deficiency, since he is incapable of either hating or loving—

For in base mind nor friendship dwels nor enmity,

conflicting forces that are hostile and favorable to true love and friendship meet in the Amoret story. In the first place, Amoret appears as the victim of lust in the House of Busirane. Rescued by Britomart from her captivity here (III, vii), she needs to be once more saved from "greedie Lust" by Belphœbe in the fourth book. "It is the young," says Aristotle, "who make friends for pleasure; like lovers, they are guided by passion." To this weakness in Amoret corresponds Scudamour's liability to suspicion. Believing

the slander of Até, he not only doubts the virtue of Amoret
but suspects the integrity of his old friend Glauce. Contrasted with this, is the suggested security against slander
of Amoret and Æmylia when attended by Arthur. They
dwelt in the very house of slander and were "followed fast"
and "reviled sore" by "the shameful hag"—

> she did annexe
> False crimes and facts, such as they never ment.

But she only illustrates an impotent rage, still barking and
backbiting,

> Though there were none her hatefull words to heare
> Like as a curre doth felly bite and teare
> The stone which passed straunger at him threw;
> So she them seeing past the reach of eare,
> Against the stones and trees did rayle anew,
> Till she had duld the sting which in her tongs end grew.

A milder form of the dark suspicion of Scudamour is
illustrated in the jealousy of Belphœbe. Able to free her
twin sister from "greedie Lust," Belphœbe is not above sus-
pecting Timias when she comes upon him tenderly caring
for the wounded Amoret. In the case of both Scudamour
and Timias there is shown the contrast between that tranquillity of mind already noted as one of the fruits of true
friendship, and the distress and anxiety which disturb the
association not grounded in complete virtue. Scudamour in
the House of Care is, thus, a companion picture to Timias
living in the wilds.

Looking broadly at Spenser's treatment of friendship
in the fourth book of the *Faerie Queene,* we might regard
as its text the sentence of Cicero: "If it be not clearly per-

ceived how great is the power of friendship and concord, it can be distinctly inferred from quarrels and dissensions." As Professor Erskine says: "The allegory of the fourth book is a variation of a few themes; it tries to put into narrative the ways by which the virtuous enter into the communion of friendship, the ease with which false friends fall out, the warfare that the devil wages against all harmony, the temporary estrangement that discord sometimes achieves between good men and women, and the relation of love to friendship."

While we have no difficulty in tracing in Aristotle and Cicero most of Spenser's ideas on friendship, it has been shown by Professor Erskine that a nearer source is probably Giraldi Cinthio's *Tre Dialoghi della Vita Civile,* upon which Spenser's friend Bryskett drew in writing his *Civil Conversations.* Following Aristotle, Giraldi had remarked that friendship, if not a virtue, is near to virtue, and, indeed, that the other virtues cannot be practised without it. Upon virtue must rest that true communion of minds which, according to Plato, constitutes true friendship. Where evil exists there can be only discord. The cause of that friendship which makes, as it were, one mind in two bodies is beauty. "According to Plato," says Giraldi, "beauty has the chief part in friendship—that is to say, the beauty of mind which is born of virtue; it binds human minds with such a knot and with so firm a consent that they become, as it were, one thing, and it appears that a single mind dwells in two bodies." In this manner, Britomart's beauty affected Arthegall. But, sometimes, as in the case of the false Florimell, a beautiful body will lead one to love a base mind; this, says Giraldi, cannot be called friendship, but rather a low and abominable union. Further on, in speak-

ing of the relation between friendship and love, Giraldi
quotes Plato as saying that friendship is a habit acquired by
long love or that friendship is a kind of inveterate love. He
recalled too that the author of the Lysis had said that
friendship contains love, though love does not necessarily
contain friendship. It would seem, for example, that though
Scudamour and Amoret were lovers, they were not true
friends; for out of their separation grew misunderstanding; whereas true friendship, according to Giraldi, should
be a communion of minds which cannot be impaired by
length of time or separation or great happiness or adverse
fortune or any other accident which befalls mankind. It is

> the band
> Of noble minds derived from above,
> Which being knit with vertue, never will remove.

Of the political allegory of the fourth book very little
can be said with confidence. Indeed it is only in the Belphœbe-Timias episode that we find an historical situation
at all clearly reflected. Its hero, whose name derives from
the Greek adjective τίμιος, meaning honorable, may be
rather confidently identified with Raleigh; and Amoret
would then be some lady for whose sake the great Sir
Walter had incurred the displeasure of his Queen. The lady
in question is probably Elizabeth Throckmorton, one of
Elizabeth's maids of honor, whose secret marriage with
the Queen's favorite in 1593 led to his banishment from
court. However, Queen Elizabeth's displeasure, like that
of Belphœbe, was not protracted; and in 1596, the year
in which Spenser published the second three books of the
Faerie Queene, Raleigh, enjoying once more the royal
favor, served as an admiral in the expedition against Cadiz.

For the story of the fourth book of the *Faerie Queene* we turn once more to Ariosto as Spenser's chief source. Here and there we shall find that the Arthegall-Britomart story still runs parallel to that of Ruggiero and Bradamante. For example, Arthegall's courtship of Britomart in *Faerie Queene* IV, vi, st. 40 ff. suggests Ruggiero's courtship of Bradamante in the *Orlando* XXII, 31–36. In each case the hero wins the love of his lady soon after they have recognized each other, and, like Arthegal, Ruggiero promises his lady to return at the expiration of three months. With this parallel in the situation there goes a difference in style which will be apparent to any one who compares with the corresponding stanzas in Spenser the following less temperate passage from Ariosto:—

XXXII

Rogero looks on Bradamant, and she
Looks on Rogero in profound surprise
That for so many days that witchery
Had so obscured her altered mind and eyes.
Rejoiced, Rogero clasps his lady free,
Crimsoning with deeper than the rose's dyes,
And his fair love's first blossoms, while he clips
The gentle damsel, gathers from her lips.

XXXIII

A thousand times they their embrace renew,
And, closely each is by the other prest;
While so delighted are those lovers two,
Their joys are ill contained within their breast.
Deluded by enchantments, much they rue
That while they were within the wizard's nest,

They should not e'er have one another known,
And have so many happy days foregone.

In other episodes Spenser none the less obviously drew
upon his Italian source. The permission granted the false
Florimell at the tournament of Satyrane to choose her own
knight may be compared with the similar favor accorded
Doralice in the *Orlando* (XXVII, 104 ff.), though Doralice's choice of the intrepid Mandricardo is very different
from Florimell's decision in favor of the cowardly Braggadocchio. Here in Ariosto the allegorical figure of Discord
corresponds to Spenser's Até. Over the strife among the
knights in Canto XXVII,

> mad Discord laughed, no more in fear
> That any truce or treaty should ensue;
> And scowered the place of combat there and here,
> Nor could stand still, for pleasure at the view.
> Pride gamboled and rejoiced with her compeer,
> And on the first fresh food and fuel threw,
> And shouted so that Michael in the sky
> Knew the glad sign of conquest in that cry.

In passages of this kind, Ariosto's merely incidental personifications are clearly inferior to Spenser's full-fledged
allegory.

Here an inconsistency in Spenser's description of Até
may be traceable to the influence of Ariosto. Having in
Canto I, st. 17 said that Até together with Duessa bore
"faire semblance in face and outward shew," he goes on in
st. 27–29 to describe her face as foul and filthy. In the
second passage he seems to have had in mind the hag
Gabrina, who in *Orlando Furioso* (Canto XX) is met by
Marphisa after she has separated from those who shared

her adventure in the land of Orontea. Of Gabrina, Ariosto wrote:

> Older than Sibyl seemed the beldam hoar,
> As far as from her wrinkles one might guess,
> And in the youthful ornaments she wore,
> Looked like an ape which men in mockery dress. (XX, 120.)

Further, we might compare Braggadocchio's cowardice at the Tournament of Satyrane (F.Q. IV, iv, st. 20) with Martano's conduct at the tournament of Damascus (O.F. XXVII, 88–90). Ariosto's narrative, it will be noticed, is much more circumstantial then Spenser's. Of Braggadocchio we are simply told that he hesitated, "as one that seemed doubtful or dismayd," and that Triamond thereupon snatched his spear from his grasp. The corresponding passage in Ariosto is as follows:—

88

> When vile Martano from his place discerned
> The fate which might be *his* with fearful eye,
> Into his craven nature be returned,
> And straight began to think how he might fly:
> But him from flight the watchful Guyphon turned,
> And after much ado, with act and cry,
> Urged him against a knight upon the ground,
> As at the ravening wolf men slip the hound;

89

> Who will pursue the brindled beast for ten,
> Or twenty yards, and, after, stop to bay;
> When he beholds his flashing eyes, and when
> He sees the grisly beast his teeth display.

'Twas thus, before those valiant gentlemen
And princes, present there in fair array,
Fearful Martano, seized with panic dread,
Turned to the right his courser's rein and head.

90

Yet he who would excuse the sudden wheel,
Upon his courser might the blame bestow:
But, after, he so ill his strokes did deal,
Demosthenes his cause might well forego.
With paper armed he seems, and not with steel,
So shrinks he at the wind of every blow:
At length he breaks the ordered champions through,
Amid loud laughter from the circling crew.

91

Clapping of hands, and cries, at every turn,
Were heard from all that rabble widely spread.
As a wolf sorely hunted makes return
To earth, to his retreat Martano fled.

A further parallel may be drawn between Spenser's
episode of Æmylia in the cave of Lust (Canto VII, 15 ff.)
and Ariosto's account of Isabella in the robbers' cave (O.F.
XII, 89 ff.). In the Italian poem Orlando, in search of his
love Angelica, observes a light shining through a fissure in
the mountain side. Guided by the flickering ray he de-
scends by a long flight of steps into a cave. In the middle of
the cave, sitting by a fire, Orlando sees a girl about fifteen
years old, who, though she was weeping, made the rugged
scene appear a paradise. She was attended by an old woman,

and the pair
Wrangled, as oftentimes is women's way.

Upon the entrance of the knight the women cease their quarreling, and Isabella tells her story. She, a Saracen girl, having fallen in love with the Christian Zerbino, could be united with him only in secret. To this end Oderic, the best friend of her beloved, meeting her in her garden by the sea, carries her off by ship. The party is shipwrecked and only she and Oderic are saved. On a lonely shore Isabella encounters a fresh peril in the importunate love-suit of Oderic, from whom she is not quite happily rescued by the robbers in whose care she has been discovered by Orlando. The old woman attending Æmylia may be compared not only with the old woman of the Isabella story but with Gabrina, already described, with some reminiscence perhaps of the housekeeper of the Orc, the terrible creature described by Ariosto in the seventeenth canto of the *Orlando*.

A few other parallels between the fourth book of the *Faerie Queene* and the *Orlando* may be briefly pointed out: —Just as Até excites Scudamour's jealousy in I, 47 ff., by charging Amoret with infidelity, so Gabrina, whose resemblance to Até has already been noted, arouses Zerbino's suspicions by similar charges against Isabella (O.F. XX, 134 ff.). Spenser's bridge guarded by Doubt in Canto X (st. 2 ff.) is similar to Ariosto's bridge guarded by Erifila or Avarice (O.F. VI, 78, 79; VII, 2-5)—a character that may be compared with the Lady Munera of the bridge in Book V of the F.Q. Finally the Gardens of Adonis in Canto X seem to be slightly reminiscent of the gardens described in the *Furioso* in VI, 19-22; X, 61-63; XXXIV, 49-51.

A few sources for the fourth book, aside from Ariosto, may finally be indicated. Upton remarked that "the Fay Agapé seems imaged from the Fay Feronia in Virgil (Æn.

VIII, 564), who had procured for her son three souls, and 'thrice he was to be slain before destroyed.' " Upton further indicated that several passages in the tournament of Satyrane echo Chaucer's *Knight's Tale*. The dove that leads Belphœbe to Timias is compared by the same editor to the bird of Venus that conducted Æneas to the golden bough in *Æneid* VI, 191. This note Miss Clara W. Crane has supplemented by calling attention to a similar detail in the old French romance of *Violette*. There to a defamed and abandoned maiden, sorrowing for the loss of her lover, is brought a lark, who, flying with the maiden's ring about his neck to the forgetful lover, brings about a reconciliation like that which takes place in the *Faerie Queene* between Belphœbe and Timias. Finally, as already noted, the Amyas-Placidas story, is reminiscent of *Amis and Amiloun,* a romance of friendship which was widely popular throughout the Middle Ages and of which a thirteenth-century Middle English version exists. The two stories have in common the exact likeness of the friends, their perfect friendship, the wooing lady, the reluctant young man, and the device of substituting one friend for the other.

REFERENCES

Albright, E. M. *"The Faerie Queene' in Masque at the Gray's Inn Revels.* Publications of the Modern Language Association, XLI (1926), 497 ff.

Ayres, H. M. *The Faerie Queene and Amis and Amiloun.* Modern Language Notes, XXIII (1908), 177–180.

Covington, F. F. Jr. *A Note on the "Faerie Queene,"* IV, iii, 27. Modern Language Notes, XL (1926), 253.

Crane, Clara W. *A Source for Spenser's Story of Timias*

and Belphœbe. Publications of the Modern Language Association, XLIII (1929), 635–644.

Erskine, John. *The Virtue of Friendship in the Faerie Queene.* Publications of the Modern Language Association, XXX (1915), 831 ff.

Joyce, P. W. *Spenser's Irish Rivers.* Fraser's Magazine, N.S., XVII (1878), 315 ff.

Osgood, C. G. *Spenser's English Rivers.* Transactions of the Connecticut Academy, XXIII (1920), 65 ff.

CHAPTER XVIII

THE FAERIE QUEENE, BOOK V

IN BOOK V Spenser repeats certain details of narrative structure already noted in Books I and II. For example, early in the first canto is introduced the motif of a quest assigned by the Fairy Queen. Just as the Red Cross Knight was to rescue the land of Una from the dragon of sin, so Arthegall was assigned the task of recovering the heritage of the lady Eirena, wrongly withheld by Grantorto. The story, thus set in its course, proceeds to three *exempla* of justice, those of Sanglier, Pollente, and the giant with the scales. These, one should note as marking here a characteristic difference of structure, are, unlike the corresponding *exempla* of temperance in Book II, in no way connected with the objective or subsequent developments of the plot. Reverting to the Florimell story in Canto III, Spenser turns that very pointedly to the account of his ethical theme by giving prominence to the punishment of Braggadocchio; but here again, as in the following story of the two brethren, there is no effort to weave this thread of narrative interest into the subsequent action of the book. So far we have but a set of *exempla* connected only by the person of Arthegall and unified only by their common theme. Nor is there any attempt, as in Books III and IV, to pattern the story by studied parallelism and contrast.

This highly episodic arrangement of rather more than

the first fourth of Book V gives way in Canto V to the continuous narrative interest of the Arthegall-Radigund-Britomart story, which, like the Florimell episode, resumes an earlier theme. But so far as Book V is concerned it is quite independent of what precedes or follows. Occupying about the same space as the purely episodic section of the book, the poet's moral intention does not here encroach to an equal extent upon his art. After being introduced by the rescue of Terpine, the story passes to the defeat and rescue of Arthegall, developing a romantic interest in the Clarin incident and providing a complication in Dolon's plot against Britomart. As emphasizing the independence of this part of Book V we should note further that Arthur, though very prominent in the last division of the book, does not here rescue the hero, and that Britomart's separation from Arthegall after she has liberated him from Radigund is very weakly motivated.

Rather more than half of the book having been thus divided into two distinct sections, the last five cantos are as sharply marked off for the exploits of Arthur and Arthegall. More fully than in any previous book Arthur here co-operates with the titular hero. Together they slay the Soudan and capture Guile in Cantos VIII and IX. Then, as in Book II, Canto IX, Arthur and Guyon go together to the House of Temperance, so here in a corresponding canto Arthur and Arthegall accompany each other to Mercilla's palace; and Arthur champions Mercilla as in the earlier book he had championed Alma. Such correspondences might suggest that Spenser had at one time in mind a structure for the fifth book similar to that which he has followed in Book II, but that the necessity of continuing the Britomart story and the exigencies of the political allegory resulted in a more patchwork arrangement than we find in any other book of the *Faerie Queene*.

Spenser's account of Justice follows the main lines of Aristotle's analysis of the virtue in Book V of the *Nicomachean Ethics*. In chapter iii of this Book Aristotle defines Justice as complete virtue, not, to be sure, "in an absolute sense, but in relation to one's neighbours." It is "more glorious than the star of eve or dawn." Some such comprehensive sense, Spenser may have had in mind in the opening lines of the first stanza of Canto VII:—

> Nought is on earth more sacred or divine,
> That gods and men doe equally adore,
> Then this same vertue that doth right define.

In the Greek sense of the term any wrong action may be called unjust; e. g., acts of cowardice or anger. It is interesting to note that Spenser shares with Aristotle one illustration of this point,—the cowardice of the man who throws away his shield in battle (Aristotle V, iv and F.Q. Canto XI, st. 46).

But clearly the poet is particularly interested in justice understood as "a part of virtue"; and this, following Aristotle, he divides into distributive and corrective justice. In Chapter V of the *Nicomachean Ethics* we read:— "There are two kinds of particular justice and of the just action which corresponds to particular justice, one consisting in the distributions of honour or wealth or any other things which are divided among the members of the community, as it is here that one citizen may have a share which is equal or unequal to another's, the other kind which is corrective of wrong in private transactions. This latter again has two subdivisions, private transactions be-

ing (1) voluntary, and (2) involuntary. Voluntary transactions are such as selling, buying, lending at interest, giving security, lending without interest, depositing money,
hiring; and they are said to be voluntary because the origin
of these transactions is voluntary; i. e., people enter upon
them of their own free will. Involuntary transactions again
are either (1) secret, as e. g., theft, adultery, poisoning,
pandering, enticing slaves away from their masters, assassination, and false witness; or (2) violent, as assault, imprisonment, murder, rape, mutilation, slander, and contumelious treatment."

In his special treatment of distributive justice in the following chapter (vi), Aristotle says that what is unjust in
this sense may be called unfair; and this kind of justice may
be considered "a sort of proportion." "That which is just
must imply four terms at least; for the persons relatively to
whom it is just are two, and the things in which it consists are two likewise. Also, if the persons are equal, the
things will be equal; for as one thing is to the other thing,
so is one person to the other person. For if the persons are
not equal, they will not have equal shares." Further on
in Chapter vii this Justice is defined as "a mean between
the violations of proportion; for that which is proportionate is a mean, and that which is just is proportionate."

While conceding (Chapter vi) that the standards of merit
will vary with the government, the democrats setting up
freedom as their standard, the oligarchs wealth or nobility,
and the aristocrats virtue, Aristotle, and Spenser following
him, sides with the aristocrats. These were entitled by
virtue of their native nobility to the wealth, powers, and
privileges that churls would wrest from them. Inimical
to the existing social order, which Spenser believed was

divinely appointed by God, were not only the forces of violence and corruption but also the misguided social idealists, who, like the Anabaptists of Munster, would create a society embodying subversive ideas of liberty, fraternity, and equality. Dealing with the subject in the third chapter of the third book of his *Governour,* Sir Thomas Elyot wrote: "The inferior persone or subjecte aught to consider, that all be it (as I have spoken) he in the substance of soule and body be equall with his superior, yet for als moche as the powars and qualities of the soule and body, with the disposition of reason, be not in every man equall, therfore God ordayned a diversitie or preeminence in degrees to be amonge men for the necessary derection and preservation of them in conformitie of livinge." If we think that the instinct of beasts whereby they choose governors and leaders is reasonable, "how farre out of reason shall we judge them to be that wolde exterminate all superiorietie, extincte all governaunce and lawes, and under the coloure of holy scripture, whiche they do violently wraste to their purpose, do endeavour them selves to bryng the life of man in to a confusion inevitable." Quite similar views Spenser might have met with in his master Chaucer, who has his Parson say:— "But for-as-muche as the estaat of hooly chirche ne myghte not hav be, ne the commune profit myghte not hav be kept, ne pees and reste in erthe, but if God hadde ordeyned that some men hadde hyer degre and som men lower, therfore was sovereyntee ordeyned to kepe and mayntene and deffende hire underlynges or hire subgetz, in resoun, as ferforth as it lith in hire power, and not to destroyen hem ne confounde."

These ideas of distributive justice Spenser has illustrated in the two episodes that constitute the second canto of the fifth book. The story of Pollente and Lady Munera deals with the acquisition of wealth by the wicked through deceit and violence. As Pollente symbolizes power, his daughter Munera, like the Lady Mede of *Piers Plowman,* represents bribery and the forces of corruption. In contrast with the true nobilty founded upon virtue, Pollente is a *parvenu,* **a** *nouveau riche,*

> Having great lordships got and goodly farmes,
> Through strong oppression of his power extort.

His daughter, too, has wrongfully amassed so much wealth that she is richer than many princes and, a land grabber, she

> purchast all the countrey lying ny
> With the revenue of her plenteous meedes.

No doubt, as has been suggested, the prototype of such a family Spenser could easily have found in Ireland. In the second episode of the Giant with the scales the poet passes from a practical to a theoretical treatment of his subject. If the economic doctrine which Spenser has here in mind is Communism, the doctrine illustrated in Plato's *Republic,* Sir Thomas More's *Utopia,* and the social experiment of the Anabaptists in Munster, he evidently misunderstands that which he undertakes to condemn. The giant on the rock argues for the equalization of property, not for the ownership of all property by the state. Rejecting the Aristotelian principle of proportionate distribution, explained above, the giant, speaking for the many-headed multitude, would reduce all things "unto equality." As in the former episode the poet attacked the newer aristocracy of wealth and power, here he assails the "vulgar," the "rascall crew," who gather about the visionary social reformer as do "foolish flies about an hony crocke." The only answers made by Spenser to the advocates of democratic principles, such as the pamphleteer Robert Crowley, who lived in the poet's time, is that the established order was divinely appointed and that the proposed reforms are contrary to the principle of the golden mean. Forgetting perhaps the July eclogue, Spenser can write in stanza 41 :—

> The hils doe not the lowly dales disdaine;
> The dales doe not the lofty hils envy.

For his social philosophy, he would argue, he can find a divine sanction. But it is Aristotle of whom he is thinking when in stanza 49 he writes :—

> it was not the right which he did seeke;
> But rather strove extremities to way,
> Th'one to diminish, th'other for to eeke:
> For of the meane he greatly did misleeke.

The logic of this contention should be referred to the seventh chapter of the fifth book of the *Nicomachean Ethics*. "That which is proportionate," says Aristotle, "is a mean, and that which is just is proportionate"; and, further on, we read, "disproportion may take the form either of excess or defect; and this is actually the case, for the author of the injustice has too much, and the victim has too little, of the good." Evidently for both Aristotle and Spenser equalization implies disproportion, and is therefore contrary to the golden mean.

If we turn now from distributive to corrective justice, we shall find that Spenser follows Aristotle in discrimi-

nating between the unjust and the unfair, or between law
and equity. In the fourteenth chapter of the fifth book of
the *Nicomachean Ethics,* Aristotle declares that justice and
equity "are not absolutely the same, nor generically different"; and, further on, that "while that which is equitable is
just, it is not just in the eye of the law, but is a rectification
of legal justice. And the reason is that all law is couched in
general terms, but there are some cases upon which it is
impossible to pronounce correctly in general terms."

To equity as to distributive justice Spenser gives both
general and particular treatment. The particular case is the
story of the two brothers in Canto IV, to whom the sea
brings respectively land and treasure. Here, again, as in the
theory of society set forth in Canto II, the case is referred
to the tribunal of God. That which, acting through the
forces of nature, God has brought about, must be right;
as it is right that there should be hills and valleys, princes
and peasants.

The theoretical statement of the principle of equity here
involved is implicit in the symbolism of Canto VII. Here
Isis stands for "that part of justice which is equity" (VII,
3), and, further, as we gather from stanzas XV and XXII,
she represents Britomart herself, while the crocodile, standing for Osiris, is also a symbol of Arthegall. The whole
relationship, then, between Britomart and Arthegall is here
conceived in terms of that between equity and justice, and
equity is understood as involving clemency (stanza 22):—

> For that same crocodile Osyris is,
> That under Isis feete doth sleepe for ever:
> To shew that clemence oft, in things amis,
> Restraines those sterne behests and cruell doomes of his.

The vice corresponding to this virtue of clemency, as Seneca pointed out in the *De Clementia,* is *misericordia* or pity, and it is this infirmity which has brought about the downfall of Arthegall in Canto V, as it was almost the undoing of Sir Guyon during his journey to the Bower of Bliss. Having overcome Radigund and unlaced her helmet, he is astonished by her beauty :—

> At sight thereof his cruell minded hart
> Empierced was with pittifull regard,
> That his sharpe sword he threw from him apart,
> Cursing his hand that had that visage mard.

Just as the defect of clemency is pity, so the vice corresponding to the firmness, the *severitas* of the upright judge, is *crudelitas* or barbarity. *Misericordia* and *crudelitas* Seneca describes as vices of the mind, a leaning, on the one hand, to weak pity and, on the other, to savageness. True justice, then, as here understood, is what Aristotle calls a state, or as Spenser says in Canto II, stanza 47 :—

> But in the mind the doome of right must bee.

Such a view of equity, or of the relation between mercy and justice, Spenser might have found expressed in the literature of his own time. It was, indeed, often invoked to support a philosophy of tolerance. In England not only Lord Bacon and Hooker but Gabriel Harvey, the poet's friend, reasoned against the intolerance of extremists. Hooker's intention in his *Ecclesiastical Polity* was "not to provoke any but rather to satisfy all tender consciences"; and Bacon recommended that every one in those troubled times should be "swift to hear, slow to speak, slow to wrath." Writing in a similar vein in his *Pierces Supereroga-*

tion, Harvey counseled a following of Aristotle's doctrine of the golden mean; for "it is neither the Excess, nor the Defect, but the Meane, that edifyeth." In France quite similar views were expressed by Michel de l'Hôpital, the author of the *Traité de la Reformation de Justice,* and Jean Bodin, who wrote among other works the *Six Livres de la République.* "Never," says de l'Hôpital, "under the pretext of mercy should we work injustice, nor under the protection of a harsh and severe justice should we be guilty of any cruelty." In the opinion of Bodin the proper temper of the magistrate may be described as "gravité douce."

Evidently Spenser in his "Legend of Justice" has represented this doctrine as the ideal of his Queen. The very name Mercilla, here assigned Elizabeth, makes the matter clear; and among those attending upon her throne are wise Eunomie, mild Eirene, and "goodly Temperance in garments clene." In the very act of enforcing justice she was "ruing" the "wilful fall" of Duessa. In another passage the queen, Mercilla, is described as holding in her royal hand a sceptre which is

> The sacred pledge of peace and clemencie,
> With which High God had blest her happie land,
> Maugre so many foes which did withstand.
> But at her feet her sword was likewise layde,
> Whose long rest rusted the bright steely brand;
> Yet when as foes enforst, or friends sought ayde,
> She could it sternely draw, that all the world dismayde.

In his consideration of corrective justice Aristotle, as already noted, had distinguished voluntary from involuntary transactions. The former are voluntary because "the origin of these transactions is voluntary; i. e., "people enter upon them of their own free will"; and the examples given by Aristotle are various forms of business transactions that would be covered nowadays by business law. An example of this type of justice is offered once more by the case of the two brothers, whose story begins with the bequests contained in the will of their father. On the other hand, Aristotle's so-called involuntary transactions, whether secret or violent, are naturally not overlooked in Spenser's allegory. Theft, here listed by Aristotle, is illustrated in the story of Guyon's horse stolen by Braggadocchio, and false witness, another item in Aristotle's list, by

> That false Duessa, which had wrought great care
> And mickle mischiefe unto many a knight,
> By her beguyled and confounded quight;

and plots of assassination by the tale of Dolon and his trap-door in Canto VI. Of the items in Aristotle's list of examples of violent injustice Spenser has illustrated murder in the story of Sanglier, both imprisonment and contumelious treatment in the episode of Arthegall and Radigund, and slander in the episode of the hags and the Blatant Beast in Canto XII.

In the thought of Jean Bodin we may find a parallel not only for Spenser's philosophy of justice but also for those views on the "woman question" which occupy so considerable a part of the fifth book. Opposed to the idealism of the third book and contrary to the views expressed by Plato and Sir Thomas More, Spenser here takes a position with which John Knox, the author of the *First Blast of the Trumpet against the Monstrous Regiment of Women,* might have agreed. Like Knox, he must have had in mind such dominant women as Margaret of Parma, Catherine de' Medici, Mary Queen of Scots, and her mother, Mary of Lorraine. As representative of the class he sets up Radegund, opposing to her Britomart, in whom had been focussed the feminine idealism of the "Legend of Chastity." The poet comments upon the type in the twenty-fifth stanza of the fifth canto :—

> Such is the crueltie of women kynd,
> When they have shaken off the shamefast band,
> With which wise Nature did them strongly bynd,
> T'obay the heasts of man's well ruling hand,
> That then all rule and reason they withstand,
> To purchase a licentious libertie.
> But vertuous women wisely understand,
> That they were borne to base humilitie,
> Unlesse the heavens them lift to lawfull soveraintie.

Taking a similar position, Bodin had written in the Republic :—"There has never been either law or custom which has exempted women from the obedience and reverence which they owe to their husbands"; again, "there is nothing greater in this world, as Euripides says, nor more necessary for the conservation of republics, than obedience of the wife to her husband."

If, seeking further light upon Spenser's ideal of justice, we turn now, as we have done before, to Cicero's *De Officiis,* we may find grounds for disagreeing with Dr. Gough in his opinion that in Canto V Arthegall's "symbolic rôle is so far forgotten that he seizes on a prospect of escape in spite of his parole, and encourages Clarinda's passion with ambiguous compliments and 'faire semblant.'" Cicero might have judged otherwise, since he writes in the tenth chapter of the first book of the *De Officiis:* "Justice is altered by an alteration of circumstances. Further, it is plain to any one's sense that such sort of promises can never be binding as are made by people overawed by fear, or over-reached by deceit." Since Spenser gives much attention to the relation between justice and deceit, let us note, further, the following passage in the thirteenth chapter of the same treatise: "In fine to close up this discourse of justice, there are two ways or methods whereby one may injure or oppress another; the one is fraud and subtlety, the other open force and violence; the former of which is esteemed the part of a fox, and the latter of a lion; both of them certainly very unworthy of a reasonable creature, though fraud, I think, is the more odious of the two. But of all injustice, theirs is certainly of the deepest die, who make it their business to appear honest men, even whilst they are practising the greatest of villanies."

The political allegory of the fifth book is more transparent than that of any other in the *Faerie Queene*. Touched lightly in the earlier cantos, it develops in great detail from Canto VI to the end. Its main themes present different aspects of the Catholic danger in England, France, the Low Countries, and Ireland. In Canto VI Dolon's plot against Britomart clearly reflects Catholic attempts against the life of the Queen. If we recall the rôle that Philip II here played, we shall be disposed to identify the character of Dolon with the Spanish king. Beneath a surface of friendly relations, represented by the treaty of 1573 and suggested in the allegory by Dolon's hospitality, Philip lent his support to the schemes of Mendoza, the Spanish ambassador, and the Jesuit mission. He seems also to have had a hand in the Throckmorton plot of 1583, that had as its purpose the assassination of Elizabeth. It has been further suggested that the two knights who seek to murder Britomart in her chamber may be identified with the Duke of Guise and his brother, the Duke of Mayenne, who had planned in 1583 to coöperate with Philip in an invasion of England.

In Canto VII the Radigund-Britomart duel is obviously to be interpreted as the conflict between Mary Queen of Scots and Elizabeth. The allegory is so far true to the historical situation that the two queens may be said to have contended not only for the advantage of their respective religions but for their lives. If the Queen of Scots had been victorious, Elizabeth would no doubt have met the fate of Mary. Furthermore, the slaughter of the Amazons by Talus will suggest the punishment of English Catholics; for example, the hundreds that were hanged after the Rising of the Northern Earls had failed.

Leaving in Canto VIII the theme of Mary's political duel with Elizabeth, Spenser returns to the subject of Anglo-Spanish relations. In the rôle of Samient, who acts as a messenger between Mercilla and the Souldan, the poet glances at the efforts of Elizabeth to adjust by diplomacy the differences between the two countries. It is significant that the hero of this episode in Spenser's story is not Arthegall but Arthur. The distortion of history in this case is noteworthy. Leicester, with whom Arthur is here as elsewhere to be identified, was, indeed, appointed by Elizabeth as the commander-in-chief of her land forces when the Spanish invasion threatened; but the great victory was of course by sea, and with that Leicester had nothing to do. Nevertheless, details of the Pagan's warlike equipment and of his fighting have been referred to the Spanish Armada; for example, the effect of Arthur's unveiled shield to that of

the English fireships sent against the Spanish galleons, and
Arthur's attack of the Souldan from behind, explained in
stanzas 31–6, to the plan of the English leaders to make a
rear attack upon the Spanish ships in the Thames. If ingenuity seems here to overshoot the mark, we might accept
as significant the parallel between the Souldan's chariot
furnished with hooks and Parma's ships held in reserve at
Antwerp, which were similarly equipped with iron spikes
and hooks.

In Canto IX the allegory shifts to Ireland. Malengin in
his unkempt appearance and in the deceit which his name
declares represents certainly the wild and elusive Irish
against whom Lord Grey had to contend. The agility and
trickery which he uses in making his escape are suggestive
of the methods of guerilla warfare employed by the Irish;
and the poet's introduction of the episode at this point
might be interpreted as meaning that the Lord Deputy's
policy was to destroy the roving bands of the wild Irish before proceeding to restore Ireland to its true allegiance and
save it from Roman dominion. The trial of Duessa, which
is a further episode in this canto, points so clearly to the
trial and condemnation of Mary, Queen of Scots, that
it called forth a well-known protest from her son, James VI.
We should not expect here historical accuracy in detail.
Elizabeth was of course not present in person at Mary's
trial, and no doubt Spenser was misleading in writing:—

> Yet in that wretched semblant, she did sure
> The peoples great compassion unto her allure.

On the other hand Arthegal's presence is supported by the
historical fact that Lord Grey was a member of the com-

mission that tried the case against the unhappy queen and later passed upon her the sentence of death. In stanza 40 Spenser has no basis in history for saying that mention was made at the trial of the many knights that Mary had "beguyled and confounded quight," but he is correct in pointing out that the sole charge brought against her was that of

> vyld treasons, and outrageous shame,
> Which she against the dred Mercilla oft did frame.

In the concluding stanza of the canto Spenser interprets the well-known indecision of Queen Elizabeth in a way to suggest that it was prompted more by sympathy than policy. However, it should be noted that among those who pleaded for Duessa was

> Daunger threatning hidden dread,
> And high alliance unto forren powre.

In compact form Canto X deals with the conflict between England and Spain in the Netherlands. As in the poet's account of the trial of Mary, Queen of Scots, Elizabeth is here represented as the merciful queen. She goes into the Netherlands as into Ireland because of her sympathy for the oppressed population. "It is greater prayse," says the poet, "to save, then spill." It is on this key that the tenth canto opens. The story proper begins with the arrival at Mercilla's court of "two springals" of the widow Belge. Of her seventeen sons all but five had been devoured by the fell tyrant Geryoneo. No allegory could be more transparent than this. The name of the distressed lady and the exact correspondence between the number of her sons and the number of the provinces which constituted the Netherlands, puts the meaning of the passage beyond the shadow of a doubt. In all probability the "two springals" who wait upon Mercilla are to be equated with the provinces that took the lead in the revolt of the Netherlands, namely, Holland and Zeeland, although Upton was of the opinion that they represented the Marquess of Havre and Adolf Meetkercke, whom the states sent as special envoys to England in 1577.

The story told by the messengers lends itself almost as easily to interpretation as the above details of the allegory. Some question might arise as to whether Geryoneo should be identified with Philip II or with the Hapsburg dynasty, which in the person of the emperor Charles V fell heir to the Netherlands on the death of Charles the Bold, Duke of Burgundy. If the latter is the husband of the Lady Belge, Charles V is the "bold tyrant" whom in her widowhood she accepted as her champion. In accord with this, the more likely interpretation, is the description of the policy of the champion in the following lines :—

> Whereof she glad, now needing strong defence,
> Him entertayn'd, and did her champion chose :
> Which long he usd with carefull diligence,
> The better to confirme her fearelesse confidence.

> By meanes whereof, she did at last commit
> All to his hands, and gave him soveraine powre
> To doe what ever he thought good or fit.
> Which having got, he gan forth from that howre
> To stirre up strife, and many a tragicke stowre,
> Giving her dearest children one by one

Unto a dreadfull monster to devoure,
And setting up an idole of his owne,
The image of his monstrous parent Geryone.

This is true to history in that the tyranny of Philip II was preceded by the wise policy of Charles V. The latter, indeed, showed "careful diligence" in unifying the Netherlands and in freeing them from the Empire. In this way he might be said to have inaugurated their independence. But later, like Spenser's champion, he "spoiled his own work," in the words of Mr. Armstrong, "by granting the Netherlands to Philip." If we accept the more common identification of the husband of Lady Belge with William, Prince of Orange, the quoted passage is less easy of explanation.

The passage in which Mercilla, having heard the story of "the springals," grants Arthur's request that he might be permitted to go to the relief of Lady Belge, is clearly based upon Elizabeth's despatch of Leicester in 1585 to the Netherlands in response to the urgent request of the provinces. Nor should we be at a loss to recognize in the poet's mention of the Lady's banishment to the moors and marshes an allusion to the topography of Holland and Zeeland, where the army of the Lowlands made a stand against Spanish tyranny. The "Citie farre up land," which had been extorted from the Lady by her strong foe, is Antwerp, which Leicester's force had arrived too late to save. In stanzas 27 ff. the allusion to the Spanish Inquisition in the Netherlands is too obvious to require comment. In its prosperous event, on the other hand, the story is as clearly unhistorical; because, far from conquering the Prince of Parma, who was Regent of the Netherlands and who is represented in the poem by Geryoneo's Seneschall, Leicester returned from the Low Countries after having accomplished virtually nothing.

The continuation of the Arthur-Geryoneo story in the first thirty-five stanzas of Canto XI, departing still farther from history, seems to take on the character of hopeful prophecy. Though Leicester was dead, England might some day conquer Philip on land as she had done on the sea; and, in destroying Spanish rule in the Netherlands, might eradicate at the same time the Catholic power in that country. In the meantime, more or less successful campaigns were being conducted against different parts of that unwieldy Spanish empire not inappropriately symbolized in the giant of the three bodies and the six hands; for example, the expedition to Portugal in 1589, that to the Azores in 1590–2, and the raid of the West Indies by Drake and Hawkins in 1595–6.

Spenser, passing abruptly in stanza 36 to the quest of Arthegall, represents him as meeting first of all in the land of Irena the good Sir Sergis, who tells him how Irena, having repaired to the shore at the appointed time to meet her champion, falls into the hands of Grantorto. Sergis is probably Sir Henry Sidney, who had served three times as Lord Deputy in Ireland, and whom Lord Grey, before entering upon the office in 1580, is known to have consulted. Grantorto is either Philip II or the Pope. Setting out to rescue Irena, Artegall and Sergis come upon a knight and a lady in the midst of a confused rout of people. After he has rescued them, Arthegall learns that the knight's name is Burbon and the lady's, Flourdelis. In the course of the fight, Burbon, to avoid exciting further the enmity of the people, has thrown away his shield, an act for which Sir Arthegall duly takes him to task. Though competently rescued, the lady, who was "wondrous faire" and "richly clad," seems neither glad nor sorry at the sight of her rescuers; and when Burbon "would have embraced her with hart entyre"—

> she backstarting with disdainefull yre,
> Bad him avaunt, ne would unto his lore
> Allured be, for prayer nor for meed.

Rebuked by the knights, Fleurdelis, though "nor well nor ill apayd," permits herself to be carried away, while Talus continues to pursue the "raskall many."

Like the episodes already considered, this of Burbon and Flourdelis is almost self-explanatory. Without doubt Burbon is Henry of Navarre, with whose accession the House of Bourbon succeeded the House of Valois on the throne of France; and his throwing away of his shield is the latter's renunciation of the Protestant faith when, on capturing Paris, he declared that the capital was worth a mass. Just as certainly Flourdelis is France, and her manner of receiving Burbon and acknowledging his services is accurately descriptive of the temper of France when Henry became king with the title of Henry IV. The "rude rout" besetting Burbon and Flourdelis is for the Protestant poet a just description of the Catholic forces in France; and the assistance rendered by Arthegall points definitely to the aid furnished by Elizabeth during the siege of Rouen. Since Lord Grey had no part in these operations, Arthegall must here stand either for Lord Willoughby, who commanded the relief force of 1589, or for the Earl of Essex, who took part in the expedition of 1591.

The theme of Arthegall's rescue of Irena, which had been introduced in Canto XI, is brought to a term in the final

canto of the fifth book. Dr. Gough's identification of Grantorto (Great Wrong) with the Pope should be preferred
to the traditional identification with Philip II; because it
was the Pope rather than Philip that took an active part in
Irish affairs. It was he who in 1577 gave James Fitz-
maurice a commission to conquer the country, who in 1579
bestowed a consecrated banner upon the small expedition
headed by Fitz-maurice and his own legate Dr. Saunders;
and who in 1580 despatched the 800 Italians and Spaniards, most of whom were put to the sword by Grey in the
well-known massacre at Fort del Oro. To this inconclusive
event of the Irish campaign Spenser gives an air of final-
ity in his account of the rescue of Irena through the defeat
and death of Grantorto. The subsequent policy of the Lord
Deputy he describes in the twenty-sixth stanza:—

> During which time, that he did there remaine,
> His studie was true Justice how to deale,
> And day and night employ'd his busie paine
> How to reforme that ragged common-weale:
> And that same yron man, which could reveale
> All hidden crimes, through all that realme he sent,
> To search out those that usd to rob and steale,
> Or did rebell gainst lawfull government;
> On whom he did inflict most grievous punishment.

Whatever we might think of Grey's "true Justice," the
stern measures which he took in order to subdue Ireland
are here clearly stated. That, however, the suspicion of un-
due severity was unwarranted the poet suggests in representing Arthegall in stanza 8 as staying the fury of Talus.
Nevertheless, it was feared from the beginning that the
Deputy's anti-Catholic zeal might carry him to extremes;

as is clear from the instructions which he took to Ireland. He was warned against being too strict in religious matters and "to have an especial care that by the oppression and insolencies of the soldiers our good subjects may not be alienated from us." The tone of these instructions is in accord with the characterization of Elizabeth by the Master of the Rolls as the "Amor Hiberniae." In the very opening stanzas of the twelfth canto, Spenser, the champion of Grey, protects himself against the imputation of criticizing the Queen by praising her clemency; but Grey doubtless would have agreed with Waterhouse's remark to Walsingham: "If the Queen will use mildness with the traitors, she would do better to discharge her army at once." Whatever differences existed between the Queen and her Lord Deputy, Grey's enemies made the most of them. At Smerwick, it was said, he was guilty of bad faith as well as cruelty because he had obtained the surrender of Fort del Oro only by promising clemency to the garrison. Burghley, Grey himself complained, lent an ear to the slanderous reports in circulation; and such an act as his execution on insufficient evidence of guilt of Nicholas Nugent, former Chief Justice of the Common Pleas in Ireland, certainly did him no good.

To the slander and detraction that led to the Lord Deputy's recall, Spenser pays his respects in the concluding stanzas of the twelfth canto. In his description of the two hags, Envy and Detraction, and of the Blatant Beast, he expresses the full measure of his contempt for Grey's enemies. They have been actuated by no high motives; it is simply their nature to "grieve and grudge" at all that they see done "prays-worthily." They sorrow over the good and rejoice over the evil of which they hear; and while concealing the good, they publish the evil far and wide. What is well meant, they misconstrue; and in common haunts they are active in gossip and slander. In stanza 37 the poet makes a good point when he argues that the very agencies of Envy and Detraction which are hostile to Grey are at the root of the Irish question. They were hostile to him because he had freed Irena from their own snares,— a suggestion that the Roman Catholics had inspired the attack on the Lord Deputy.

Spenser's chief source in the fifth book of the *Faerie Queene* is once more Ariosto. First of all, in the story of Pollente in the second canto he draws upon Ariosto's tale of Rodomonte, which, introduced in *Orlando Furioso* XXIX, is continued in cantos XXXI and XXXV. The Italian tale properly begins with the importunate courtship of the afflicted Isabella by Rodomonte, the Saracen King of Algiers. True to the memory of her dead lover, Zerbino, Isabella resists these unwelcome attentions to the point of planning her own death. She offers Rodomonte in lieu of her love an ointment so potent, she says, as to make him invulnerable; he may, if he wishes, try it on her. Having, accordingly, anointed her body, she offers her neck to the Saracen's sword and is forthwith decapitated. So remorseful is Rodomonte that he now builds a tomb in honor of Isabella by the deep river that flows in front of his castle and that is crossed by a narrow bridge without railings. At the approach of any knight a watchman stationed in a neighboring tower sounds a horn, which gives to Rodomonte the signal to come forth and contest the passage with the stranger. If he is victorious, Rodomonte hangs the armor of the defeated knight as a trophy upon the tomb of Isabella. The Saracen has his first fight with the mad Orlando, who, after dragging his enemy into the river, makes good his escape. Then Brandimart, in quest of Orlando, is conducted by Flordelis to the perilous passage (Canto XXXI). In this case, after both knights have been hurtled into the river, Brandimart and his steed, at a great disadvantage, stand "rooted in the mud"; whereupon the Saracen's lady intercedes successfully for the Christian knight. Finally (Canto XXXV) Bradamante, in turn conducted to the bridge by Flordelis, overcomes Rodomonte, just as Arthegall defeats Pollente.

In adapting this episode, Spenser, intent upon his allegory, has made several obvious changes. The three conflicts he has reduced to one, and the motivation of the episode he has necessarily changed. Pollente is merely a strong robber making the most of the advantage offered by the location of his castle. Instead of keeping Ariosto's watchman in a tower, Spenser develops his theme of robbery by introducing

> a groome of evill guize,
> Whose scalp is bare, that bondage doth bewray,
> Which pols and pils the poore in piteous wize.

Similarly, to focus attention further upon the central ethical theme, the Saracen's lady, who intercedes for the overthrown Brandimart, is transformed into Lady Munera. Then, to make more of the theme of trickery, Spenser introduces the detail of the trapdoors in the bridge. In general, in his more compact and moralized treatment of the theme he has contrived to turn it to good allegorical account.

Like the tournament of Sir Satyrane in the fourth book, the tournament in Canto III derives from that of King Norandino of Damascus in the seventeenth canto of the

Orlando Furioso. To celebrate the escape of himself and his bride Lucina, after three months' imprisonment in the cave of the orc, Norandino at the end of every third month proclaims a tournament. At the one described, the most formidable champion is Gryphon, who appears in the lists attended by Martano. While the former proves his prowess in every encounter, the latter is only prevented by Gryphon's exertions from fleeing the place of battle. When at the close of the fighting Gryphon falls asleep at a neighboring inn, Martano plots with his paramour Origille to steal the victor's horse and armor in order that he might appear before Norandino as the true victor of the tournament. Having deceived the King, he not only receives all the honors due to the triumphant knight, but he even brings about the disgrace of Gryphon before he is himself detected and punished.

In this episode as in the preceding, Spenser has made the narrative more compact. The detection of Braggadocchio is quickly effected by Arthegall's simple expedient of showing his own wounds and battle-scarred sword. Then, too, the theft of the horse and armor is done away with by having Arthegall, to conceal his identity, exchange shields with Braggadocchio before they enter the tournament. In Spenser's story the false Florimell takes the place of Martano's paramour, Origille.

The remaining debt to Ariosto in the fifth book will be found in the Britomart-Radigund story. It has been already shown that Britomart is modeled after Ariosto's Bradamante. Radegund is compounded of suggestions derived from Ariosto's Orontea, whose story is told in O.F. XX and of the Pagan Marfisa, who is contrasted in the Italian epic with the Christian Bradamante. Further, Arthegall's subjugation to Radegund will suggest the classical story of Hercules and Omphale.

Ariosto's story of Orontea is that of a company of ladies who, after they have been deserted by their lords, vow eternal vengeance on all men who may come to their shores, saving of these only enough to propagate the race. Of this company Orontea is the chief. Like her, Spenser's Radegund (Canto IV, stanza 30) has "vow'd to doe all the ill which she could do to knights"; but the motivation in Spenser's story, though similar, is not the same as that in Ariosto's. Radegund's hostility to men is due not to desertion but to Bellodant's failure to reciprocate her love.

In the case of the Marfisa story we shall find in the seventh canto of the *Faerie Queene* a much closer parallel with Ariosto. The conflict between Bradamante and Marphisa in Canto XXXVI is the prototype of the Britomart-Radegund duel in Spenser. The differences to be noted are that in the former Rogero, who corresponds to Arthegall, is present with conflicting feelings during the fight and tries to separate the combatants; for Bradamante, Rogero's "love was fury, fire," for Marphisa, " 'twas rather fondness than desire." Then, unlike the termination of Spenser's episode, Ariosto's heroine does not slay her opponent; instead, the hostility in the *Orlando* is brought to an end by a voice from the tomb of their common mother declaring that Rogero and Marphisa are brother and sister. Finally, Ariosto is disposed characteristically to introduce into his story an element of the burlesque, which is quite foreign to Spenser's manner. Rogero, having vainly entreated the women to stop fighting, attempts by force to part them :—

When he entreaties unavailing found,
The youth prepared by force to part the two:
Their poniards snatched away, and on the ground,
Beneath a cypress-tree, the daggers threw.
When they no weapons have wherewith to wound,
With prayer and threat, he interferes anew:
But vainly; for, since better weapons lack,
Each other they with fists and feet attack.

If one now compares Ariosto's description of Bradamante's love and jealousy (Canto XXXII) with the corresponding passage in the *Faerie Queene* (Canto VI), the
difference between the dramatic and the descriptive treatment of a situation will be at once evident. In the *Orlando*
almost the whole passage is a soliloquy, whereas in Spenser
only the dialogue with Talus is in direct discourse; and the
rhetoric of Ariosto is much more passionate, as the following stanza illustrates:—

But, woe is me, alas! and, what can I
Save my irrational desire lament?
Which makes me soar a pitch so passing high,
I reach a region, where my plumes are bent;
Then, unsustained, fall headlong from the sky;
Nor ends my woe; on other flight intent,
Again I imp my wings, again I soar;
To flame and fall, tormented evermore.

There is nothing in Spenser as energetic as this. Perhaps
the best passage there is stanza 14, in which Britomart is
compared to a wayward child; but this, however true to the
abstract theme of jealousy, may be criticized as subtract-
ing something from the dignity of Britomart's character.

In Ariosto a Gascon knight, corresponding to Talus, brings Bradamante news of her love ; and in both stories the jealous woman impulsively arms herself and sets out in quest of the absent knight.

Corresponding to the pleasing passage in which Britomart is described as standing at a window that looked to the west and sending her winged thoughts to her lover, is a situation much more circumstantially treated in Ariosto (XXXII, st. 14 ff.). Bradamante

> oft ascended
> A turret, from whose top she might survey
> Gay champaign, wood, and, mid the wide expanse
> A portion of the road, that led to France.
>
> When shining arms at distance she perceives,
> Or any thing that speaks a cavalier,
> 'Tis her desired Rogero, she believes ;
> And her fair eyes and brows are seen to clear.
> If footman, or unarmed, the maid conceives,
> It is a courier from the youthful peer ;
> And, though fallacious every hope she feeds,
> Another and another aye succeeds.

Additional correspondences between the fifth book of the *Faerie Queen* and the *Orlando* may here be briefly noted. With Arthegall's sword Crysaor (I, st. 9–10) may be compared Orlando's Durindane (Canto XXX, 59) ; with Arthur's shield (VIII, 37–38), that of Atlante (II, 55), (Cp., also, the shield of Apollo described in *Iliad* XV, 308 ff.) ; and with the net employed by Malengin (IX, 96–99), that employed by the giant Caligorante for a similar purpose (XV, 44–45). Further, a general resemblance may be noted between Arthegall's rescue of Lady Belge (X) and Orlando's rescue of Olimpia, a lady of Holland (O.F. IX).

REFERENCES

Gough, A. B. Ed. *The Faerie Queene,* Book V. Oxford, 1918.

Bhattacherje, Mohinimohan. *Studies in Spenser.* Calcutta, 1929; Chapter I, Justice.

Gough, A. B. *Who was Spenser's Bon Font?* Modern Language Review, XII (1917), 140 ff.

Greenlaw, Edwin. *Spenser and British Imperialism.* Modern Philology, IX (1912), 347 ff.

Hughes, M. Y. *Spenser and Utopia.* Studies in Philology, XVII (1920), 132 ff.

Knowlton, E. C. *The Genii of Spenser.* Studies in Philology, XXV (1928), 439 ff.

Padelford, F. M. *Spenser's Arraignment of the Anabaptists.* Journal of English and Germanic Philology, XII (1913), 434 ff.

Padelford, F. M. *Talus: The Law.* Studies in Philology, XVIII (1921), 334 ff.

CHAPTER XIX

THE FAERIE QUEENE, BOOK VI

IN the matter of structure Book VI has its points of like-ness with those already criticized. For example, as often before, a transition from the preceding book is made by bringing the respective protagonists together in the open-ing canto. Here, in Calidore's conversation with Arthegall, the main objective of the action is, according to Spenser's original plan, brought clearly before us :—

> "The Blattant Beast," quoth he, "I doe pursew,
> And through the world incessantly doe chase,
> Till I him overtake, or else subdew :
> Yet know I not or how or in what place
> To find him out, yet still I forward trace."

There is, too, a rescue by Arthur in the eighth canto; it is not, however, the hero who is there saved, but the persons of a minor episode—Timias and Mirabella.

Less in accordance with the original plan is the rela-tion of the hero to the plot. In this respect we may compare the sixth book with the third. During about half of the ac-tion the principal character is, in each case, off the stage. In Canto III of the sixth book, Sir Calidore, leaving Serena to the care of Calepine, goes in pursuit of the Blatant Beast ; and it is not until Canto IX that the poet's team returns to the furrow which it has left unploughed (Canto IX, stanza 1).

Looking broadly at the narrative of Book VI, we may note that it falls into three main parts. The first, extending to the 27th verse of the third canto, presents Sir Calidore as the champion knight of courtesy; the second, reaching from this point to the ninth canto, replaces him in this rôle with Arthur and Timias; and the third, bringing the book to an end, restores him to his place as the chief character in the action.

The "Legend of Sir Calidore" opens with *exempla* of discourtesy and courtesy, illustrating in Briana the discourtesy of women and in Crudor that of men. The contrast here between the virtue and the vice gains point by placing Sir Calidore and the discourteous knight of the Sir Tristram episode in similar situations; for in each case the knight comes unexpectedly upon a couple in a "covert shade," (II, 16 and III, 21). Pursuing the Blatant Beast, Sir Calidore now passes for a time out of the story, leaving the wounded Serena to the care of her lover Calepine.

The Calepine-Serena episode here introduced constitutes the main interest of the second part of the book. Once again, the discourtesy of both women and men is illustrated in the persons of Mirabella and Turpine. To match Calidore's hurried exit from the story in pursuit of the Blatant Beast is Calepine's equally impetuous departure in pursuit of a bear that is carrying off a child; and then, taking her turn, Serena, having seen Timias overcome, "fled away with all the speed she mought." Further use of similarity and contrast appears in setting the savage who befriends Calepine and Serena over against the hostile savages who in Canto VIII take Serena captive. The gentle savage, be it noted, illustrates no democratic or equalitarian faith on Spenser's part; but, on the contrary, the conviction maintained throughout the book that blood will tell (Canto V, 1 and 2).

In its progress from the first adventures of Calepine and Serena to their reunion in Canto VII the story of this second part, through the separation of its characters, radiates in a fan-like structure along several lines of interest. Out of the Calepine-bear episode grows the Matilda-Bruin story. Then the savage man, Serena, Arthur, and Timias, first grouped together at the hermitage, pair off, the Serena-Timias adventures leading first to the Mirabella story; then, in turn, Serena, separated from Timias, has her experiences with the savages. In the meanwhile, Arthur and the savage man develop the Turpine story. With the close of this well-defined section Arthur and Timias and Calepine and Serena are once again united.

The last main division of the "Legend of Courtesy" occupies a third of the book. The Blatant Beast, who has had his place in the Calepine-Serena story, plays here no part in the episode of Pastorella; and it is not until the final canto is well advanced that Calidore returns to the quest. Unwilling to repeat in the case of Pastorella the story of Serena's capture, Spenser characteristically repeats another motif which he had employed in the previous section. The gentle blood of Pastorella like that of the "salvage man" declares itself through all misfortunes; and as in the other case savages who were really savages served as a foil, here, too, we have in Coridon the rustic who is truly the rustic. Beyond this we may compare Pastorella's restoration to her parents with the bringing of Aladine and Priscilla home in the Tristram story of Part I. Further, the capture of Serena by the savages may be compared with the capture of Pastorella by the Brigands. There is, indeed, throughout the book enough of parallelism and contrast to show that Spenser has once more employed a favorite method of unifying his story.

In his treatment of the ethical allegory of Book VI Spenser was at the disadvantage of having anticipated his subject. Indeed, since the declared purpose of the *Faerie Queene* was to "fashion a gentleman or noble person in vertuous and gentle discipline," courtesy, it should be evident, was the subject of the whole work; so that at almost every turn in the preceding books the poem had offered some illustration of a virtue that was really its central theme. Particularly, as has been explained above, was temperance shown to be salient to the manners of a true gentleman. What remained for the poet was to exhibit in his allegory certain articles in that familiar creed of courtesy which had been stated and expounded in many doctrinal treatises of the Renaissance, and to oppose to the ideal of the gentleman the forces which were hostile to its realization.

It is impossible to find among the private moral virtues "as Aristotle hath devised" one that at all closely corresponds to courtesy. Nevertheless, one may compare the Aristotelian gentleness or good temper, a virtue opposed not only to irascibility but to sullenness and sternness as well. "A good-tempered person," says Aristotle, "is in effect one who will be cool and not carried away by his emotion but will wax wroth in such a manner, on such occasions, and for so long a time, as reason may prescribe. But it seems that he will err rather on the side of deficiency; for a good tempered or gentle person is inclined to forgiveness rather than to revenge" (IV, ch. ii). The spirit of forgiveness here illustrated in the good-tempered man animates the conduct of Calidore after his defeat of Crudor in Canto I. In lines worthy of quotation he states his principles clearly:—

> In vaine he seeketh others to suppresse,
> Who hath not learnd him selfe first to subdew.

and further,

> Who will not mercie unto others shew,
> How can he mercy ever hope to have?

Again, Aristotle in Book IV, ch. 12 describes a virtue for which he can find no name but which is comparable to that for which Sir Calidore stands. It is a mean between obsequiousness and surliness. A person having this virtue will not seek to be merely complaisant, and he will avoid being either a flatterer or a contentious person. The virtue thus described "most nearly resembles friendliness," but "it differs from friendliness in being destitute of emotion or affection for the people with whom one associates, as it is not friendship or hatred that makes such a person assent to things in a right spirit but his own character. For he will so act alike to strangers and acquaintances, and to persons with whom he is or is not intimate; only in each case his action will be suitable; for it is not natural to pay the same regard to strangers as to intimate friends, or to be equally scrupulous about causing them pain." Speaking in general terms, Aristotle declares that "such a person will associate with other people in a right spirit." Further, "he will never lose sight of what is noble and expedient. For it seems that he has to do with such pleasures and pains as occur in human society." Again, this man "will not associate in the same spirit with people of high position and with ordinary people, or with people whom he knows well and whom he knows only slightly, and so on as other differences may occur; but he will render to each class its proper due." One is reminded of the opening stanza of Canto II:—

What vertue is so fitting for a knight,
Or for a ladie whom a knight should love,
As curtesie, to beare themselves aright
To all of each degree, as doth behove?
For whether they be placed high above,
Or low beneath, yet ought they well to know
Their good, that none them rightly may reprove
Of rudenesse, for not yielding what they owe:
Great skill it is such duties timely to bestow.

Thirdly, in Aristotle's virtue of truthfulness (IV, xiii) one may note an element of courtesy. The truthful man he here opposes to the pretentious or the boastful. On the other hand, those who depreciate themselves and whom he calls ironical people "show a more refined character, for it seems that their object is not to make gain but to avoid pomposity."

Finally, among the mean states which "are all concerned with the association of people in certain words and deeds," are those concerned with amusements. One who regards "a manner of intercourse which is in good taste" and who accordingly remembers that "there are right things to say and a right way of saying them," will avoid buffoonery and boorishness. To the mean state in respect of fun Aristotle gives the name tact, and he describes the person of tact as "one who will use and listen to such language only as is suitable to an honorable gentleman; for there is such language as an honorable gentleman may fitly use and listen to in the way of fun, and the fun of a gentleman is different from that of a slavish person, and again, the fun of a cultivated person from that of one who is uncultivated" (IV, xiv). All of this goes to make what Aristotle calls "the moral state of the refined gentleman."

Turning from Aristotle to Cicero, we may compare the latter's concept of *honestas* with Spenser's virtue of courtesy. Honesty, like courtesy, is comprehensive enough to include all that becomes a gentleman; the cardinal virtues —i. e., prudence, justice, fortitude, and temperance—being the four elements into which it may be divided. Considering "the excellence of the nature of man," Cicero wrote in the fourth chapter of the first book of the *Offices:* —"It is another, and that too no mean prerogative of our reasonable nature, that man alone can discern all the beauties of order and decency, and knows how to govern his words and actions in conformity to them. It is he alone that, of all the creatures, observes and is pleased with the beauty, gracefulness, and symmetry of parts in the objects of sense; which nature and reason observing in them, from thence take occasion to apply the same also to those of the mind; and to conclude that beauty, consistency, and regularity, should be much more kept up in our words and actions; and therefore command us, that nothing be done that is effeminate or unbecoming; and that so strict a guard be kept over every thought and action, as that no indecency be either conceived or practised by us."

However interesting may be these parallels from classical philosophy, we shall have to seek elsewhere the source of Spenser's ideal of courtesy. Strictly speaking, this derives from a well-defined literary tradition which is concerned with the theory and practice of nobility. On the one hand, it looks back to the mediæval knight, and, on the other, it looks forward to the cavalier of the seventeenth century. Besides draughting a code of manners and outlining a course of education, the books of the gentleman often theorized on such subjects as the origin and the essence of true nobility. In part, the doctrine on this subject, as expounded in the manuals of the Renaissance, had been for centuries a commonplace of the poets. Already in the *Romance of the Rose* (*cir.* 1275) Jean Clopinel had written (section xcix) :—

> An upright heart
> Doth true nobility impart,
> But mere nobility of birth
> I reckon as of little worth.
> The nobleman who lives to-day
> Before his fellows should display
> Those qualities which his forbears
> Won bright renown in former years.

Expressing himself in a similar vein, Chaucer wrote in the *Balade of Gentilesse:*—

> The firste stocke, fader of gentilesse,
> What man desireth gentil for to be
> Must folowe his trace, and alle his wittes dresse
> Vertu to love, and vyces for to flee;
> For unto vertu longeth dignite,
> And nought the reverse, savely dar I deme,
> Al were he miter, croune, or dyademe.

This traditional view once more finds expression in the *Wife of Bath's Tale,* 1113 ff. It was voiced also after

Chaucer by the Scottish poets, Gawain Douglas and Henryson.

Now, though Spenser transmits this democratic doctrine, he cannot be said to emphasize it in the sixth book of the *Faerie Queene*. The aristocratic idea, in which he is there more interested, is that blood in spite of everything will tell. However, in the fourth stanza of the prologue to the Legend of Courtesy he wrote that comely courtesy

> though it on a lowly stalke doe bowre,
> Yet brancheth forth in brave nobilitie,
> And spreds it selfe through all civilitie.

And, then, the poet draws a contrast between the true courtesy of "plaine antiquitie" and the "fayned showes" of the "present age," reminding us of those old men mentioned in Castiglione's *Cortegiano* who "praise the Courts of time past because there were not in them so vicious men as some that are in ours" :—

> But in the triall of true Curtesie,
> Its now so farre from that which then it was,
> That it indeed is nought but forgerie,
> Fashion'd to please the eies of them that pas,
> Which see not perfect things but in a glas;
> Yet is that glasse so gay that it can blynd
> The wisest sight, to thinke gold that is bras.
> But Vertues seat is deepe within the mynd,
> And not in outward shows, but inward thoughts defynd.

With these lines we should compare the stanza in the *Teares of the Muses* in which Clio, speaking of the "mightie peeres," complains :—

But they doo onely strive themselves to raise
Through pompous pride, and foolish vanitie;
In th'eyes of people they put all their praise,
And onely boast of armes and auncestrie:
But vertuous deeds, which did those arms first give
To their grandsyres, they care not to atchive.

One should further recall for their connection with the subject of Book VI the justly celebrated description of the perfect courtier in *Mother Hubberd's Tale*, 717 ff., and the account of the short-comings of the court in *Colin Clouts Come Home Againe*, 680 ff.

There is no difficulty in finding parallels to the views of the poets in the many books of the gentleman produced within the period of the Renaissance. The English books of this class derive most of their ideas, even when they do not translate their texts, from Italian originals. Examples are Elyot's *Governour* (1531), the anonymous *Institucion of a Gentleman* (1555), Lawrence Humphrey's *The Nobles, or of Nobility* (1563), William Segar's *The Booke of Honor and Armes* (1590), the same author's *Honor Military & Civil* (1602), and Peacham's *Complete Gentleman* (1634). Of these the *Institucion of a Gentleman,* while sharing with the other manuals the debt to Italian sources, reveals such a vein of English sympathy as gives a special character to Ascham's *Schoolmaster*. For example, in reviewing the familiar doctrine of the gentleman it quotes with approval Chaucer's *Gentilesse,* and later on in recommending archery on patriotic grounds it invokes the authority of Ascham. Quite in harmony with the ideas of Chaucer's *Balade* is the following passage from the *Institucion:* —"No other thing old knighthood had wont to bee then a degree geven unto a soldier for his worthines in the warres above others. Therfore no man ought to contempne or dispyse that man whom virtue hath set up more higher than his parents were before him. . . . Not by lineage made noble but by his own knowledge, labour, and industry becometh gentle, where unto Tully consenteth and saith non domo dominus, sed domino domus homestanda est." Elyot, too, in the fourth chapter of the second book of the *Governour,* contended that, as in the case of money, "it appeareth that the estimation is in the metal, and not in the print or figure"; and that "nobility is not after the vulgar opinion of men, but is only the praise and surname of virtue." Similarly, Roger Ascham wrote in the first book of the *Schoolmaster:* "nobility without virtue and wisdom, is blood indeed, but blood truly without bones and sinews."

While recognizing the importance of virtue as the true foundation of nobility, the courtesy books are traditionally in favor of the view that gentle birth and nobility of character together create the most favorable conditions. For example, the author of the *Institucion,* writing of those whom he calls *gentle gentle,* declares that "such noblemen deserve to be called not only Gentle Gentle, but also they shall be esteemed xv fold Gentle, as men in whom we may discern the perfect shape of nobility"; and Elyot, in the chapter cited above, says: "the longer it continueth in a name or lineage, the more is nobility extolled and marveled at." To the same purpose writes Ascham: "nobility, governed by learning and wisdom, is indeed most like a fair ship, having tide and wind at will, under the rule of a skilful master." In accord with this widespread doctrine is Spenser's opinion that, although courtesy may flourish on a lowly stalk, it is principally the ornament of the nobly born.

However, in utilizing a familiar idea of folk-tale and romance he has carried the aristocratic contention to the point of maintaining that blood in all circumstances will tell. This is the view that we find illustrated in the episode of Serena and the Salvage Man.

The ground of true nobility is, of course, only one topic in the courtesy books. The outline of the *Institucion* may be regarded as typical: "Herein is declared who is gentle and who is ungentle: what offices, conditions, qualities and manners ought to be in a gentleman, and how he should differ from other sorts of men, as well in conditions and behavior as also in apparel, and ornaments to his body belonging, not leaving unrehearsed what games and pastimes be fit for a gentleman and how they ought to be used. Finally of honor and worship therein is somewhat rehearsed of which no man is worthy but he that by his deeds deserveth the same."

Our best source of knowledge for "the courtier's, soldier's, scholar's eye, tongue, sword" is certainly Baldassare Castiglione's *Libro del Cortegiano,* first published in 1528 and translated into English by Thomas Hoby in 1561. The book is cast in the form of conversations carried on by the lords and ladies of the brilliant court of Urbino. From these conversations may be gathered the requirements of the true courtier. We learn among other things that he should have by nature "not only a wit, and a comely shape of person and countenace, but also a certain grace and (as they say) an air that shall make him at the first sight acceptable and loving unto who so beholdeth him." Like Spenser's knight, the "principal and true profession" of Castiglione's courtier is in "feates of arms." In the pursuit of this calling "he should be known among other of his hardines, for his achieving of enterprises, and for his fidelity toward him whom he serveth. And he shall purchase himself a name with these good conditions, in doing the deeds in every time and place, for it is not for him to faint at any time in this behalf without a wondrous reproach." However, that peace has its virtues as well as war neither Castiglione nor Spenser has forgotten. "Whereas in war," says Castiglione, "the courtier should be fierce, bitter, and evermore with the first," he should be everywhere else, like Sir Calidore among the shepherds, "lowly, sober, and circumspect, fleeing above all things bragging and unshameful praising himself." It is further recommended that he should have skill in wrestling, horsemanship, and hunting. The general goodness of the courtier should be set off by some knowledge of letters, music, and painting.

These refinements of the courtly ideal that should accompany its moral probity and its knightly prowess, Spenser has pointedly symbolized in his description of the dance of the nymphs and graces about Colin's love, while the poet shepherd plays upon his pipe. After the dancers have vanished upon Calidore's approach, Colin himself furnishes the best commentary on the passage:—

> These three on men all gracious gifts bestow,
> Which decke the body or adorne the mynde,
> To make them lovely or well favoured show,
> As comely carriage, entertainement kynde,
> Sweete semblaunt, friendly offices that bynde,
> And all the complements of curtesie:
> They teach us, how to each degree and kynde
> We should ourselves demeane, to low, to hie,
> To friends, to foes; which skill men call civility.

To this general correspondence between Castiglione and Spenser we may now add a few particulars. In his many conflicts Sir Calidore of course fully and obviously illustrates the virtues of the knight in action. Quite as well does the Meliboe episode furnish illustration of the "lowly, sober, and circumspect" character of the courtier and knight in retirement. One should note not only the speech of Meliboe on the familiar theme of the tried estate, with its suggestions of the type of the country gentleman, who was already recognized in the books of courtesy, but more particularly the behavior of Sir Calidore among the rustics. In the words of Castiglione his "lowliness is much to be commended," seeing that he is "a gentleman of prowess and well seen in arms." During his sojourn with Meliboe he has a chance to prove his skill in wrestling and hunting, activities which are both recommended for the gentleman by Castiglione. A passage in the conversation of the second book bears more directly upon Calidore's wrestling bout with Coridon. Sir Frederick remarks that the courtier "ought to have a great consideration in presence of whom he sheweth himself, and who be his better matches. For it were not meet that a gentleman should be present in person and a doer in such a matter in the country, where the lookers on and the doers were of a base sort." In opposing this opinion the Lord Gasper Pallavicin cites the more democratic practice of Lombardy; there, he says, "you shall see the young gentleman upon the holidays come dance all the day long in the sun with them of the country, and pass the time with them in casting the bar, in wrestling, running and leaping. And I believe it is not ill done. For no comparison is there made of nobleness of birth, but of force and slight, in which things many times the men of the country are not a whit inferior to gentlemen, and it seemeth this familiar conversation containeth in it a certain lovely freeness." Sir Frederick cannot approve "this dancing in the sun," but he goes on to say, "who so will wrestle, run, and leap with men of the country, ought (in my judgement) to do it after a sort: to prove himself and (as they are wont to say) for courtesy, not to try mastery with them: and a man ought (in a manner) to be assured to get the upper hand, else let him not meddle withal, for it is too ill a sight and too foul a matter and without estimation, to see a gentleman overcome by a carter, and especially in wrestling." Calidore might so far have satisfied Sir Frederick that he accepted the challenge of Coridon in the assurance of victory and in the belief that

> courtesie among the rudest breeds
> Good will and favour.

Then, Calidore's unselfishness and good humor are con-contrasted throughout with Coridon's envious and surly disposition. The courtier, says Castiglione, should be "no envious person, no carrier of an evil tongue in his head: nor at any time given to seek preferment or promotion any naughty way, nor by the meane of any subtil practise." In Canto IX, stanza 39, Spenser points the contrast between the courteous Calidore and the rude Coridon:—

> And ever when he came in companie
> Where Calidore was present, he would loure
> And byte his lip, and even for gealousie
> Was readie oft his owne hart to devoure,
> Impatient of any paramoure:
> Who on the other side did seeme so farre

From malicing, or grudging his good houre,
That all he could, he graced him with her,
Ne ever shewed signe of rancour or of jarre.

Evidently, too, Sir Calidore, though, in the words of Castiglione, "he perceived himself excellent and far above others, yet showed that he esteemed not himself for such a one." Witness his generosity (stanza 42) in transferring to Coridon's head the flowery garland with which Pastorella had crowned him.

Only a few of the characters in the sixth book can be confidently identified with historical figures. The hero, Sir Calidore, stands traditionally for Sir Philip Sidney, whom Spenser in the *Shepheardes Calender* had described as

> the president
> Of noblesse and of chevalree.

The plausibility of this identification is strengthened by the certainty that Meliboe is Sir Francis Walsingham, prominent as a member of the Privy Council and as a Secretary of State under Elizabeth. He is remembered now chiefly for his exposure of the Babington Conspiracy and for the aid he rendered in the prosecution of Mary, Queen of Scots. Under the name Meliboe, Spenser had already sung his praises in the *Ruines of Time,* 435 ff :—

> Therefore in this halfe happie I doo read
> Good Meliboe, that hath a poet got
> To sing his living praises being dead,
> Deserving never here to be forgot,
> In spight of envie, that his deeds would spot:
> Since whose decease, learning lies unregarded,
> And men of armes doo wander unrewarded.

The poet here alluded to is Thomas Watson, who sang the living praises of the famous statesman in his Latin eclogue entitled *Melibœus*. Spenser himself addressed to him one of the sonnets dedicatory of the *Faerie Queene,* in which Watson is praised as the "great Mecenas of this age." The poet's "lowly Muse" craves "protection of her feeble-nesse" :—

> Which if ye yield, perhaps ye may her rayse
> In bigger tunes to sound your living prayse.

The promise of the sonnet would seem to be fulfilled in the sixth book of the *Faerie Queene*.

If Melibœ is Walsingham, Pastorella may be accepted as his daughter Frances, to whom Sir Philip Sidney (Calidore), after some opposition from the Queen, was married in 1583. The relations between Melibœ and Calidore in Spenser's allegory no doubt represent faithfully the cordial terms upon which Walsingham stood with his son-in-law. For two years after his marriage Sidney was one of the household at Barn Elms, the country estate of the Walsing-hams. In his retirement there we might suppose that Walsingham, though not yet fifty, philosophized in some such vein to his young son-in-law as that in which Melibœ addresses Calidore. In representing Pastorella as the adopted daughter of the old shepherd, Spenser was, of course, departing from historical fact in order to conform to the type story outlined above.

Of the traditional identifications noted above only one has been called into serious question. Dr. Percy Long has argued that the Earl of Essex, not Sir Philip Sidney, is the real hero of the book. This contention gains some support from the fact that Essex, the second husband of Frances

Walsingham, was Spenser's last noble patron. Overlooking perhaps the contrasted requirements of the two poems, Dr. Long points out that whereas Sidney in Astrophel is described as "a slender swaine" (l. 15), the hero of the "Legend of Courtesy" is "full stout and tall" (I, 2) and "strong and mightily stiffe pight" (IX, 44), and that the poet's praise of Calidore for military prowess suits Essex better than Sidney. Further, in representing the death of Meliboe as contemporary with Calidore's courtship, the poet, it is argued, describes a situation into which Essex chronologically fits more easily than Sidney. The latter was married in 1583, whereas Walsingham's death and the second marriage of his daughter both occurred in 1590. If one insists upon chronological accuracy or correspondence in allegory, one might point out further with Dr. Long that Spenser could not have talked about his lady love with Sidney, as Colin does with Calidore, since the poet's courtship of Elizabeth Boyle did not begin until after Sidney's death. Again, the supposed difference in social status between Pastorella and Calidore is thought to favor the Essex theory, since "in 1500 when Walsingham's fortune was broken, the match between his dowerless daughter and one of the chief earls of England constituted a *mésalliance*." Those who approve Dr. Long's conjecture will be disposed with him to regard the sixth book of the *Faerie Queene* as a fulfilment of the promise contained in the dedicatory sonnet addressed to the Earl of Essex :—

> But when my Muse, whose fethers, nothing flitt,
> Doe yet but flagg, and lowly learne to fly,
> With bolder wing shall dare alofte to sty
> To the last praises of this Faery Queene,

> Then shall it make more famous memory
> Of thine heroicke parts, such as they beene.

If the identification of Meliboe with Walsingham is virtually certain, that of Corydon with Watson is very doubtful. To be sure, Watson in the preface to his English version of *Meliboeus* had said: "I figure myself in Corydon," and it is quite possible that Spenser had Watson in mind when he wrote in *Colin Clout,* ll. 382–3 :—

> Corydon, though meanly waged,
> Yet hablest wit of most I know this day.

On the other hand, the only ground for associating the author of *Meliboeus* with the daughter of Walsingham is the dedication to her of the English version of his pastoral. Moreover, the character of Sir Calidore's rival is opposed to the identification. Such a characterization, which is out of harmony with the praise in *Colin Clout,* would have been, besides, a poor return for Watson's praise of Spenser in *Meliboeus.*

A few other identifications may be added to those suggested above. As Belgard Castle in Canto XII is in all probability Belvoir Castle, Sir Bellamour we may understand to be the Earl of Rutland, and the Prince of Picteland the King of Scotland. Ben Jonson's notion that the Blatant Beast stood for the Puritans is now generally discredited, though we may grant that Spenser had Puritan extremists in mind when describing in Canto XII the despoiling of a monastery.

The debt of the sixth book of the *Faerie Queene* to Ariosto is not considerable. Most noteworthy, perhaps, is the likeness between Spenser's Turpine and Ariosto's Pinabello, that knight "of over-weening pride and little

fame" (O.F. XXII, 50), who, on account of the ancient
rivalry between his house and that of Bradamante, contrives (O.F. II) to imprison the latter in a vault, where she
meets Melissa and hears the prophecy of her descendants.
In Canto XX he is overthrown by Marphisa at a riverside,
and his lady's clothes given to the hag Gabrina. His lady,
described as "so wayward that she is without a peer" (O.F.
XII, st. 49), offers points of similarity and contrast with
Spenser's Blandina. The infamous custom devised by this
meretrice to vent her spleen, and described in O.F. XX,
may be compared with the inhospitality of Turpine in refusing stranger knights admission to his castle, and will
suggest, further, the Malbecco episode. In Ariosto's story
every knight coming to Pinabello's castle was deprived of
horse and armor, and if a lady accompanied him, she was
stripped of her clothing. It should be noted, however, that
Blandina, unlike the *meretrice,* pleads for the stranger. A
further parallel between the Turpine and the Pinabello
stories will be found in Turpine's enlistment of two knights
to pursue and attack Prince Arthur and Pinabello's forcing
four knights to maintain his custom (O.F. XXII, 53 ff.).
Another instance in Ariosto of the inhospitable custom has
been already pointed out in the story of Tristram's Tower,
recounted in the thirty-second canto of the *Orlando.*

Apart from this parallelism between the Turpine and the
Pinabello stories, attention has been called to the likeness
of the naked and invulnerable "salvage man" of the sixth
book of the *Faerie Queene* to the mad Orlando, whose
story we read in Cantos XXIII and XXIX of Ariosto's
poem; to a similarity of *motif* in Mirabella's story and in
the allusions (during the conversation of Astolpho and the
Spirit in O.F. XXXIV) to the punishment accorded the

heartless Lidia and Anaxarete; to the similarities in the pictures of the nude Olympia, freed from the Orc of *Orlando* in Canto XI, and Serena stripped by the savages in F.Q. Canto VIII, stanzas 42, 43. Further, Pastorella in the robbers' den offers a general likeness to Isabella in the cave of the robbers (*Orlando Furioso,* XI, 91 ff.). Finally, with the opening stanza of the seventh canto in the *Faerie Queene* we may compare the following stanza from Ariosto (XXXVI, stanza 1) :—

> Where'er they be, all hearts of gentle strain
> Still cannot choose but courtesy pursue;
> For they from nature and from habit gain
> What they henceforth can never more undo.
> Alike the heart that is of churlish vein,
> Where'er it be, its evil kind will shew.
> Nature inclines to ill, through all her range,
> And use is second nature, hard to change.

To students of the sources of the sixth book of the *Faerie Queene* special interest attaches to the Meliboe-Pastorella episode. Professor Greenlaw has shown that its typical plot, employed by Sidney and Shakespeare as well as by Spenser, develops from the Greek romance of *Daphnis and Chloe* through the medium of the Italian and Spanish pastoral romances,—such as Boccaccio's *Ameto,* Sannazaro's *Arcadia,* and Montemayor's *Diana,*—into the form that we find in Sidney's *Arcadia* and Spenser's *Faerie Queene.*

In the early Greek story the lovers are both foundlings, brought up by rustics whom they regard as their parents. As in the *Faerie Queene,* there is a rude and cowardly countryman who is the hero's rival in love; but the Greek romance differs from the English poem in having the girl attacked not by a real animal but by the rival disguised as a wolf. The hero, of course, rescues her. When, later, wicked men attempt to kidnap Daphnis, his rival is slain. After the heroine, in turn, has been captured by outlaws and later liberated, the lovers are recognized by their wealthy parents and in due course reunited.

The change in this simple story, necessitated by its introduction into such a chivalric romance as the *Arcadia* or the *Faerie Queene,* was to represent the hero as a young knight sojourning among shepherds and adopting their dress and manner of life. In the latter as in the earlier form of the story, after the usual rescues from a wild animal and from pirates or outlaws, the girl's high birth is revealed and she marries the hero. The most important addition made by the Italian and Spanish romances is a character who has no part in the plot but who has chosen to pass his time in peaceful, if sometimes sorrowful, retirement among the shepherds. In both the *Arcadia* and the *Faerie Queene* he is the author himself,—named Philisides in Sidney's prose romance and Colin Clout in Spenser's poem. In the other particulars in which Sidney's version departs from the traditional story it does not agree with Spenser's.

Other stories which may be noted as more or less remote analogues rather than as actual sources are Greene's *Dorastus and Fawnia* and the episode of Erminia in Cantos VII and XIX of Tasso's *Gerusalemme Liberata.* In the former we have the story of a prince who becomes a shepherd in order to win the love of a maiden living with an old shepherd whom she regards as her father. It should be noted here that Fawnia's disguise does not deceive Dorastus. In Tasso's tale of Erminia the parallel with Spenser appears in the account of the old shepherd who discourses like Meliboe on the relative merits of town and country life and who, like Meliboe, has been a gardener in the city. The heroine, Erminia, after leaving the shepherds is captured by outlaws, but her story has nothing else in common with Pastorella's.

REFERENCES

Bhattacherje, Mohinimohan. *Studies in Spenser.* Calcutta, 1929; Chapter V, Courtesie.

Greenlaw, Edwin. *Shakespeare's Pastorals.* Studies in Philology, XIII (1916), 122 ff.

Hall, E. A. *Spenser and Two Old French Grail Romances.* Publications of the Modern Language Association, XXVIII (1913), 539 ff.

Harrison, T. P. *The Faerie Queene and the Diana.* Philological Quarterly, IX (1930), 51 ff.

Koeppel, E. *Archiv für das Studium der neueren Sprachen und Litteraturen,* XCV (1895), 164–168.

Long, P. W. *Spenser's Sir Calidore.* Englische Studien, XLII (1910), 53 ff.

Rowe, K. T. *Sir Calidore: Essex or Sidney?* Studies in Philology, XXVII (1930), 125 ff.

CHAPTER XX

THE FAERIE QUEENE, MUTABILITIE CANTOS

THE so-called *Cantos of Mutabilitie* were first printed by Matthew Lownes in the 1609 Folio of the *Faerie Queene,* with the title, *Two Cantos of Mutabilitie: Which, both for Forme and Matter, appear to be parcell of some following Booke of the Faerie Queene, Under the Legend of Constancie. Never before imprinted.*—The cantos published are numbered six and seven, and to these are added two stanzas of an eighth.

That the "Legend of Constancie" in some form was designed for the *Faerie Queene* has been generally assumed on the grounds of Lownes's declaration, of its metrical form, and of the following lines from stanza 37 of Canto VI :—

> And were it not ill fitting for this file,
> To sing of hilles and woods, mongst warres and knights,
> I would abate the sternenesse of my stile,
> Mongst these sterne stounds to mingle soft delights.

However, there has been some disagreement with this prevailing opinion. For example, T. J. Wise (*The Faerie Queene,* 1897, I, lxxix) thought that *Mutabilitie* is a fragment of a "second projected or attempted epic," and Sebastian Evans (Macmillan's Magazine, XLII, 1880, pp. 145 ff.) argued that the *Cantos* "form, in fact, a complete and highly-finished poem, with a distinct beginning, middle, and end of its own, though similar in form to the *Faerie Queene,* utterly different from it in matter and in aim." He thought that Lownes himself could not have had "any authoritative information on the subject"; otherwise, he would not have said merely that the *Cantos "appeare* to be parcell of some following booke of the *Faerie Queene"*; and he remarks, further, that although there are "lengthy and fantastic digressions" in Spenser, "there is no single canto, much less two consecutive cantos, of the *Faerie Queene* entirely destitute as these cantos are of any reference to the business or to any one character of the poem."

About the date of composition of the *Mutabilitie Cantos* there can be no certainty. If we remember that Spenser began his residence at Kilcolman about 1589, we may argue that the description, in VI, 36 ff., of the scenery surrounding his castle establishes a probability that the fragment was written after that date. Furthermore, the following quotation from VI, 40, points directly to a passage in *Colin Clouts Come Home Againe*—l. 104 ff.—the dedicatory letter of which is dated December, 1591 :—

> Amongst the which there was a nymph that hight
> Molanna, daughter of old Father Mole,
> And sister unto Mulla, faire and bright,
> Unto whose bed false Bregog whylome stole,
> That Shepheard Colin dearely did condole.

On the face of it, this passage would seem to fix the date of *Mutabilitie* some time after 1591.

We should not, however, overlook other possibilities. In the first place, the lay of the Bregog and the Mulla might have existed independently of *Colin Clout* and later been introduced into that poem, as the *Epithalamium Thamesis* was incorporated in the *Faerie Queene*. Another possibility is that the passages descriptive of Irish scenery in *Mutabilitie* were a later addition to a "Legend of Constancie" of which we have only a fragment preserved. In favor of the former conjecture is the request of the "bony boy" in *Colin Clout* that Spenser "record" to the company "that lovely lay againe"; and what has been called "the obviously digressive character" of the passage in *Mutabilitie* may be supposed to favor the latter. Not forgetting that the *Faerie Quene is* full of digressions, we should give due weight to the suggestion that the first line in the passage quoted above is in the nature of a "frank apology for the incongruity" of the following stanzas in both matter and tone. However, the localization of the action in the Kilcolman country is introduced in the stanza (xxxvi) preceding the apologetic line and in Canto VII, stanzas four and eleven, there are further allusions to Arlo Hill and Mole (the mountains about Kilcolman). If we reject the hypothesis of interpolations, it seems not unreasonable to suppose that Spenser's proprietary interest in Kilcolman led to his choice of the setting for the trial scene in *Mutabilitie,* and that accordingly the stanzas should be dated after 1589.

Against this conclusion Miss Albright has cited the evidence of one of Gabriel Harvey's letters to Spenser, which, though undated, seems from its place in Harvey's *Letter Book* (pp. 82–88) to have been written in 1579. Harvey here alludes to the poet's "last weekes letter, or rather bill of complaynte" as delivered "at myne hostisses by the fyerside, beinge fasteheggid in rownde abowte in every side with a company of honest good fellowes, and at that tyme

reasonable honest quaffers." After Harvey had read aloud
the poet's "bill of complaynte" to the "honest quaffers," the
company definitely condemned as insufficient the argument
upon which it stood. A reply was then concocted, in which
the poet was frankly told that his "newe complaynte of the
newe worlde is nye as owlde as Adam and Eve." The
"complaynte" alluded to seems to be that succinctly stated
by Spenser in *Mutabilitie* VI: 5, where he declares that all
things which Nature had "established first in good estate,
and in meet order ranged," Mutability had perverted, "and
all their statutes burst"; she had altered quite "all the
worlds faire frame," and

> made them all accurst
> That God had blest, and did at first provide
> In that still happy state for ever to abide.

To this, it is argued, Harvey replies pointedly in the following passage of his letter:—"Nature herself is changeable
and most of all delighted with vanitye; and art, after a
sort her ape, conformeth herself to the like mutabilitye."
In opposition to Spenser's retrospect of the Golden Age,
Harvey accepts Jean Bodin's opinion that the present is
better than any preceding time. Again, the letter (pp. 84,
85) is thought to offer criticisms of the idea expressed in
VII: 17 ff., that Mutability governs all the elements,—
earth, air, fire, and water. Perhaps, too, it alludes to other
poems of Spenser. The following passage at least, reminds
us of Erato's complaint in the *Teares of the Muses* and of
the *Hymne in Honour of Love:* "You suppose most of these
bodily and sensual pleasures to be abandoned as unlawfull
and the inward contemplative delightes of the mind more
zelously to be imbracid as most commendable." The poet's

Platonism proceeds, Harvey thinks, from "sum strange mellancholy conceites and speculative imaginations discoursed at large in your fansye and brayne."

If one looks in the *Nicomachean Ethics* for the ethical theme of Spenser's fragmentary seventh book, he will find in Aristotle's virtue of steadfastness, already illustrated in the second book of the *Faerie Queene,* the nearest correspondence to the Constancie of the *Mutabilitie Cantos.* However, in this case as in his treatment of love in the *Hymnes,* Spenser has celebrated as a cosmic principle what elsewhere he has regarded as a virtue of practical ethics. To understand the poet's philosophy of constancy and change, it will be necessary to recall certain theories of the universe expounded by the philosophers of the ancient world.

The fundamental question was posed very early in the history of Greek philosophy. In the fifth century before Christ there were already two sharply opposed schools of thought, the Eleatic and the Ionic. The former, best represented by Parmenides of Elea, a Greek city of lower Italy, based its teaching upon the contention that there was absolute, self-existing being, which was the subject of true knowledge, as distinct from phenomenal nature, which was the province of mere opinion. In sharp contrast to this philosophy was that of Heraclitus, representing the Ionic school, for whom there was nothing constant except change, —a philosophy of the flux and flow. The old debate is in substance revived by Spenser in his opposition of Mutability to Jove, who, obviously representing the absolute and the permanent, defends heaven against the assaults of the Titans.

The philosophy of the character Mutability in Spenser's "Legend of Constancie" is obviously not Eleatic but Heraclitan, and as such it obviously bears some relation to the *De Rerum Natura* of Lucretius (99–55 B. C.), a disciple of Epicurus and justly famous for his exposition of the atomic theory in Latin verse.

To the mind of Lucretius all creation consisted of atoms and void, and the objects of sense have been made by combinations of the primordial substances determined by natural law. From the operations of this law the gods stand aloof. Though Lucretius has given us the most celebrated work of science in verse, the motive of his book is obviously more moral than scientific. By freeing men from faith in the gods and from belief in the immortality of the soul, he would free them also from superstitious fears and bring them "to look on all things with a mind at peace."

Evidently Spenser knew Lucretius. It was long ago pointed out that the hymn to Venus (F.Q. IV, X, 44–47) is a paraphrase of the invocation to Aphrodite at the beginning of the first book of the *De Rerum Natura;* and it seems possible that he had in mind the philosophy of Lucretius when in *Faerie Queene* III, VI, he described Time as the enemy of all things (D.R.N.I, 225–229), when he offers an account of the origin of organic life (D.R.N. I, 188 ff.), when he describes the growth of all things in Nature's garden (D.R.N. I, 795–819), when he touches upon its orderly arrangement (D.R.N. II, 1097–1092), and when he speaks of changes in the "hew" and "sondry formes" of substances (D.R.N. II, 1002–1006). One might note, further, that the pitying gods of Spenser (F.Q. III, vi, 40), like the gods of Lucretius (D.R.N. II, 1171 ff.), are far removed from the world of human affairs.

A comparison of the fifth book of the *De Rerum Natura* with *Mutabilitie* confirms, it has been argued, the impression of Lucretian influence produced by the parallels which have been cited in the preceding paragraph. "The whole attempt of Mutability, detailed in the preceding canto and here brought to trial," writes Professor Greenlaw, "may be regarded as an argument for a materialistic conception of the world as against all supernaturalism." (*Spenser and Lucretius,* p. 145.) Further on in the same article he declares that "the *Mutabilitie Cantos* are charged with true Lucretian scepticism." In view of the situation in *Mutabilitie,* which represents the Titaness as making war against Jove, attention is called particularly to the comparison by Lucretius of his attack on supernaturalism with the attempt of the Titans to cast Jove from his seat. Again, Mutability in elaborating her argument follows "in chronological order the points developed in the fifth book of Lucretius, using only the ones that fit her theme."

Though one accepts the evidence of Lucretian influence upon the Garden of Adonis and *Mutabilitie,* one need not believe that Spenser at any time had adopted a Lucretian philosophy of life. The context of the hymn to Venus in Book IV and the association of Amoret with the Garden of Adonis can only mean that the poet connected this philosophy of change with the lower forms of love, which he is never tired of contrasting with the ideal love of a Britomart. His awareness of mutability like his awareness of despair or idle mirth is sufficiently vivid, but the spiritual affirmation in the last stanza of the final canto of *Mutabilitie* is none the less emphatic.

Thus affirming his faith in permanence beyond a world of change, Spenser naturally came to occupy himself with problems of becoming and being. For these problems he has offered a Platonic solution in the *Four Hymnes.* In the

Mutabilitie Cantos, on the other hand, as well as in the Garden of Adonis passage, he has been thought to show the influence of Empedocles of Agrigentum, who attempted before Plato to reconcile the two schools of thought represented respectively by Parmenides and Heraclitus. Empedocles believed that the elements are eternal Being, unoriginated, imperishable, and unchangeable. What we call origination is a combination, and what we call destruction is a separation of these elements, which are moved by forces of attraction and repulsion, or, as Empedocles would say, by love and hate.

Miss Albright, taking into consideration the *Hymnes,* the *Mutabilitie Cantos,* the Garden of Adonis passage, *Colin Clouts Come Home Againe* (799 ff.), and the Proem to Book V of the *Faerie Queene,* has made the following comparison of Empedocles and Lucretius with Spenser :—

1. Lucretius is an atomist. Spenser starts with the elements, following Empedocles, whom Lucretius has rejected.

2. Lucretius is opposed to the principle of two-fold couplings of elements which Spenser takes from Empedocles as creative activities.

3. Lucretius has no place for such forces as Love and Strife in conflict in creation, as has Spenser, following Empedocles.

4. Aside from abiogenesis, which Empedocles has also, Spenser's notion of animal creation shows no resemblance to Lucretius's.

5. The one modern note in Lucretius, the approach to a definite doctrine of "survival of the fittest," does not appear in Spenser.

6. Lucretius's ruling force in creation is Chance. To this

Spenser is opposed. Lucretius sees no design; Spenser sees a goal of perfection.

7. Lucretius denies God as creator, as divinity, and as revealed in Nature. Spenser affirms all this.

8. Lucretius denies immortality of soul, including pre-existence, after life, and ability of soul to exist apart from the body. Spenser believes in all these.

9. Lucretius has no heaven; Spenser has.

10. Lucretius is a materialist, opposed to all that is mythical or mystical, or supernatural. Spenser revels in the ideas which Lucretius regards with disgust or contempt.

So far as the evidence of the *Mutabilitie Cantos* goes, there can be little doubt of Spenser's position. Although Nature argues as persuasively as either Despair or Phædria, the case is decided in favor of Jove:—

> Ah! whither doost thou now, thou greater Muse,
> Me from these woods and pleasing forrests bring?
> And my fraile spirit (that dooth oft refuse
> This too high flight, unfit for her weake wing)
> Lift up aloft, to tell of heavens king
> (Thy sovereaine sire) his fortunate successe,
> And victory in bigger noates to sing,
> Which he obtain'd against that Titanesse,
> That him of heavens empire sought to dispossesse?

In accord with this is the quatrain at the head of Canto VII, in which Nature's doom is called righteous. If it is objected that the case is decided by Nature instead of Jove, we might answer that Jove is a party to the suit and that it is *bold* Alteration who presumes to appeal "from Jove to Nature's

bar." That Nature is on Jove's side in the conflict between
Mutability and Constancy should not surprise the careful
student of Spenser's philosophy. This position is wholly
in accord with the cosmogony of the *Hymnes* and with the
Christian philosophy of the first book of the *Faerie Queene*.
If we recall what is said of the Law of Nature in the
first book of Hooker's *Ecclesiastical Polity,* we may almost
consider it the official position of the national church.

As a further source for the *Mutabilitie Cantos,* Ovid's
Metamorphoses has been adduced. Of the two elements,
argument and masque, that are combined in the fragment,
the latter suggests some comparison with Ovid. With the
trial scene in *Mutabilitie* Professor Greenlaw has compared
the passage in the second book of the *Metamorphoses* in
which "Ovid tells how Phaethon goes to the palace of the
sun to complain to his father Apollo. Phœbus is seated on
a splendid throne, made of emeralds and other brilliant
gems. On his right hand and on his left the Days, the
Months, the Years, the Ages, and the Hours are all ar-
ranged at corresponding distances and the fresh Spring is
standing crowned with a chaplet of blossoms; Summer
stands naked except for garlands made of ears of corn;
Autumn is besmeared with the trodden-out grapes; next
comes icy Winter rough with his hoary hair."

Miss Albright has reminded us that a more striking analogue is a debate in the *Constancy* of Lipsius (1547–1606),
a Flemish scholar, whose stoicism offers more than one
interesting parallel with the philosophy of Spenser. In this
case the subject of the debate is the same as that in Spenser
and here, too, the victory, based on a decision of Nature,
is won by God. The doctrine of Lipsius is like Spenser's:—
"Nature's laws and Nature's Order, and the Necessity or

Fate that rules the changing affairs of this world are seen as an expression of the will of God who works as omniscient and overruling Providence." As Miss Albright has remarked, it is the aim of both Lipsius and Spenser "to justify the ways of God to man."

Still another author whom students of Spenser have tried to bring into some kind of relation with the *Mutabilitie Cantos* is Giordano Bruno (1550?–1600), a free-thinker of the Renaissance, to whom the philosopher Spinoza was indebted for some of his ideas. Bruno, it should be remembered, spent two years in England and dedicated to his friend Sir Philip Sidney two of his works. To a writer in the Quarterly Review (1902) the "broken cantos 'On Constancy' recall some of the 'Spaccio' in their machinery and other works of Bruno in their ruling idea." The parallels, however, are not particularly striking. In the *Spaccio* Jove, feeling age coming upon him, fears that he himself may be subject to the universal law of change. To obviate this misfortune he reforms and, having called a meeting of the gods, he gives them to understand that they, also, are to turn over a new leaf. In another work, the *Eroici Furori,* Bruno dwells upon the unending, universal alteration in Nature, much as Mutability does in Spenser's poem. It is clear enough that Spenser is no more a disciple of Bruno than he is of Lucretius. On the contrary, it has been suggested by Sebastian Evans in the article noted above that the poem is an "indirect refutation" of some of Bruno's doctrines; particularly that expressed in the following quotation from the *Trattato de la Causa, Principio et Uno* (1584) :—"Wherefore," remarks one of the parties of this dialogue to another, "in your ears will not sound ill the opinion of Heraclitus, who said that all things are One, the which by Mutability hath in itself all things; and because all forms are in it, consequently all definitions agree with it, and so far contradictory propositions are true." Upon this Mr. Evans comments: "Spenser admits that all things in nature change but change is not therefore an attribute of Deity." Aristotle had taught that "change is necessarily determined both at its beginning and its end, and cannot be eternal, consequently cannot be divine. God is God, says Bruno in effect, in virtue of His infinite mutability. Not so, answers Spenser; God is God in virtue of his infinite stability."

Finally attention may be called to a general resemblance between Spenser's Nature and the corresponding figure in Alanus's *De Planctu Naturæ*, to which Spenser alludes in *Mutabilitie* VII, stanza 9. The correspondence is here so slight that one may suspect that the allusion was taken from Chaucer's *Parliament of Birds*, which in the passage cited is associated with Alane's *Plaint of Kinde*.

REFERENCES

Albright, Evelyn M. *Spenser's Reasons for Rejecting the Mutability Cantos.* Studies in Philology, XXV (1928), 93 ff.

Albright, Evelyn M. *Spenser's Cosmic Philosophy and His Religion.* Publications of the Modern Language Association, XLIV (1929), 715 ff.

Albright, Evelyn M. *On the Dating of Spenser's "Mutability" Cantos.* Studies in Philology, XXVI (1929), 482 ff.

Belden, H. M. *Alanus de Insulis, Giles Fletcher, and the "Mutabilitie" Cantos.* Studies in Philology, XXVI (1929), 142 ff.

Bush, Douglas. The Date of Spenser's *Cantos of Mutability*. Publications of the Modern Language Association, XLV (1930), 954 ff.

DeMoss, W. F. *The Influence of Aristotle's "Politics" and "Ethics" on Spenser*. Chicago, 1918, 49 ff.

Elton, O. *Modern Studies*. London, 1907.

Evans, S. *A Lost Poem by Edmund Spenser*. Macmillan's Magazine, XLII (1880), 145 ff. (Compare, *Spenser as a Philosophic Poet,* Edinburgh Review. Vol. 161, Jan. 1885; and Edinburgh Review, Vol. 201, 1905, 164 ff.)

Falkiner, C. L. *Essays Relating to Ireland*. London, 1909. 26 ff.

Greenlaw, Edwin. *Spenser's Influence on Paradise Lost*. Studies in Philology, XVII (1920), 320 ff.

Greenlaw, Edwin. *Spenser and Lucretius*. Studies in Philology, XVII (1920), 439 ff.

Greenlaw, Edwin. *Some Old Religious Cults in Spenser*. Studies in Philology, XX (1923), 216 ff.

Greenlaw, Edwin. Spenser's *"Mutabilitie."* Publications of the Modern Language Association, XLV (1930), 684 ff.

Lemmi, C. W. *The Allegorical Meaning of Spenser's Muiopotmos*. Publications of the Modern Language Association, XLV (1930), 732 ff.

Levinson, R. B. *Spenser and Bruno*. Publications of the Modern Language Association, XLIII (1928), 675 ff.

Padelford, Frederick M. The *Cantos of Mutabilitie:* Further Considerations Bearing on the Date. Publications of the Modern Language Association, XLV (1930), 704 ff.

CHAPTER XXI

DAPHNAÏDA

IN 1591 [1] Spenser published his elegy lamenting the death of Douglas Howard, the daughter of Henry Lord Howard and the wife of Arthur Gorges. The poem was dedicated to Lady Helena, Marquesse of Northampton, one of Douglas's aunts. The couple had been married on October 14, 1584, when Douglas was in her thirteenth year. So strong was the opposition of her father to the match that after her marriage he charged the groom before the Star Chamber with the theft of his daughter. About four years after the marriage their child Ambrosia was born, and less than two years later, on August 13, 1590, Douglas died after a long illness and before she had reached her nineteenth birthday.

Under the pastoral name Alcyon, which he bears in the *Daphnaïda,* Spenser had already accorded in *Colin Clouts Home Againe* (384–391) more than his due praise to Arthur Gorges :—

> And there is sad Alcyon, bent to mourne,
> Though fit to frame an everlasting dittie,
> Whose gentle spright for Daphnes death doth tourn
> Sweet layes of love to endlesse plaints of pittie.
> Ah! pensive boy, pursue that brave conceipt,

[1] For the date of Daphnaïda, see Chapter XXII.

In thy sweet *Eglantine of Meriflure,*
Lift up thy notes unto their wonted height,
That may thy Muse and mates to mirth allure.

The eulogy and the elegy were accorded Gorges not so
much in his own right as in that of Sir Walter Raleigh, who
was a maternal first cousin of Gorges's mother. The kins-
men were closely associated over a long period of years,
perhaps from the time of their boyhood in Devonshire and
later at Oxford and in public life. Together they served
in Parliament and according to Camden they were both
on the Channel fleet in the year of the Armada (1588). As
captain of Raleigh's ship, the Wastspight, Gorges accompanied the great explorer to the Azores in 1597. In
his *History of the World* Raleigh takes note of his cousin's
part in the landing at Fayal, and a record of the expedition
is preserved in Gorges's best-known work, *The Islands
Voyage,* which was printed by Purchas in 1625. His poems
mentioned in *Colin Clout* have all been lost, but there are
still eleven items constituting his extant works, which
besides *The Islands Voyage* are: 1. *Observations and
Overtures for a Seafight uppon our owne Coasts.* Un-
printed. 2. *Observations and Overtures concerning the
Royall Navye and Seaservice.* 3. *A Forme of Orders and
Directions . . . (for) Conducting a Fleete through the
Narrow Seas.* 4. *A Breefe Discourse tending to the Wealth,
and strength of this Kingedome of Greate Brittayne.* Un-
printed. 5. *New Year's Verses to the King, the Queen, and
the Prince with devices exquisitely drawn and illumined.*
Printed in Brydges, *Restituta,* 1816, IV, 506 ff. 6. *The
Publique Register for generall Commerce.* 7. *The Olympian
Catastrophe,* 1612. Printed in 1925 by Randall Davies.

Subject: The death of Prince Henry written in pseudo-Spenserian style. Prefatory and concluding verses by Gorges. 8. *Lucan's Pharsalia. Translated into English verse.* 9. *Francis Bacon's The Wisedome of the Ancients. Done into English.* 1619. 10. Bacon's *Moral Essays. Translated into French.* 1619.

In the lament for Dido in the November eclogue Spenser, following Marot, produced his first elegy. There, it was noted, he used the structure of the classical type in dividing the poem into two parts—one expressive of unrelieved sorrow, and the other, of consolation and hope. The *Daphnaïda* shows no such fidelity to the traditional form. Its first division is narrative, recounting the poet's meeting with the man in black, who was plunged in sorrow but unwilling at first to reveal the cause of his grief. It is not until we reach the end of this division that we learn of Daphne's death. The following seven divisions of the poem, moving to a climax of strong emotion and leading up to a brief conclusion, have as their subjects the lady's beauty, her death-bed address to her husband, the latter's contrast between past joys and present sorrows, his expression of bitterness and resentment, and the voicing of his hatred of all things to which his sorrow has led. Here and there passing allusions to sheep and shepherds associate the *Daphnaïda* loosely with the pastoral; and at more than one point there are details of description and lyrical turns suggesting the poet of the *Shepheardes Calender* and the *Faerie Queene*. Particularly noteworthy are the descriptions of evening at line 22 ff., and of the shepherds' dance at 309 ff.

Combined with its debt to the pastoral tradition are *Daphnaïda*'s obvious borrowings from Chaucer's *Book of the Duchess*. In the earlier poem the vogue of the love-vision was adapted to the requirements of the elegy. In *Daphnaïda* Spenser does away with the device of the vision but, following his predecessor, he represents the author of the poem, himself in sorrow, as meeting by chance a man in black, who hesitates to declare the cause of his grief. In each case, the man in black tells the story of his courtship and rails against a cruel Fortune that has bereft him of his love. With Chaucer's game of chess, employed by the afflicted lover as an indirect means of telling his story, should be compared Spenser's story of the capture of the White Lioness, suggested by the lion on the armorial bearings of the Howards. Perhaps, too, the name Alcyon, very rare in pastoral poetry, was taken from the story of Ceyx and Alcyon with which Chaucer begins the *Book of the Duchess*.

On the score of its rhetoric and metrical form *Daphnaïda* invites still further consideration. It will at once recall the poet's early work in its free use of such rhetorical devices as the rhetorical question, the apostrophe, and the pathetic fallacy. Characteristic, too, of his early poetry is such weaving of alliteration and assonance, of repeated words and phrases, as we find in the following quotation :—

> She is the rose, the glorie of the day,
> And mine the primrose in the lowly shade:
> Mine? ah, not mine! amisse I mine did say:
> Not mine, but his which mine awhile her made.

Those special forms of repetition known as anaphora and doubling, which are found in the *Calender* and elsewhere, also recur in *Daphnaïda*. For example :—

> Out of the world thus was she reft awaie
> Out of the world, unworthie such a spoyle;

and,

> Thus when he ended had his heavie plaint,
> The heaviest plaint that ever I heard sound.

A more skilful art of repetition, which is suggestive of Elizabethan music with its counterpoint and undersong, is illustrated in the following beautiful stanza:—

> She fell away in her first ages spring,
> Whil'st yet her leafe was greene, and fresh her rinde,
> And whil'st her braunch faire blossoms forth did bring,
> She fell away against all course of kinde:
> For age to die is right, but youth is wrong;
> She fell away like fruite blowne downe with winde:
> Weepe, Shepheard, weepe, to make my undersong.

Apart from such forms of repetition, one can hardly miss in *Daphnaïda* that overwrought rhetoric of melancholy in which the *Teares of the Muses* is largely written, and of which the best illustration in sixteenth century English literature is offered by Sackville's *Induction* to the *Mirrour for Magistrates*. In *Daphnaïda* the poet invites not only the Fatal Sisters, but the "queene of darknes" and "grisly ghosts" to hearken unto his song. It is in the "gloomie evening" that he meets the man in black, he himself the most miserable man alive, his thoughts full of "this worlds vainnesse and life's wretchednesse." The "dying paines" of the man in black are multiplied by his "huge anguish," and not only would he have the birds "silent on the naked spray," but, in harmony with his melancholy mood, he would have "the shady woods resound with dreadfull yells," the air should "be filed with noyse of dolefull knells," and Nature should bring forth "hideous monsters full of uglinesse." From such hollow rhetoric it is pleasant to turn to the graceful description, at line 309 ff., of Daphne leading the dance of the shepherds' daughters or to that lyric stanza, quoted in the preceding paragraph, which carries the accent of a sorrow truly felt.

The *Daphnaïda* deserves higher praise for its meter than for its rhetoric. Here Spenser has achieved a notable success by a slight variation of Chaucer's seven-line rhyme-royal stanza. The variation consists in the transposition of one rhyme, so that instead of ababbcc, the result is ababcbc. The effect of this arrangement is, in the words of Professor Dodge, a "haunting cadence, almost as beautiful as the stanza of 'October.'" Within the stanza we find usually one strong pause, almost always at the end of a line. Here and there special effects are produced by multiplying the pauses and placing them more freely; for example, in the following stanza beginning at line 183:—

> Then sighing sore, 'Daphne thou knewest,' quoth he;
> 'She now is dead': ne more endured to say,
> But fell to ground for great extreamitie;
> That I, beholding it, with deepe dismay
> Was much appald, and lightly him uprearing,
> Revoked life, that would have fled away,
> All were my self through griefe in deadly drearing.

With this might be compared the stanza beginning at line 288. On the whole, however, the meter of the poem leaves with us that impression of ease and fluidity which is broadly characteristic of Spenser's versification.

REFERENCES

Renwick, W. L. *Daphnaïda and Other Poems.* London, 1930.

———

Erskine, J. *The Elizabethan Lyric.* N. Y. 1903. 176 f.

Nadal, T. W. *Spenser's Daphnaïda and Chaucer's Book of the Duchess.* Publications of the Modern Language Association, XXIII (1908), 646 ff.

Sandison, Helen E. *Arthur Gorges, Spenser's Alcyon and Raleigh's Friend.* Publications of the Modern Language Association, XLIII (1928), 645 ff.

CHAPTER XXII

COLIN CLOUTS COME HOME AGAINE

COLIN CLOUTS COME HOME AGAINE, published by Ponsonbie in 1595 with Astrophel and the other elegies commemorating Sidney's death, is introduced by a letter addressed to Sir Walter Raleigh and dated "from my house of Kilcolman, the 27 of December, 1591." "It was obviously written," writes Professor Dodge, "not long after his return to Kilcolman and sent to his friend as soon as done." There are, however, difficulties in the way of accepting this inference. As Dr. Long has reminded us, the dating of *Colin Clout* from Kilcolman is our only proof that Spenser returned to his Irish estate in 1591. In the way of crediting what at first will seem sufficient proof, is the dating of *Daphnaïda* from London, according to the old calendar only five days later, January the first, 1591. To avoid the supposition of so incredibly speedy a round-trip, some editors of Spenser have assumed that the dating of *Daphnaïda* conforms not to the old calendar but to the new, which makes January the first instead of the tenth month of the year. An alternative explanation is that the dating of *Colin Clout* is a literary device designed to heighten the verisimilitude of the poet's pastoral fiction. "It was for London readers," writes Dr. Long, "that *Colin Clout* was written. How delicately Spenser couches this flattery in a recital feignedly made far away at his homecoming! So appropriately and with such a consistent sense of decorum that he feignedly dates the poem from his Irish home at Kilcolman, being in reality—where? Where his poem would be fully appreciated, in London, where he was five days later, when he dedicated the 'Daphnaïda.' "

That Spenser regarded *Colin Clout* as a sequel of the *Shepheardes Calender* is evident not merely from its title and pastoral setting but from its return to the familiar Hobbinol and Rosalind themes. Moreover, its plan will at once recall that of the September eclogue. In each case, Hobbinol, after commenting upon the long absence of a returned traveler, requests some account of his experiences in the place of his sojourn and in each case he learns of the corruption that prevails there. Furthermore, in *Colin Clout* as in the *Shepheardes Calender,* Colin sings one of his songs in compliance with the request of a fellow-shepherd, the Queen is given exalted praise, and much is made of the contrast betwen base and ideal love. The poet resumes, too, the familiar theme of the mean estate, for which Harvey had been the spokesman in the *Calender*. The amplification of this theme involved praise of the simple life in Ireland as contrasted with the complicated, corrupt life of the court. Colin is, accordingly, moved

> to warne yong shepheards wandring wit,
> Which, through report of that lives painted blisse,
> Abandon quiet home, to seeke for it.

Upon this there follows a passage thoroughly in line with traditional satire of the court. What avails there is

> a guilefull hollow hart,
> Masked with faire dissembling curtesie.

There one learns that "each mans worth is measured by his weed," and that the "vaunted vanitie" of the courtiers is

> Nought else but smoke, that fumeth soone away.

As for love,—

> His mightie mysteries they do prophane.

All of this is in the key of Diggon Davie's discourse upon the loose living of popish prelates.

In this passage Spenser has changed the relations between court and country as we find these explained elsewhere in the poem. Where, as at l. 308 ff., he is moved to sing the praises of the Queen and the courtly circle, Ireland ceases to be the conventional pastoral land of peace and the "quiet home" and takes on the harsher aspect of reality. Now, with Elizabeth

> all happie peace and plenteous store
> Conspire in one to make contented blisse.

There he has found the best of shepherds and such nymphs as Urania, the sister of Astrofell, "faire Marian, the Muses' only darling," and Mansilia,

> Best knowne by bearing up great Cynthiaes traine.

All this praise of the life of courts, reflecting such ideals as Castiglione set forth in the *Cortegiano,* is here contrasted with "the land of wailing and wretchedness, of bloody issues and leprosies, of grisly famine, the raging sword, nightly bodrags, and the hue and cry." Here, as Thestylis of the poem says, is the

barrein soyle,
Where cold and care and penury do dwell.

So, in dealing with both court and country, Spenser, the idealist, and Spenser, the satirist, meet in *Colin Clout*. If the poem appears to contradict itself, we may refer that apparent contradiction to the ethical principle expressed in the following lines :—

all good, all grace there freely growes,
Had people grace it gratefully to use :
For God his gifts there plenteously bestowes,
But gracelesse men them greatly do abuse.

With this compare the words of the *Hymne in Honour of Beautie,* l. 157 ff. :—

Nothing so good, but that through guilty shame
May be corrupt, and wrested unto will.
Nathelesse the soule is faire and beauteous still,
How ever fleshes fault it filthy make.

Evidently *Colin Clouts Come Home Againe,* though pastoral in setting, is not attuned throughout to the shepherd's pipe, and is reminiscent of other poems than the *Shepheardes Calender.* Colin's praise of Raleigh and the dominion of Elizabeth over land and sea recalls the note of imperialism in the *Faerie Queene* as, for example, in the prologue to Book II ; and Colin's song of the Mulla and the Bregog will remind every one of the marriage of the Thames and the Medway in the eleventh canto of the fourth Book. Very explicit, too, is the allusion to the sixth canto of Book III in what is said at line 799 ff. of the birth of Cupid and the Gardens of Adonis ; nor can any one miss the parallel to the *Hymnes* in Colin's account, at line 835 ff., of the creation of the universe through love.

Among the noteworthy passages of *Colin Clout* is that beginning at l. 376, in which Spenser pays his respects to twelve contemporary poets. His list was certainly not made out with sole reference to literary merit, and a number of those included are very difficult to identify. In two cases the poets for some reason are given their own names: William Alabaster, a very indifferent poet, who had at least so much in common with Spenser that he had undertaken and failed to finish a poem of epic proportions in honor of the Queen, entitled *Eliseis* and intended to run to twelve books; and the infinitely more gifted Samuel Daniel, whose accent most excels "in tragick plaints and passionate mischance." Of the others we can certainly identify the Shepherd of the Ocean as Raleigh, Astrofell as Sidney, and Alcyon as Arthur Gorges, in commemoration of whose wife Spenser had written *Daphnaïda*. For the other seven poets various identifications have been suggested. The most considerable effort to establish identifications was made by Malone in the second volume, pp. 226 ff., of his edition of Shakespeare (1821). His equation of Aëtion with Shakespeare has been approved by Sidney Lee, J. M. Robertson, and W. J. Rolfe; another suggestion and one more in favor now is that Aëtion stands for Michael Drayton, l. 447, referring to his pseudonym Rowland (see Dodge's note); Miss Stopes has suggested an identification with Thomas Edwards, the author of *Cephalus & Procris,* and Le Franc (in *Sous le masque de Shakespeare*) has detected under the fanciful name the person of William Stanley. Amyntas is identified by Malone, McKerrow, Miss Stopes, and Le Franc as the brother of this William Stanley, namely Ferdinando, Earl of Derby. For Harpalus, suggested identifications are Churchyard (Malone), Barnaby Googe (Todd), Thomas Sackville (Collier and Dodge), George Puttenham (Nicholson, N. & Q., 5th Series), George Turberville (Koeppel and J. E. Hankins). In support of the final suggestion is the following from Turberville's "He Sorrowes Other to Have the Fruites of his Service" :—

> Even so fare I poore Harpalus
> Whome Cupids paines devour.

Corydon—Abraham Fraunce (Malone), Sir Edward Dyer (Fleay) ; Palin—Peele (Malone), Thomas Challoner (Dodge) ; Alcon—Thomas Lodge (Malone), Thomas Watson (Dodge) ; Palaemon—Golding (Malone), Thomas Churchyard (Dodge).

Following the list of poets is one of the ladies of the court. The first mentioned, Urania, sister unto Astrofell, is, of course, Mary, Countess of Pembroke. Theana is doubtless Anne Russell, widow of Ambrose Dudley, Earl of Warwick (Dodge) ; Marian—Margaret, Countess of Cumberland (Dodge) ; Mansilia—Helena, Marchioness of Northampton, to whom Spenser had dedicated *Daphnaïda* (Dodge, Sandison) ; Galathea and Neæra are not yet identified ; Stella—Lady Rich ; Phyllis, Charillis, Amaryllis —Elizabeth, Anne, and Alice Spenser respectively, daughters of Sir John Spencer of Althorpe.

Viewed in its larger aspects, *Colin Clout* may be felt to mark the culmination in Spenser's poetry of one line of stylistic development, which may be referred to both Chaucer and Marot, and which he employed in both the plaintive and satiric vein. In the *Calender* he had judged

that the *naïveté* appropriate to the pastoral would be promoted by a rustic idiom; but this, it will be remembered,
Sir Philip Sidney could not "allow." In *Colin Clout* the poet
might seem to have accepted and justified Sidney's criticism
by eschewing the affectation of a pseudo-dialect and falling
back for his effect upon an apparently artless idiom, which
like Chaucer's is in reality an achievement of art. Throughout there is a notable gain over the *Calender* in the rhetorical
ease of his narrative and discursive style. The same may be
said for the metrical form of *Colin Clout,* which shows, as
Mr. Greg has remarked, "a considerable advance in smooth-
ness and command of rhythm over the non-lyrical portions
of the *Calender."* In fine, style and metrical form in
Colin Clout are so well accommodated to the poet's theme
and so well attuned to his mood that the result is what Mr.
de Selincourt has justly described as "the triumph of the
familiar style, in which so few writers have excelled."
"To write thus," the same critic adds, "is only possible to
one who is both artist and gentleman."

Not that the whole poem is pitched in the same key. The
tone of ardent patriotism and exalted eulogy interchanges
with the quieter notes of reflection and the harsher accents
of satire; but dominant throughout is that minor key, which
in contrast to the overwrought rhetoric of melancholy
illustrated in the *Ruines of Time,* the *Teares of the Muses,*
and *Daphnaïda,* we have already observed in the *Shepheardes Calender.* "In the spring of the great age of English
song," writes Mr. Greg, "Spenser's note is like the voice of
autumn, not the fruitful autumn of cornfield and orchard,
but a premature barrenness of wet and fallen leaves—

The woods decay, the woods decay and fall.

REFERENCES

Courthope, W. J. *History of English Poetry*, III, 9 ff.

Greg, W. W. *Pastoral Poetry and Pastoral Drama*. London, 1906, 98 ff.

Hankins, John E. The *Harpalus of Spenser's Colin Clout*. Modern Language Notes, XLIV, 164 ff.

Long, P. W. *Spenser's Dating of "Colin Clout."* The Nation, N. Y., LXXXIII (Nov. 1, 1906), 368 ff.

Sandison, Helen E. *Spenser's Mansilia*. London Times Literary Supplement (September 8, 1927), 608.

Malone, E. *Works of Shakespeare*, 1821. II, 226 ff.

CHAPTER XXIII

ASTROPHEL

PUBLISHED in 1595 in the same volume with *Colin Clouts Come Home Againe, Astrophel* is Spenser's belated tribute to the memory of Sir Philip Sidney. That the elegy was written after 1590 we may conclude from Spenser's statement in his dedication of the *Ruines of Time* that he had not yet "shewed anie thankefull remembrance" to his former patron. The name here given Sidney is, of course, that which he had himself assumed in his famous sonnet sequence, and the story of his love for Penelope Devereux, the daughter of Essex and the wife of Lord Rich, which he had there recounted, is here further idealized. As a matter of fact, the historical Stella did not, of course, "make untimely haste" to follow "her mate," when she knew him to be dead. On the contrary, she lived long enough to marry again. It has been plausibly maintained that another poetic version of the Sir Philip-Penelope story is Ford's *Broken Heart,* in which the heroine is named Penthea; this is within a letter of one of Spenser's designations for the flower into which Astrophel and Stella were together transformed. Noting the general likeness of the play to the poem, Professor Sherman remarked that "when Ford made Penthea die of a broken heart, he simply repeated the poetical fiction of Spenser."

In the volume of 1595, *Astrophel* introduces a group of

obituary poems commemorating the death of Sidney. Following the *Astrophel* is a second contribution by Spenser, usually entitled the *Doleful Lay of Clorinda*. The others by Bryskett, Matthew Roydon, and Sir Walter Raleigh were perhaps all composed more punctually than *Astrophel*. At least the *Mourning Muse of Thestylis* by Bryskett was entered upon the Stationers' Register in August, 1587. Although *Astrophel* compares favorably with the other commemorative poems in the volume, it occupies no very distinguished place in the long tradition of the elegy that extends from the age of Theocritus to modern times.

Whatever its quality, the *Astrophel* at least shows Spenser working more independently than in either of his other two elegies. The Lament for Dido of the November eclogue follows, very closely it will be remembered, a poem by Marot, and in the *Daphnaïda* the influence of Chaucer's *Book of the Duchess* is not inconsiderable. The story of the boar-hunt in *Astrophel* will, in its turn, at once suggest Bion's *Lament for Adonis,* but a comparison of the two elegies reveals only the most general likeness. Professor Erskine has felt that its "general tone is Greek" and it has even suggested to him the Homeric Hymns.

To others *Astrophel* will suggest more promptly the plaintive vein of the *Shepheardes Calender*. Written in the fluid, six-line stanza of "January," "July," and "December," it employs, too, their familiar alliterative and repetitious rhetoric. For example,

> Stella the faire, the fairest star in skie,
> As faire as Venus or the fairest faire,
> (A fairer star saw never living eie).

As he resumes in *Astrophel* his praise of Sidney, Spenser
describes far less effectively than he had done in *Mother
Hubberds Tale* the "president of noblesse and of chivalry."
It is only lightly that he touches upon Sir Philip's "good-
nesse and grace," his "joyance innocent," his charm for
the nymphs "of wood and brooke," and his devotion to
manly exercise. He establishes a slight parallel with Bion's
famous *Lament* by making the fatal boar-hunt of Adonis
symbolize the campaign in the Netherlands, in which Sidney lost his life. Lacking the accents of tragic emotion, the
poem is at its best when it attunes some idyllic fancy to
the minor measures of its pathos :—

> His palled face, impictured with death
> She bathed oft with teares and dried oft:
> And with sweet kisses suckt the wasting breath
> Out of his lips like lillies pale and soft:
> And oft she cald to him, who answerd nought,
> But onely by his lookes did tell his thought.

Here and there an attenuated charm is refined to true
felicity :—

> Whilest none is nigh, thine eyelids up to close,
> And kisse thy lips like faded leaves of rose.

As clearly as anywhere the Greek tone or the refinements
of Alexandrian fancy may be detected in those stanzas in
which taking a hint from Greek story the poet describes
the transformation of the lovers, there lying on the field,
into a flower both red and blue—"it first growes red, and
then to blew doth fade." The star-like center is as radiant
as Stella in the fresh days of her youth :—

And all the day it standeth full of deow,
Which is the teares that from her eyes did flow.

.   .   .   .

.   .   .   .

And when so ever thou it up doest take,
Do pluck it softly for that shepheards sake.

REFERENCES

Erskine, J. *The Elizabethan Lyric*. N. Y. 1903.

Shafer, R. *Spenser's Astrophel*. Modern Language Notes, XXVIII (1913), 224 ff.

Sherman, S. P. *Stella and the Broken Heart*. Publications of the Modern Language Association, XXIV (1909), 285 ff.

CHAPTER XXIV

THE DOLEFUL LAY OF CLORINDA

THIS poem, which immediately follows *Astrophel* in the anthology of obituary poems written in commemoration of Sidney's death, was long thought to have been written by Sidney's sister, the Countess of Pembroke. Recently the elegy has been assigned to Spenser in view of certain metrical and rhetorical characteristics. Dr. Long goes so far as to maintain that it is an integral part of *Astrophel,* occupying a position similar to that of Alcyon's lament in *Daphnaïda.* He calls attention to the fact that it has no separate title or pagination, being separated from the preceding stanzas only by an ornamental capital and a band, that its stanza form is that of *Astrophel,* and that the only evidence for Mary Sidney's authorship is found in the transition beginning at line 211, in which, however, Spenser says that he will "rehearse" the verse "as she it sung." Further, the *Lay* bears no likeness to the original poems of the Countess; for example, the pastoral attributed to her in Davison's *Poetical Rhapsody.*

Internal evidence for Spenser's authorship Dr. Long finds in the frequent placing of a colon after the second line of the stanza. This he regards as "a trademark of Colin," frequently illustrated in the *Calender,* as in "January" and "December." There are eleven cases in the sixteen stanzas of the *Lay* as compared with thirty-four cases in the thirty-nine stanzas of *Astrophel*. To this Professor Osgood has added that "almost every phrase, combination, and mannerism in it (the *Lay*), not to say the little thought which it contains, is found elsewhere in Spenser, especially in his elegiac verse." In sum the *Lay* may be regarded as "in its finest fibre Spenserian." He points out that only three words not found in the *Spenser Concordance* occur in the poem. And yet Professor Osgood thinks that Spenser has "attempted a qualification and cloaking of his natural tone to something more feminine and tenuous— 'least I marre the sweetnesse of the verse, In sort as she it sung.'" As an illustration he cites the following lines in which "with exquisite effect" the poet's "usual energy is tempered" :—

> In bed of lillies wrapt in tender wise,
> And compast all about with roses sweet,
> And daintie violets from head to feet.

REFERENCES

Long, P. W. *Spenseriana*. Modern Language Notes, XXXI (1916), 79–82.

Osgood, C. G. *Doleful Lay of Clorinda*. Modern Language Notes, XXXV (1920), 90 ff.

CHAPTER XXV

AMORETTI

IN 1595 there was printed for William Ponsonby a volume bearing the title *Amoretti* and *Epithalamion written not long since by Edmunde Spenser*. It was dedicated to the Right Worshipfull Sir Robert Needham, Knight, doubtless the same person who is mentioned in the *Calendar of State Papers* (*Ireland,* 1592–1596, p. 519) as "a very young soldier" who "prays to be satisfied of his arrearage." In the words of Ponsonby's dedicatory letter it was to gratulate this young soldier's safe return from Ireland that Spenser's sweet conceited sonnets were published. "This gentle Muse," continues Ponsonby, "for her former perfection long wished for in England, now at length crossing the seas in your (Needham's) happy company (though to your self unknown), seemeth to make choice of you, as meetest to give her deserved countenance, after her return." From the above it would seem that Needham, returning to England perhaps in the interest of his "arrearage," brought Spenser's sonnets with him, though Spenser's poetry—or Spenser himself (?)—was unknown to him. Earlier in the letter Ponsonby speaks of having "confidently presumed" to publish the poet's verses in his absence. Although the letter is not clear throughout, it would convey the idea that the printer has brought out the volume without the supervision of the poet.

It should be noted further that the letter, while mentioning specifically the sweet conceited sonnets, has nothing to say about the *Epithalamion,* and that the latter is supplied with a separate title page. Unless we assume that the term sonnet is here used loosely, there is, then, some reason to suppose that the sonnet sequence and the marriage hymn, though entered together on the Stationers' Register, November 19, 1594, and though having at the beginning a title page in common, were at first intended for separate publication.

So far as we may be guided by Ponsonby's letter and the separate title page, we should hardly think of the *Epithalamion* as a sequel of the *Amoretti*. This, however, is the traditional and prevailing opinion. The sonnet-sequence, we are told, is the story of Spenser's courtship of Elizabeth Boyle (or Elizabeth Peace) and thus appropriately precedes his wedding song. From l. 265 ff. of the *Epithalamion* we conclude that the poet was married on St. Barnabas' Day, June 11, and the "not long since" on the title page of this 1595 volume points to the year 1594. Working back from June 11, 1594, we can, then, on the traditional hypothesis, find in sonnets 62 and 4 poems commemorative of the New Year Days of 1594 and 1593 respectively, and can conclude that the poet's courtship covered a period of some eighteen months. If this explanation is accepted, the *Amoretti* would hold the unique position of an English sonnet sequence celebrating a serious courtship which led to marriage.

It is, however, not perfectly clear that the *Amoretti* is entitled to this unique position. For one thing, the sequence, concluding with the separation of the lovers, does not lead up easily to the marriage hymn. If the latter was regarded as the sequel of the former, it seems strange, too, that there should have been introduced between them the four poetic trifles in the manner of Anacreon. Finally, would Spenser have written line 427 of the *Epithalamion,* in which the word "ornaments" [1] seems to allude to his poetry, if he were publishing in the same volume with it a long sonnet sequence dealing with the progress of his courtship? We must conclude that we know nothing certainly about the lady of the *Amoretti* except that her name was Elizabeth (*see* sonnet 74).

Dr. Long's alternative hypothesis to the traditional one is that the lady of the sonnets is not Elizabeth Boyle but Elizabeth Carey, whom with her sisters Spenser had highly praised and compared with Sidney's Stella in *Colin Clouts Come Home Againe* (536 ff.), to whom he had ardently dedicated *Muiopotmos,* and in whose honor he had written one of the dedicatory sonnets prefixed to the *Faerie Queene.* This sonnet, which is one of two in that group addressed to ladies, has been described as "intimately personal and gallant" and as constituting a marked compliment to a "lady of comparatively inferior rank." It concludes with something like a promise that the poet will at some opportune time honor her still further in his verse. Is the *Amoretti* a fulfillment of that promise?

The problem of the sonnets considered above involves in some sense the question of their style. In a matter of this sort opinions easily differ, even after all the available facts are known. Many critics have detected in the *Amo-*

---

[1] "Ornaments" may mean wedding presents, for which we may suppose the bridegroom had sent to London, but which for some reason did not reach Ireland in time for the wedding. In lieu of these the poet wrote the *Epithalamion.*

retti a clearer note of personal feeling than what can be found in the usual complimentary series addressed to a poet's official mistress. For example, Professor R. E. N. Dodge thinks that "behind the graceful banalities of fancy, the imitations of previous imitators of Petrarch, almost inevitable in an Elizabethan sonnet sequence, one may read the history of a genuine courtship as clearly as in a set of old letters"; and Mr. E. de Selincourt, writing in a similar vein, declares that "amid much that is borrowed from the stock-in-trade of the French sonneteers, and recounts the emotions incident to every courtship, real or feigned, there is much also that, to the sympathetic reader at least, seems circumstantial in detail, both in the progress of his suit and in the character of his mistress." On the other hand, Sidney Lee maintains that "Spenser, no less than Sidney, to a large extent handled the sonnet as a poetic instrument whereon to repeat in his mother-tongue what he regarded as the finest and most serious examples of poetic feeling and diction in Italy and France"; and Dr. Janet G. Scott, a careful student of the Elizabethan sonnets, while allowing for originality here and there, finds that the series as a whole is largely conventional. Whatever might be the correct view of the style of the *Amoretti,* the facts upon which we should found an opinion are chiefly those which concern Spenser's sources.

It was hardly possible for Spenser, sharing the revived vogue of the sonnet which was stimulated in 1591 by the publication of Sidney's *Astrophel and Stella,* not to come under the influence of foreign models. His friend Gabriel Harvey in *Pierces Supererogation* (1593) places him among the Petrarchists; and, indeed, there can be no doubt

of his ultimate debt to the great Italian master of the sonnet form, even though, as Dr. Scott says, Petrarch was
not the principal creditor of Spenser's Muse. Fashionable
conceits of the Petrarchists are not far to seek. For example, in sonnets 34 and 63 Spenser compares himself to
a ship beset by storms; in 30 he dwells upon the paradox
of the lover's fire that hardens instead of melting ice; and
in 12 and 57 he rings the familiar changes upon the military metaphors of the ambush in his lady's eyes and of
his lady as a sweet warrior. In other cases, where we might
seem to have found Spenser's immediate source, we no
doubt have to do merely with an analogue. Among the
closer French analogues are sonnets of Desportes, a poet
who exercised a noteworthy influence upon the English
sonneteers of the sixteenth century. "The *préciosité* of
the Abbé de Tiron," writes Dr. Scott, "was without doubt
the quality which aroused the enthusiasm of the sixteenth
century in England"; moreover, as she reminds us, the
French of Desportes was easy to read, and his poems were
accessible in many editions. Of Ronsard's influence it is
hard to speak definitely; an instance of correspondence at
least may be noted between Spenser's 64 and Ronsard's
Amours I, 140, and Spenser's 88 and Ronsard's *Amours,*
II, 62. Dr. Scott thinks a certain affinity of Spenser for
Ronsard appears in the burning verses of love and sensu-
ality with which Spenser addresses his mistress. In the
case of Desportes the following parallels should be noted:
Amoretti, 18, Desportes' *Hippolyte,* 51; *Amoretti,* 15,
Desportes' *Diane* I, 32; *Amoretti* 68, Desportes' *Diane*
II, 46.

To facilitate a comparison of Spenser with the French

sonneteer whom he seems to have known best, number 51
of *Les Amours D'Hippolyte* is here placed by the side of
Amoretti, 18:—

<table>
<tr><td>Desportes—Les Amours
D'Hippolyte, 51</td><td>Amoretti, 18</td></tr>
</table>

Desportes—*Les Amours D'Hippolyte, 51*	*Amoretti,* 18
L'eau tombant d'un lieu haut goute à goute a puissance	The rolling wheele, that runneth often round,
Contre les marbres durs, caver finablement;	The hardest steele in tract of time doth teare:
Et le sang du lion force le diamant,	And drizling drops, that often doe redound,
Bien qu'il face à l'enclume et au feu resistance,	The firmest flint doth in continuance weare:
La flamme retenüe enfin par violance	Yet cannot I with many a dropping teare
Brise la pierre vive, et rompt l'empeschment;	And long intreaty, soften her hard hart,
Les aquilons mutins, soufflans horriblement,	That she will once vouchsafe my plaint to heare,
Tombent le chesne vieux, qui fait plus de deffance.	Or looke with pitty on my payneful smart.
Mais moy, maudit Amour, nuict et jour soupirant,	But when I pleade, she bids me play my part,
Et de mes yeux meurtris tant de larmes tirant,	And when I weep, she sayes teares are but water,
Tant de sang de ma playe, et de feux de mon ame;	And when I sigh, she sayes I know the art,
Je ne puis amollir une dure beauté,	And when I waile, she turns hir selfe to laughter.
Qui, las! tout au contraire accroist sa cruauté	So do I weepe, and wayle, and pleade in vaine,
Par mes pleurs, par mon sang, mes soupirs et ma flame.	Whiles she as steele and flint doth still remayne.

The greater liveliness in Spenser's treatment of the conventional theme is here too obvious for comment.

For students of the *Amoretti* Tasso occupies among the Italian sonneteers a place even more important than that of Desportes among the French. His attraction for Spenser both here and in the *Faerie Queene* is traceable, as Dr. Scott has suggested, to his Platonism and to the combination in his poetry of a free painting of physical beauties with a deep appreciation of moral beauty. In the following list are brought together the English and Italian sonnets that invite comparison. References are to Solerti's edition:—
Spenser 3, Tasso II, p. 52; Spenser 5, Tasso II, p. 54; Spenser 21, Tasso II, p. 115; Spenser 13, Tasso II, p. 316; Spenser 31, Tasso, *Rime* 4, 14; Spenser 43, Tasso 164, 166; Spenser 47, Tasso 88; Spenser 49, Tasso 74; Spenser 54, Tasso 712; Spenser 56, Tasso 1022; Spenser 67, Tasso II, p. 429; Spenser 72, Tasso II, p. 98; Spenser 73, Tasso II, p. 319; Spenser 76, 77, Tasso III, p. 133; Spenser 79, Tasso III, p. 142; Spenser 81, Tasso II, p. 25; Spenser 84, Tasso II, p. 194; Spenser 89, Tasso II, p. 439. Of these 31, 72, and 73 of the *Amoretti* are near enough to the Italian to be regarded as translations. The following sonnets in parallel columns may be compared in detail:

Tasso 2, 47	Amoretti, 72
Ritorno dal cielo alla sua donna	
L'alma vaga di luce e di bellezza,	Oft when my spirit doth spred her bolder winges,
Ardite spiega al Ciel l'ale amorose;	In mind to mount up to the purest sky,
Ma si le fa l'umanità gravose,	It down is weighd with

Che le dechina a quel, ch'in
terra apprezza.

E de' piaceri alla dolce esca
avvezza,
Ove in sereno volto Amor la
pose
Ira bianche perle e mattutine
rose,
Par che non trovi altra mag-
gior dolcezza.

E fa quasi augellin, ch'in alto
s'erga,
E poi discenda alfin ov'altri il
cibi;
E quasi volontario s'im-
prigioni.
E fra tanti del Ciel graditi
doni,
Si gran diletto par che in voi
delibi
Ch'in voi solo si pasce, e solo
alberga.

thoght of earthly things,
And clogd with burden of
mortality:
Where, when that soverayne
beauty it doth spy,
Resembling heavens glory in
her light,
Drawne with sweet pleasures
bayt, it back doth fly,
And unto heaven forgets her
former flight.
There my fraile fancy, fed
with full delight,
Doth bath in blisse, and mant-
leth most at ease;
Ne thinks of other heaven,
but how it might
Her harts desire with most
contentment please.
Hart need not wish none
other happinesse,
But here on earth to have
such hevens blisse.

Whoever may have been the lady of the *Amoretti* and
whatever its debt to foreign literature, the element of personal interest in these sonnets is considerable. In several
of them this element is explicit. For instance, 33, addressed
to Lodowick Bryskett, apologizes for the great wrong the
poet does the "most sacred empresse" in not finishing "her
Queene of Faëry"; 80 informs us that six books of his
Faerie Queene are finished; 60 notes the duration of the
courtship and gives the poet's age; and 74 acquaints the

reader with the name of his mother and mistress. Even
more revealing than these sonnets, which place a stamp
of reality upon the sequence, are those which acquaint
us with Elizabeth's character and bring before us apparently actual situations. "Whatever fancies the poet may
have borrowed," writes Professor Dodge, "he has not borrowed the temperament of his mistress: it may please him
to mention little except her pride; but her pride is clearly
her own." Associated with it is true humility:—

> Most goodly temperature ye may descry:
> Myld humblesse mixt with awfull majesty.

Her pride, too, is not an affectation of superiority or a
social weapon of defense; it is a natural expression of
her ideals.

> For in her lofty lookes is close implide
> Scorn of base things, and sdeigne of foule dishonor.
> But that same lofty countenance seemes to scorne
> Base thing, and thinke how she to heaven may clime.

Appearing as self-assurance, her pride is not only an integral part of her character but a directing principle of
her conduct. She is like a steady ship that "keepes her
course aright."

> Such selfe assurance need not feare the spight
> Of grudging foes, ne favour seek of friends:
> But in the stay of her owne stedfast might,
> Nether to one her selfe nor other bends.

Though fearing to lose her liberty, once her heart sur-
renders, she is "goodly won":—

> So let us love, deare love, lyke as we ought:
> Love is the lesson which the Lord us taught.

Besides Elizabeth's more serious qualities suggested above, the *Amoretti* celebrate here and there her lighter moods. For example in 29, "depraving his simple meaning," she playfully turns gainst him an allusion to the Phoebus-Daphne myth; and in 18, instead of the haughty and cold-hearted mistress of the tradition, she figures as the amused and ironical critic of the poet's extravagant love-making :—

> But when I pleade, she bids me play my part,
> And when I weep, she sayes teares are but water,
> And when I sigh, she sayes I know the art,
> And when I waile, she turnes hir selfe to laughter.

With this might be compared 54, in which the poet, an actor on the world's stage, is taken none too seriously by his mistress.

The impression of reality produced by Elizabeth's character as delineated in the sonnets is confirmed by the verisimilitude of those sonnets that deal with definite situations. For example, one gets from 46 and 75 the effect of a personal record, the former in humorous vein describing the poet's detention at his mistress's house by a downpour of rain and the latter, however conventional the situation, commemorating with accents of personal feeling the grave mood of the lovers as they walked together by the sea.

A sensitive French critic contrasting Spenser's *Amoretti* with Sidney's *Astrophel and Stella* describes the former sequence as "a history of tenderness without sin or remorse surrounded by a pure atmosphere and bathed in a white light." No doubt this is essentially true and no doubt we might agree with Mr. Légouis that Spenser's "maidenliness," as Coleridge would have it, is his "love for what is virginal in woman." Nevertheless, we must bring into our reckoning the frank though inoffensive sensuousness of such sonnets as 76 and 77, even while opposing to their wanton mood the Platonism of the closely following 79. If to this opposition we bring to bear the lessons of 72 (based on Tasso) and 87 we may conclude that in our poet's conflict between the body and the soul the latter achieved no absolute, no unnatural victory. Spenser's Platonism, as Professor Fletcher has reminded us, is the modified Platonism of the Renaissance. Accordingly his love "though largely ideal is by no means abstract." In the absence of his mistress he can commune with her in spirit, "beholding the idea playne"

> Through contemplation of my purest part
>
> .   .   .   .
> .   .   .   .
>
> But with such brightnesse whylest I fill my mind,
> I starve my body, and mine eyes doe blynd.

Like the bird in the sonnet of Tasso upon which he based 72, he willingly returns to earth from the purest sky, his spirit forgetting its former flight to heaven,

> Ne thinks of other heaven, but how it might
> Her harts desire with most contentment please.
> Hart need not wish none other happinesse
> But here on earth to have such hevens blisse.

The independence shown by Spenser in his handling of the conventional Petrarchan rhetoric appears more strikingly in the rhyme arrangement which he adopted for the *Amoretti*. He had already illustrated the Shakespearian form in an "Epigram" contributed to the *Theatre for Worldlings* and later in the early sonnets as revised for the *Complaints* volume. This volume also offers in sonnet 7 of the *Visions of Petrarch* and in the dedicatory sonnet prefixed to *Virgils Gnat* early instances of the *Amoretti* rhyme-scheme.

Certain features of the Spenserian sonnet were, of course, familiar before Spenser. The Italian sonnet and the French type that imitated it were like the Spenserian form in being constructed on a system of five rhymes. Moreover, when Wyatt and Surrey introduced the Italian sonnet into England, they showed a fondness for a concluding couplet, which in Italy was a very uncommon variation. Spenser, alternating his rhymes after the English fashion, departed from the Shakespearian form which he had early cultivated by binding his quatrains together with a common rhyme. This device, perhaps suggested to him by the linked quatrains of Marot, he had already used in the April and November eclogues of the *Shepheardes Calender*. In this connection we should observe that a fair proportion of the *Amoretti* sonnets are marked off by full pauses into three quatrains and a couplet; but wherever the pauses, the linked quatrains insured a compact structure, which, though a mark of the Italian octave with its repeated rhymes, was quite foreign to the 7-rhyme Elizabethan or Shakespearian form. In two instances—10 and 25—we have sonnets that close with an Alexandrine like the stanza of the *Faerie Queene*.

REFERENCES

Fletcher, J. B. *Mr. Sidney Lee and Spenser's Amoretti.* Modern Language Notes, XVIII (1903), 111 ff.

Kastner, L. E. *Spenser's "Amoretti" and Desportes.* Modern Language Review, IV (1908), 65 ff.

Lee, Sidney. Ed. *Elizabethan Sonnets.* N. Y. n. d.

Lee, Sidney. *The Elizabethan Sonnet.* Cambridge History of English Literature. Cambridge, 1909, III, 250 ff.

Long, P. W. *Spenser and Lady Carey.* Modern Language Review, III (1908), 257 ff.

Long, P. W. *Spenser's Sonnets "As Published."* Modern Language Review, VI (1911), 390 ff.

Macintire, Eliz. J. *French Influence on English Classicism.* Publications of the Modern Language Association, XXVI (1911), 521 ff.

Smith, J. C. *The Problem of Spenser's Sonnets.* Modern Language Review, V (1910), 273 ff.

Scott, Janet G. *The Sources of Spenser's Amoretti.* Modern Language Review, XXII (1927), 188 ff.

Scott, Janet G. *Les Sonnets Elisabéthains.—Les Sources et L'Apport Personnel.* Paris, 1929.

CHAPTER XXVI

THE ANACREONTICS

THE four poetic trifles that intervene between the *Amoretti* and the *Epithalamion* belong to a type of lyric poetry which derives from Anacreon and which was much cultivated in the Alexandrian period of Greek literature. Examples of the type are to be found already in Clément Marot's so-called "Epigrammes," and it was particularly cultivated by Ronsard and other poets of the *Pléiade*. The edition by Henri Estienne of a unique manuscript supposed to contain the poems of Anacreon (1554) gave an impetus to the vogue, which was further promoted by Remy Belleau's translation of these poems into French in the following year. In England the best Anacreontics of the sixteenth century will be found in the poetry of John Lyly. For three of the four poems in the *Amoretti* volume the following parallels have been found in French poetry:—

Marot, *Epigramme, 64. De Diane* (1524).

L'enfant Amour n'a plus son arc estrange,
Dont il blessoit d'hommes et cueurs et testes:
Avec celluy de Diane a faict change,
Dont eile alloit aux champs faire les questes;
Ilz ont changé, n'en faictes plus d'enquestes,
Et si on dict: A quoy les congnois tu?

Je voy qu'Amour chasse souvent aux bestes,
Et qu'elle attainct les hommes de vertu.

> Marot, *Epigrammes,* 103. *De Cupido et de
> sa Dame* (1527).

Amour trouva celle qui m'est amere,
Et je y estois, j'en sçay bien mieulx le compte:
"Bon jour," dict il, "bon jour, Venus, ma mere";
Puis tout à coup il veoit qu'il se mescompte,
Dont la couleur au visage luy monte,
D'avoir failly honteux Dieu scait combien:
"Non, non, Amour, ce dy je, n'ayez honte":
"Plus clersvoyans que vous s'y trompent bien."

> Ronsard, *Odes* IV. 16

Le petit enfant Amour
Cueilloit des fleurs à l'entour
D'une ruche, où les avettes
Font leurs petites logettes.
Comme il les alloit cueillant
Une avette sommeillant
Dans le fond d'une fleurette,
Luy piqua la main douillette.
Si tost que piqué se vit,
Ah! je suis perdu (ce dit)
Et s'en-courant vers sa mere
Luy monstra sa playe amere:
Ma mere, voyez ma main,
Ce disoit Amour tout plein
De pleurs, voyez quelle enflure
M'a fait une esgratignure.
Alors Venus se sou-rit
Et en le baisant le prit,
Puis sa main luy a souflée
Pour guarir sa playe enflée.

Qui t'a, dy moy, faux garçon,
Blessé de telle façon?
Sont-ce mes Graces riantes
De leurs aiguilles poignantes?
Nenny, c'est un serpenteau,
Qui vole au Printemps nouveau
Avecque deux ailerettes
Cà et là sus les fleurettes.
Ah! vrayment ie le cognois
(Dit Venus) les villageois
De la montagne d'Hymette
Le surnomment Melissette.
Si doncques un animal
Si petit fait tant de mal,
Quand son halesne espoinçonne
La main de quelque personne,
Combien fais-tu de douleur
Au prix de luy, dans le cœur
De celuy en qui tu iettes
Tes amoureuses sagettes?

REFERENCES

Lee, Sidney. *The French Renaissance in England*, N. Y.
1910; 197 f.

CHAPTER XXVII

EPITHALAMION

S PENSER'S *Epithalamion* belongs to a literary *genre* which may be traced back through Latin and Greek literature to the works of Hesiod and Homer and of which illustrations may be found in the Old Testament (e. g., the forty-fourth Psalm and the Book of Canticles). Already in Hesiod's *Shield of Herakles* one finds many elements of the later epithalamies; such as, the bringing home of the bride, the bridal-song, and the young men and maidens dancing by the light of blazing torches to the shrill music of the flutes. Similar accounts occur in the eighteenth book of the *Iliad,* in the *Birds* of Aristophanes, and in the eighteenth Idyl of Theocritus. For Latin literature may be cited Catullus 61 and 62 and the epithalamies of Statius, Claudian, and Seneca. In French literature a good example is Remy Belleau's *Epithalame de Mgr. le duc de Lorraine et de Madame Claude, fille de Roy Henry II.*

As an illustration of the type, the *Epithalamion* is noteworthy for its blending of narrative, descriptive, and lyric elements; and for its reminiscences of those folk-festivals in which the marriage hymn took its rise. As in Catullus 61 and in the *Epithalamion* from Seneca's *Medea,* Spenser opens his poem with an invocation, and in both Catullus and Spenser the virgins are invited to

351

sing the bride's praises. In each, too, the bride is brought home with much rejoicing, the boys shouting "Hymen! Iö Hymen!" We may further compare with Spenser's invocation to the night a similar passage at the close of Belleau's poem. However, for all his indebtedness to the tradition of the marriage hymns, Spenser's *Epithalamion* achieves a certain independence and reality by his allusions to his earlier work in the opening passage, by his adoption of an Irish setting, and by his introduction of native folk-lore. Furthermore, some of the marriage customs described in the poem, such as crowning the bride with a garland, lighting her way with torches, and strewing her threshold with flowers, were still in use in Spenser's day.

No poem of Spenser's has elicited more enthusiastic comment than his famous marriage hymn. Mr. de Selincourt considers it his "highest poetic achievement," and M. Légouis thinks it surpasses in fullness and splendor all compositions of the kind. Carried through the day, from morning to night, on the tide of its "great and gracious stanzas," one is impressed first of all by the wealth of the poet's fancy and the range of his music. Laying aside much that we had come to regard as characteristic of his verse, Spenser gives to his fluid rhetoric a strong undercurrent of indubitably personal feeling. In a plaintive vein he had paid to Rosalind those lyric tributes into which had passed all that was most tender and wistful in the love of his youth. There, too, for all the conventional phrase and image, one is conscious of the note of sincerity. When in the *Amoretti* he resumes the lyric theme of love, Spenser is already forty years old, and for the new sentiment or passion he has found

in Petrarchan rhetoric an ampler opportunity than was offered by the pleasant vein of Marot. Coming after the
lyrics of the *Shepheardes Calender* and the *Amoretti,* the
Epithalamion marks the culmination of his development
in the personal and intimate poetry of love.

The *Epithalamion,* as already noted, is richly diversified.
In the first place it achieves a dignity of movement through
its formal pageantry. That the poem is conceived in terms
of the Masque as well as the Hymn, is clearly suggested
by lines 25–26:—

> for Hymen is awake,
> And long since ready forth his maske to move.

It is, indeed, a Masque of Hymen; so that we properly
refer its qualities to the pictorial, musical, and dramatic
features of that composite *genre*. Striking details of the
pictured setting are the flower-strewn way, the pageant
of the Morning leaving Tithone's bed, the open temple
gates, the altar with angels round about, the curtained
bridal chamber with its Arras coverlets, the moon looking
through the open window. Peopling the picture are not
only the water-nymphs, the light-foot maids of the mountain, three handmaids of the Cyprian Queen, but also
Christian angels; and while the Graces dance, boys are
running up and down the street and young men of the town
are ringing the bells.

With all its pictured background and studied graces, the
Epithalamion is never merely decorative. Here and there
a quaint or homely fancy will lend the effect of reality to
the arrangements of its art. The nymphs who inhabit Mulla

are warned to make their toilet carefully before coming into the presence of the bride, and the charmingly human angels about the altar forget their service while they peer into her face.

However pictorial the poem may be, the appeal of the *Epithalamion* is by no means wholly to the sense of sight. The effect of the refrain, skilfully altered at the middle point of the poem, the recurrence of the song with its answering echo, is to attune the whole to a musical accompaniment. It is, indeed, sound more than sight or thought that links the stanzas one to another and that here and there with "sweet consent" or with "strong, confused noyce" usurps the place of the poem's pictorial art. When the poet comes to his contrast between night and day, he thinks less of the "sable mantle of the dark" than of the silence which keeps the watches of the night. The voices of the night, unpleasant in themselves, are further unwelcome, because now the soul of the dark is for the poet lover the spirit of things unuttered rather than of things unseen. The day, filled with music and expansive with joy, has now drawn into itself and deepened into the stillness of the long-awaited hours, whose approach was announced by the evening star.

Until the close, the quickening spirit in this incomparable symphony of day and night is one of enthusiasm and eager expectancy. The apostrophes recurring in almost every stanza—to the Muses, to the nymphs of Mulla, to the poet's love herself, to the Hours, to the boys attendant upon the groom, to the merchant daughters, to all who are there to hear and see—create the impression of ceaseless activity and busy preparation. Nevertheless, the poem, so charged with the impatience and importunity of desire, nowhere loses its dominant ceremonial tone; and the poet's passion, for all its candor and reality, is never unmindful of the homage due to the mild modesty and comely womanhood of his mistress. Finally, to his theme of a close and intimate love he imparts added dignity by placing it in the long perspective of time and eternity; for he thinks in the very consummation of his happiness not only of the earthly generations which are to follow him, but of those which go to increase the count of blessed saints.

In conclusion, some comment should be made upon the metrical form of the *Epithalamion*. This is based freely upon the canzone, which passed into Italian poetry from the Provençal literature of the twelfth century. The refrain derives from the classic *epithalamium*. Dante, who well illustrated the canzone, described it as *vulgarium poematum supremum*. In the more restricted sense of the term, the canzone, according to Dante, is a poetic composition of carefully unified stanzas. Like the Italian sonnet, it is in strict usage divided into two main sections, the *fronte* and the *sirima,* which may be further subdivided into *piedi* and *volte* respectively. Since Spenser did not concern himself with these conventional features of the metrical form, we need not consider them further. What, however, should be noted, is that the *Epithalamion* is much longer than the canzoni of Dante and Petrarch, which extend from four to ten stanzas only. In the length of his stanzas, Spenser has preferred the longer type, the stanzas in Italian ranging from 13 to 20 lines. As in Dante and Petrarch, short lines in the *Epithalamion* replace the longer verses, and the whole concludes with a short stanza technically known as the *tornata* or *commiato*.

REFERENCES

Van Winkle, Cortlandt. Ed. *Epithalamion*. N. Y., 1926.

———

Case, R. H. *English Epithalamies*. London, 1896.
Erskine, J. *The Elizabethan Lyric*. N. Y., 1903; 189 ff.
Saintsbury, George. *History of English Prosody*, I, 362.

CHAPTER XXVIII

FOWRE HYMNES

SPENSER'S *Fowre Hymnes,* published in 1596, were dedicated jointly to Margaret, Countess of Cumberland and Mary, Countess of Warwick. The former had previously been praised in *Colin Clout* as

> Faire Marian, the Muses onely darling:
> Whose beautie shyneth as the morning cleare,
> With silver deaw upon the roses pearling—

and to her Samuel Daniel had addressed a poem of philosophic tenor in which occur the oft-quoted lines :—

> And that unless above himselfe he can
> Erect himselfe, how poore a thing is man!

The second lady mentioned in the dedication, whose true name was not Mary but Anne and who was the wife of Ambrose Dudley, the brother of Leicester, Spenser had already described in the *Ruines of Time* as "a noble spouse and paragon of fame." The two were daughters of Francis Russell, second earl of Bedford, who, having suffered imprisonment for his faith during the reign of the Bloody Mary, joined the Privy Council after the accession of Elizabeth and took an active part in the religious settlement.

The first two *Hymnes,* as we learn from their dedication,

were composed "in the greener times" of the poet's youth. These, it seems, "too much pleased those of like age and disposition, which, being too vehemently caried with that kind of affection, do rather sucke out poyson to their strong passion, then hony to their honest delight." The result was that one of the two daughters of Francis Russell moved Spenser "to call in the same." Unable to do this because "many copies thereof were formerly scattered abroad," he "resolved at least to amend and by way of retractation to reforme them, making instead of these two hymnes of earthly or naturall love and beautie, two others of heavenly and celestiall."

The meaning of the quoted passage from the Dedication, as has often been noted, is not quite clear. Did the amendment and "retractation" consist in changing the poems originally published or merely in adding two which would prove more acceptable to the religious tastes of the critic? If the latter hypothesis is accepted, one is left to wonder why the poet should have given further publicity to the objectionable poems by reissuing them. If we assume that the first two *Hymnes* preserve their original form, an objection might conceivably have rested upon the paganism of certain stanzas; as, for instance, the description of the paradise of joys at the conclusion of the *Hymne of Love*. Although it is hard to believe that such stanzas would have been dangerously seductive to the most susceptible youth, it is clear that the Platonism of the first two *Hymnes,* though "in mind to mount up to the purest sky," is weighed down "with thought of earthly things"—

Drawne with sweet pleasures bayt, it back doth fly.

Now, to use Spenser's own words, it was "in stead of" the *Hymnes* of earthly or natural love and beauty that he made "two others of heavenly and celestiall." Apparently the latter were to offset rather than develop the earlier ones. Instead of pursuing the Platonic quest from the point at which the first two *Hymnes* had left off, the idealization of the poet's mistress, the second two make a fresh start in the contemplation of nature, from which the Christian Platonist passes through the recognized stages of his mystic ascent to the very throne of the eternal. Moreover, the heavenly love of the third *Hymne* is in no sense an outgrowth, but rather a contradiction, of human love. To judge from the wording of the second stanza in *Hymne* III, the first two *Hymnes* are to be included among the poet's "many lewd layes" . . .

> In praise of that mad fit which fooles call love.

The earlier *Hymnes,* runs the Dedication, were written "in the greener times" of his youth and they "too much pleased those of like age and disposition." Similarly, the "lewd layes," he writes,

> I have in th'heat of youth made heretofore,
> That in light wits did loose affection move.

In contrasting the two pairs of *Hymnes,* one might, no doubt, put too fine a point upon the poet's words. It is difficult to believe that Spenser seriously repented the first two poems; and it may even be, as Dr. Long has argued, that the phrase, "the greener times of my youth," does not certainly point back to the days of the *Shepheardes Calen-*

der. May we not here, as in the December eclogue, have to do with a feigned chronology? In view of this meter, which is the same as that of the *Ruines of Time,* it has been maintained, on account of the absence of archaisms marking Spenser's earlier work, and because there is no mention of the *Hymnes* before 1590, that the first two poems of the series were probably written early in the last decade of the poet's life. If this chronology is admitted, one might argue further with Dr. Long that the first stanza of the Prologue to the Fourth Book of the *Faerie Queene* contains an allusion to *Hymnes* I and II, and that it was accordingly these poems to which Lord Burghley objected, with the result that Spenser's pension promised by the Queen was for a long time withheld. The wording of the stanza deserves comparison with the wording of the dedication of the *Hymnes* and with that of the passage already quoted from the *Hymne to Heavenly Love:*—

> The rugged forhead that with grave foresight
> Welds kingdomes causes and affaires of state,
> My looser rimes (I wote) doth sharply wite,
> For praising love, as I have done of late,
> And magnifying lovers dear debate;
> By which fraile youth is oft to follie led,
> Through false allurement of that pleasing baite,
> That better were in vertues discipled,
> Then with vaine poemes weeds to have their fancies fed.

Whether *Hymnes* I and II are dated early or late, they belong with the Rosalind eclogues, the *Amoretti,* and the *Epithalamion* to the record of the poet's loves. It may be added that their Platonism has the limitations that mark the Platonism of the *Amoretti* in that it does not carry the lover of beauty far beyond its human associations. Spenser tells us in the Petrarchistic rhetoric which blends with the Platonism of the first two *Hymnes* that the poems were written with a view to easing his bitter smart and in the hope

> That she, whose conquering beautie doth captive
> My trembling hart in her eternal chaine,
> One drop of grace at length will to me give.

In contrast to this personal note is the more general and purely doctrinal treatment of his subject in the *Hymnes on Heavenly Love and Beauty*. The poet's point-of-view, then, as well as his procedure serves to emphasize contrast rather than continuity as we pass from the earlier to the later poems in the series.

For the type of poem illustrated broadly in Spenser's *Hymnes* as well as for their philosophy one turns to ancient literature. Professor Osgood has reminded us that each one of these poems justifies its general title in being addressed to some divinity, and that a parallel for their philosophical character may be found in the Orphic hymns. The deities celebrated in turn by Spenser are Cupid, Venus, Christ, and God himself, God in the final poem of the series sharing the honors with Sapience, the Queen of Heaven. To exalt the persons thus honored Spenser associates with them the Platonic or neo-Platonic philosophy of love and beauty. While it is difficult to ascertain at every turn the immediate source of the poet's ideas, they obviously derive in the main from the Platonic dialogues entitled the *Symposium* and the *Phædrus* through the neo-Platonism of the Florentine Academy, which is best represented in Ficino's commentary upon the *Symposium*. Furthermore, Spenser seems to have used the *De gl'heroici furosi* of Giordano Bruno, a distinguished contemporary, who passed two years in England and dedicated the book above mentioned to Sir Philip Sidney; and also Jerome Benivieni's *Canzone della Amore celeste et divino,* which was published near the end of the fifteenth century. A follower of Ficino, Benivieni based his poem on that scholar's Commentary upon the *Symposium.* Possibly Spenser used further the commentary upon Benivieni's *Canzone,* written by that prodigy of the Florentine Academy, Pico della Mirandola; and it is not unlikely that he was acquainted with Pietro Bembo's *Gl'Asolani.* Nor could he have failed to be influenced by Bembo's discourse on love in Book IV of Castiglione's *Cortegiano.* To these sources Professor Padelford has shown that we must add for *Hymnes* III and IV the *Institutes* of Calvin. Since in these various works there is necessarily much in common, one cannot always be sure which in the particular passage the English poet was following.

What is of more importance than the indebtedness of particular passages in the *Hymnes* to individual writers is the broad outline of their traditional Platonism. Their doctrine, at once personal and cosmic, gives in the earlier poems a religious significance to the theme of human passion. The creative and regulative agency of love—so runs the familiar lore—in the beginning called order out of chaos and established peace among the warring elements. To love is, therefore, to enter harmoniously into the universal order. Plato in the *Symposium* had declared that Love was both the oldest and the youngest of the gods, and Ficino had explained away this contradiction by saying that Love, having created the angels, was necessarily older than they, and, on the other hand, younger because it binds these celestial beings to their creator. This true love which we share with angelic beings is opposed to the unruly passion of lust, in that while the latter strives only to quench its flame, the former is moved to seek immortality. In its posterity, Diotima of the *Symposium* had said, the mortal body partakes of immortality. Clearly, while Spenser discriminates between the higher and the lower forms of love, the limits of his romantic Platonism exclude his developing Plato's subject of creative souls, and the requirements of chivalry, here combined in generous proportions with Platonism, forbade him to "abate his violent love of the one in order to become the lover of all beautiful forms." Indeed, the lover of the first *Hymne* hardly passes beyond the second stage of that pilgrimage of the soul which is outlined in section 210 of Plato's *Symposium*. The poet has learned to love one beautiful form and from that he has created beautiful thoughts. Nevertheless he affirms with Plato the divinity of beauty, and he is at one with him in maintaining that the love of beauty is both a dedication and a discipline. Through the illumination of his spirit the lover seeks to embrace what "seems on earth most heavenly"; and to win to his reward he needs to be schooled in steadfastness, truth, and loyalty. Under the influence of his disciplined passion he ascends from his Hell and Purgatory to his Paradise—

> above the native might
> Of heavie earth, up to the heavens hight;

and his purified mind is fashioned to a fairer form, "its image printed in his deepest wit."

Passing from this first *Hymne*, in which Platonism, as in

the *Amoretti* and generally among the Petrarchists, came to terms with traditional chivalry, we find in the second an account of the origin, nature, and proper uses of that beauty which is the exciting cause of love. It outlines the æsthetic of Italian Platonism. Taking an idea this time from the *Timaeus* of Plato, Spenser tells of the great work-master who, in fashioning the world, kept before his eyes the perfect pattern or heavenly archetype of beauty. His creations are therefore beautiful insofar as they partake of the heavenly type. Explaining his subject in a different manner, Spenser, like Giordano Bruno, then affirms that beauty is not bodily, not a mixture of colors fair, but a thing of the spirit. Still following the Italian Platonists, he explains further that the inner form or shaping force of beauty is the soul, which, except in the case of stubborn matter, fashions a body which is a fitting tenement for the beautiful spirit. It is this indwelling spirit rather than its outward form which kindles true love, which in turn preserves the natural correspondence destroyed by lust between the beauty of the soul and that of the body. Accordingly, the Platonic art of love, as contrasted with the Ovidian, recommends that ladies should strive to win love by revealing the riches of their minds. Once more according to Italian neo-Platonism, they should have in view such a spiritual union as might be supposed to exist between those born under some happy conjunction of the stars or those made of the same mould. Marriages, in a sense, are made in heaven:—

> For love is a celestiall harmonie
> Of likely harts composd of starres concent,
> Which joyne together in sweete sympathie,

To worke ech others joy and true content,
Which they have harbourd since their first descent
Out of their heavenly bowres, where they did see
And know each other here belov'd to bee.

Containing a much larger proportion of Platonism or neo-
Platonism, the second *Hymne* still falls far short of a
clearly systematic account of Plato's philosophy of beauty.
As Miss Winstanley has pointed out, it virtually leaves
out of consideration the doctrine of memory that motivates
love; that is, our recognition of earthly beauty as divine
is due, Plato says, to our memory of the heavenly archetype.

With *Hymnes* III and IV we pass into the realm of
Christian Platonism. Instead of the love and beauty of
woman we are here concerned with the beauty of nature
and the love and beauty of Christ. The soul, no longer
bound by an earthly tie, is now free to reach the goal of its
quest. With the stages of its progress more sharply defined,
it rises from the level of visible forms to the very throne of
the eternal.

Corresponding to the cosmogony of *Hymne* I, the *Hymne
of Heavenly Love* describes the genesis of all created
things. Beginning and ending with lyrical passages based
upon Plato, the poem as a whole shows relatively little
direct borrowing from either Plato or the Platonists. In
place of the eternal idea of beauty, there is God, who,
loving his own beauty, gave birth to the Son; then these
two in turn became the parents of the Holy Ghost. As
Alcuin had said, Christ was born without a mother in
heaven and without a father on earth. Then there followed
in course of time through the same love the creation of the

angels. In passages corresponding to Milton's explanation in Books VI and VII of *Paradise Lost,* Spenser goes on to account for the creation of man. It was, Spenser and Milton agree, in order to supply the place of the fallen angels that he was made in God's image. Man in turn falling from grace is redeemed by the son of God, who thus offered the highest example of devoted, self-sacrificing love. The redeemed are asked to reciprocate fully the love of God by setting aside all other loves, so that they might devote themselves absolutely to the eternal lover of mankind.

In the final *Hymne* of the series the lover of beauty, bound on his celestial journey, rises from an observation of earthly forms to dwell in contemplation of "th' immortall sky." "The true order of going or being led by another to the things of love," Diotima had said in the *Symposium,* "is to use the beauties of earth as steps along which he [the lover] mounts upwards for the sake of that other beauty, going from one to two, and from two to all fair forms, and from fair forms to fair actions, and from fair actions to fair notions, until from fair notions he arrives at the notion of absolute beauty, and at last knows what the essence of beauty is." This Platonic gradation Spenser combines with the Ptolemaic scheme of the celestial spheres and with the *Celestial Hierarchy* of the pseudo-Dionysios. In the ascent to God the soul passes through the realm of the Platonic Ideas before reaching the Dionysian realms of Powers and Dominions, Cherubim and Seraphim. In the highest heaven of all sits Sapience or Wisdom by the side of God.

For this elevation of Wisdom Spenser had found some reason in Plato's observation that "Wisdom is a most beautiful thing, and love is of the beautiful; and there-

fore Love is also a philosopher or lover of wisdom." But
the English poet's symbolism evidently goes beyond anything to be found in the Greek philosopher. Closer approxi-
mations to his conception appear in the Hebrew personifications of Wisdom to be found in *Proverbs, Job,* and
the apocryphal books of *Wisdom, Sirach,* and *Baruch.*
Spenser's Queen of Heaven, sharing the throne of God
with the Eternal, might be considered a symbolic crystalli-
zation of such passages as the following:— "Then was
I [Wisdom] with him as a nourisher; and I was daily his
delight rejoicing always before him" (*Proverbs* 8: 30);
"In that she [Wisdom] is conversant with God, it commendeth her nobility; yea, the Lord of all things loveth
her" (*Wisdom* 8: 3, 4); "Wisdom which sitteth by thy
throne" (*Wisdom* 9: 4); "Send her out of thine holy
heavens, and send her from the throne of thy majesty"
(*Wisdom* 9: 10). Like Spenser, Hebrew literature also
represents Wisdom as adorned with gems and bearing rule
over heaven and earth. In view of such parallels Professor Osgood thinks we may properly abandon "all consideration of the Virgin Mary in connection with Spenser's
Sapience."

Professor Saurat, giving more precision to Professor
Osgood's *rapprochement* of Spenser and Hebrew litera-
ture, suggests that the true prototype of the Sapience of
the Fourth *Hymne* is the Schekhina or Matrona of the
Cabala. It is not here maintained that Spenser knew the
Cabala at first hand, but it is suggested that his knowledge
might have come to him through such intermediaries as
Reuchlin, Agrippa, or Pico Mirandola. However this may
be, the correspondences between Spenser's Sapience and
Schekhina are sufficiently numerous to give weight to

Professor Saurat's suggestion. Schekhina is identified with Beauty, she is adorned like Spenser's Wisdom; the creation is her work, or, as Spenser expressed it, all creatures were "first made through observation of her high beheast"; it is ecstasy to look upon either Schekhina or Sapience and both are represented as mediating between God and man. Finally we are to note that the *Cabala* describes as sexual the relations between God and Schekhina.

If the first two *Hymnes* offer an example of Platonism blended with chivalry, the second two give us an illustration of that doctrine blended with Christian and Hebrew lore. It is not only, as we have seen above, that they bring together Greek and Hebraic elements but they seem further to have been influenced by the thought of Calvin. In the last two *Hymnes,* as Professor Padelford points out, "Platonic and neo-Platonic origins are construed to the satisfaction of Calvinism and disciplined to its creed." The distinction between *Hymnes* III and IV is what Calvin describes as the distinction between God's works of the first and the second class; that is to say, his revelation of himself "in external nature and his revelation in the treatment of mankind." In the one case there is revealed God omnipotent; in the other, the wise Providence, at once just and merciful. Calvin had written:— "The most direct path and the fittest method is not to attempt with presumptive curiosity to pry into his essence, which is rather to be adored than minutely discussed, but to comtemplate him in his works, by which he draws near, becomes familiar, and in a manner communicates himself to us." But Calvin adds that "the invisible Godhead represented by such displays we cannot see until our eyes are enlightened through faith by internal revelation from God"; just as Spenser said of Sapience, that none are worthy of looking on her except

> those whom shee
> Vouchsafeth to her presence to receave,
> And letteth them her lovely face to see.

Turning aside from the romantic Platonism of the earlier *Hymnes,* the Spenser of the later poems of the series, trying to reconcile his Platonism with his Puritanism, repudiates those loves

> with which the world doth blind
> Weake fancies, and stirre up affections base.

What formerly he had expected from the love of woman he now knows can be attained only through the love of Christ and Wisdom. It is a case of Calvin's "sovereign mercy" rescuing man from the condition of "a worm, abominable and vain, drinking in iniquity like water."

REFERENCES

Winstanley, Lilian. Ed. *The Fowre Hymnes.* Cambridge, 1907.

Bhattacherje, Mohinimohan. *Studies in Spenser.* Calcutta, 1929; chapter II, Spenser and Pico della Mirandola; chapter IV, Spenser and Bruno.

Courthope, W. J. *Cambridge History of English Literature.* III, 243–247; 275–276.

Fletcher, J. B. *A Study in Renaissance Mysticism: Spenser's "Foure Hymnes."* Publications of the Modern Language Association, XXVI (1911), 452 ff.

Fletcher, J. B. *Benivieni's "Ode of Love" and Spenser's "Foure Hymnes."* Modern Philology, VIII (1911), 545 ff.

Greenlaw, Edwin. *Spenser's Influence on Paradise Lost.* Studies in Philology, XVII (1920), 345 ff.

Harrison, John S. *Platonism in English Poetry,* N. Y. 1903. Chapter II.

Lee, R. W. *Castiglione's Influence on Spenser's Early Hymns.* Philological Quarterly. VII, 65 ff.

Long, P. W. *The Date of Spenser's Earlier Hymns.* Englische Studien, XLVII (1913), 197 ff.

Osgood, C. G. *Spenser's Sapience.* Studies in Philology, XIV (1917), 167 ff.

Padelford, F. M. *Spenser's Foure Hymnes.* Journal of English and Germanic Philology, XIII (1914), 418 ff.

Saurat, D. *Les Idées Philosophiques de Spenser.* Arsbok, 1924. Yearbook of the New Society of Letters at Lund, 251 ff.

Saurat, D. *La Sapience de Spenser et la Schekina de la Cabale.* Revue de Littérature Comparée, VI (1926), 5 ff.

CHAPTER XXIX

PROTHALAMION

THE *Prothalamion* was composed in honor of the double marriage at Essex House of Lady Elizabeth and Lady Katherine Somerset, daughters of Edward Somerset, Earl of Worcester, to Master Henry Gilford and Master William Peter. The latter, according to Burke's *Peerage,* was the second Baron Peter, who was born 24 June, 1575, and who at one time represented the county of Essex in Parliament. The father of Elizabeth and Katherine was the fourth Earl of Worcester, who was born in 1553 and died in 1628. According to the *Dictionary of National Biography* he was considered "the best horseman and tilter of his time," and in spite of his Roman Catholicism he became a favorite with Elizabeth. The Queen said that he "reconciled what she believed impossible, a stiff papist to a good subject." In contrast to the happy occasion commemorated in *Prothalamion* was a scene enacted at Essex House about four years later. The time was that of the abortive Essex rebellion. Somerset, having been sent with others to discover the reason for the large gathering at Essex House, was detained there as a prisoner while the Earl was trying to stir up London to revolt. Later, Somerset served as a member of the court which heard the charges of high treason.

Some suggestions for Spenser's "spousall verse" might

have come from *A Tale of Two Swannes* by W. Vallans,
which was entered in the Stationers' Register in 1590. The
poem was published in Hearne's edition of Leland's *Itiner-
ary*. In Vallans's blank-verse *Tale,* as outlined by Mr.
Wickham Flower in the *Athenæum,* "the heroines (if one
may so call them) are two cygnets who, at the command of
Venus, were fetched surreptitiously by Mercury from
Cayster—'a river in Boëtia, where the fairest and largest
swans do breed'—and they were brought by Mercury to
Venus, who was reclining on the banks of the river Lee at
a town in Hertfordshire, Ware. Then, at the request of
Venus, Jove ordained that the cygnets should be the king
and queen of the river, and that all the swannes—yea,
the verie Thames—should be replenished for ever by their
princely race. This was, according to the story, the origin
of all the English swans. From them were descended all
the swans that live in Severn, Humber, and Trent—'the
chiefest floods that water English ground.'" And three
times, the poem tells us, did Venus use them to draw her
ivory chariot through the air. The poet next describes the
assembling of the swans for the purpose of the procession
down the river. And so assembled they repaired together
to the river head and thence passed in state down its course.
There is not in the *Tale of Two Swannes* any such picturesque procession of water-nymphs and birds as is contained in the *Prothalamion,* but, in place of this, charming
descriptions are given of the various towns and places that
are passed by the procession. The tale ends with the marriage of the rivers—Thames and Lee—

> A Swan of Thames invites the King and Queen
> Upon a day prefixt, to see and celebrate

The marriage of two rivers of great name,
Which granted every one departs his way,
The King and Queen again into their Lee.

Vallans's preface to his poem is of interest, as was pointed out by Mr. Robert Case in a contribution to the *Athenæum,* on account of the suggestion it contains of friendly relations between the two poets. "Hereby I would animate or encourage," writes Vallans, "those worthie Poets who have written 'Epithalamion Thamesis' to publish the same. I have seen it in Latine verse (in my judgment) wel done, but the Author, I know not for what reason, doth suppresse it. That which is written in *English,* though long since it was promised, yet is it not performed. So as it seemeth, some unhappy Star envieth the sight of so good a work; which once set abroad, such trifles as these would vanish, and be overshadowed, much like the Moon and other Starres, which after the appearing of the Sunne are not to be seen at all." It would appear from this that Vallans was acquainted as early as 1590 with both the Latin and a projected English version of *The Wedding of the Thames and the Medway.*

Similar to the *Tale of the Two Swans* is Leland's *Cygnea Cantio,* an antiquarian Latin poem published with a full commentary by the author in 1545. Professor Osgood gives the following account of it:— "In his dedicatory address to Henry VIII, Leland explains that this is his swan-song to the Muses before turning to more serious antiquarian studies. He then cites a multitude of Latin authors in verse and prose to support the tradition of the swan-song. The swan whose song constitutes the poem lives in the island of the divided Isis at Oxford. It tells how it was seized with a desire of roving, and, summoning other swans,

chose twelve companions, made a farewell speech, and proceeded on its way, reviewing the beauties and antiquities of
various sites down along the Thames—Reading, Windsor,
Eton, Richmond, Kew, London, Greenwich, and Deptford. Then, from speaking of England's ships and prowess
by sea, it begins a eulogy of Henry VIII, and a review of
his works and exploits, which occupy the rest of the poem.
At the end, the swan bids its mates farewell, in preparation
for its journey to heaven."

The following passages quoted by Professor Osgood
from Leland's poem will suggest similar passages in the
Prothalamion:—

> (1) Aptantes capiti meo coronam,
>   Baccatam nitidis et hinc et illinc
>   Gemmis, ac niveum aureae catenae
>   Collum multiplici orbe circinantes
>   Postremoque vale vale canentes.

> (2) Quid magnas referam aedium nitelas
>   Multarum, radiant suo emicanti
>   Quae nunc lumine, clivus adjacet qua
>   Ripae excelsior, aspicitque lymphas
>   Nymphae caeruleas sibi faventis?

> (3) Hinc templi veteris ruïna sensim
>   Frontem attollere coepit excitata.

Still another poem which belongs to this class is the
fragmentary *De Connubio Tamis et Isis,* preserved in Camden's *Britannia* and probably written by Camden himself.
Once again, I follow Professor Osgood's convenient summary:— "The fragments tell how Isis, on his way to his
wedding, passes Radcot Bridge, where Sir K. Vere, Earl

of Oxford, was defeated in Richard II's time. As he proceeds, he is arrayed for his wedding by Zephyr and Flora. Meanwhile Thames, hurrying from her hills to meet him, passes Tame and Dorchester. Their union is attended by rejoicing nymphs, satyrs, birds, Echo, and Cupids, while Britona sings of how she became an island, and was visited by Hercules, Ulysses, Brutus, and Cæsar. Then, united as Thamesis, they hasten to the sea, passing historic Runnimede, and later old Sheen, new named Richmond by Henry VII, where died Edward III of noble memory. Here Thames meets the tide, and boasts that all rivers 'vail to him.' No other river so regularly renews its waters except Scheldt and Elbe."

Of the three motives illustrated in these poems—the journey of the swans, the marriage of the rivers, and the topographic or antiquarian review of the shores—the first, as Professor Osgood remarks, is exquisitely blended with the second in the *Prothalamion* "by transferring the wedding theme from rivers to swans with a passing intimation" of the third motive in the eighth stanza.

The metrical form of the *Prothalamion* derives from the Italian canzone in which 7-syllable and 11-syllable verses interchange. To Spenser is due the refrain of five stresses. Most of the stanzas are constructed with seven rhymes; in a few cases the poet keeps to six. The rhyming words are more often adjacent than interlaced, and in a single instance a rhyme carries over from one stanza to another (st. vi and vii). The exquisite beauty of the *Prothalamion* in Professor Saintsbury's opinion is in large part derived "from the unerring modulation of the variously lengthened and shortened lines, and of the rhymes now single, now double." He considers it, "up to its date in England, the most beautiful thing of its own prosodic kind." He thinks it "even more beautiful than the *Epithalamion* itself in the gravity and delicate management of the refrain."

REFERENCES

Hales, J. W. *Longer English Poems.* London, 1892. Contains an annotated edition of the *Prothalamion*.

———

Flower, W., J. W. Hales, Robert Case, and others. A series of letters contributed to the *Athenæum*, 1897. I, 378, 415–16, 446–47, 480–82, 510, 544, 577–78.

Osgood, Charles G. *Spenser's English Rivers.* Transactions of the Connecticut Academy of Arts and Sciences. January, 1920, pp. 100–106.

CHAPTER XXX

A VIEW OF THE PRESENT STATE OF
IRELAND

BY internal evidence Spenser's *A View of the Present
State of Ireland* may be dated 1594–1597. Sir William Russell, alluded to in the dialogue as "the honorable
gentellman that now governeth there," served as Lord
Deputy in Ireland from August, 1594 to May, 1597. On
April 14, 1598, the book was entered for publication by
Matthew Lownes, "upon condition that hee gett further
aucthoritee before yt be prynted." Whether or not the
authority was granted, the *View* was not published until
1633, when it appeared in Sir James Ware's *Historie of
Ireland, collected by Three Learned Authors.*

The *View* is of interest for both its form and its content. Written in very competent prose, it is perhaps the
best example of the expository dialogue in sixteenth century English literature. As such it may be compared with
Sir Walter Raleigh's *Perogative* (sic) *of Parliament in
England. Proved in a Dialogue between a Counsellour of
State and a Justice of the Peace* (1628), or with George
Buchanan's *Dialogue concerning the Rights of the Crown
of Scotland, Translated into English* . . . by Robert Macfarlan. Of the two interlocutors, Eudoxus and Irenæus,
the second is obviously Spenser himself, his name here
having been borrowed from a Latin dialogue on Ireland,

copiously quoted by Holinshed and written, we are told, by "one M. Alan Cope, or some other that masketh under his visours."

While the *View* lacks any such picturesque setting or dramatic characterization as we find, for example, in the Platonic dialogues, the author holds our attention throughout by virtue of his lively and varied interest in his subject. The questions and objections of Eudoxus, though contributing little to our information, are not perfunctory, and indeed serve well to point the many topics and exhibit the structure of the work as a whole. The composition is methodical. Near the beginning Irenæus succinctly states his main topics and then proceeds to develop them in orderly fashion. Before outlining his projected reforms, he would declare, under the main headings of the laws, the customs, and religion, the evils which seem "most hurtful to the common-weale of that land." In developing these topics, Irenæus takes occasion to introduce descriptions of the Irish country and not a little antiquarian lore.

Spenser's dialogue on Ireland has, then, a somewhat varied character. From one point of view, as Dr. Carpenter remarked, "it was a sort of informal state-paper and presentation of a proposed policy for Ireland, representing the best views of certain men of experience in Ireland, and, as its appeal was to those in authority in England, it doubtless kept very close to facts as Spenser saw them." In part its tone is not unlike the poet's *Brief Note of Ireland,* which was his official report to the Queen on the Tyrone rebellion. One should remark in this connection the carefully statistical character of parts of the dialogue; for example, the passages containing specifications for the placing and maintenance of garrisons.

Sometimes the *View* suggests comparison with a book like Robert Payne's *Brief Description of Ireland* (1589), which was written with the definite purpose of attracting undertakers. In its blending of the *dulce* with the *utile,* the prospective settler would no doubt have found alluring the following description of the northern part of the island: "a most beautifull and sweet country as any is under heaven, seamed throughout with many goodly rivers, replenished with all sorts of fish, most abundantly sprinkled with many sweet Ilandes and goodly lakes, like little Inland seas, that will carry even ships upon theyr waters, adorned with goodly woodes fitt for building of howses and shippes." Again, when Eudoxus remarks that no one will care to live in the wild country between Dublin and Wexforde, Irenæus replies that "though the whole tracke of the countrey be mountayne and woodye, yet there are many goodlye valleyes amongest them; fitt for fayre habitations, to which those mountayns adjoining wil be a greate increase of pasturage; for that countrey is a very greate soyle of cattell, and verye fitt for breede: as for corne," he concedes, "it is nothing naturall, save onely for barley and otes, and some places for rye, and therefore the larger penniwoorthes may be allowed unto them, though otherwise the wildness of the mountayne pasturage doe recompence the badness of the soyle, so as I doubt not but it will fynde inhabitantes and undertakers enoughe."

Though a large part of the *View* is devoted to a description of actual conditions and to specific recommendations for their reform, the dialogue is not without its background in political theory. Here Spenser has much in common with the French publicist, Jean Bodin, whose *Six Livres de la République* was well known in England. "You cannot step into a scholars studye," writes Harvey, "but (ten to one) you shall litely finde open ether Bodin de Republica or Le Royes Exposition upon Aristotles Politiques or sum other like Frenche or Italian Politique Discourses." In Bodin, then, so ready to his hand, Spenser might be supposed to have found certain political ideas on record in the *View*. For example, the English poet apparently shares with the French publicist the contractual view of the state. Referring to the submission of the Irish to the rule of England, Eudoxus asks, "Doth not the act of the parent, in any lawfull graunt or conveyaunce, bind the heyres for ever thereunto? Since then the auncestours of those that now live yeelded themselves then subjectes and liedgemen, shall it not tye their children to the same subjection?" With this might be compared a passage in the eighth chapter of the first book of Bodin's *Republic:* "The people or the nobles of a republic can give the sovereign power purely, simply, and perpetually to some one, who according to his pleasure may dispose of property, persons, and the whole state and then bequeathe it to whomsoever he will, precisely as the owner of property can dispose of it absolutely."

If this point were not conceded, one might appeal with both Bodin and Spenser to what the French author calls *Monarchie seigneuriale,* that is to power acquired by conquest, according to a principle which takes precedence over that underlying contract. "All is the conquerours," says Irenæus quoting Cicero; "therefore (me seemes) insteede of so great and meritorious a service as they bost they performed to the King, in bringing all the Irish to acknowledge him for their Leige, they did great hurt unto his title, and have left a perpetuall gall in the mynds of that

people whoe, before being absolutely bound to his obedience, are now tyed but with termes, wheras els both theyr
lives, theyr landes, and theyr libertyes were in his free
power to appoynt what tenures, what lawes, what conditions he would over them which were all his: against which
could be no rightful resistaunce, or yf there were, he might,
when he would, establish them with a stronge hand." A
similar view is expressed by Bodin in the second chapter
of his second book. "According to the opinion of all peo-
ples," he says, "what is acquired in a just war belongs
to the conqueror, and the conquered should be the slaves
of the conqueror."

In the third place, Spenser and Bodin agree in maintaining that those who have put themselves beyond the pale of
the law cannot in justice appeal to it. "The Irish," says
Irenæus, "in the violence of theyr furyes, treade downe
and trample under foote all both divine and humane
thinges, and the lawes themselves they doe specially rage
upon, and rend in peeces, as most repugnant to theyr
libertye and naturall freedome, which in theyr madnesse
they affect. . . . Soe as it is in vayne to speake of planting of lawes, and plotting of pollicyes, till they are altogether subdued." With the implications here we should
compare the observation of Bodin that "human laws have
always separated brigands and corsairs from real enemies,
who maintain their states and republics in the way of
justice, which the brigands and corsairs seek to overthrow."

Furthermore, we find Spenser and Bodin agreeing on
the subject of religion in its relations to the state. "For
religion litle have I to saye," Irenæus remarks, "my selfe
being (as I sayd) not professed therein, and it selfe being

but one, soe as there is but one waye therin; for that which is true onelye is, and the rest are not at all, yet in planting of religion thus much is needfull to be observed, that it be not sought forcibly to be impressed into them with terrour and sharpe penalties, as nowe is the manner, but rather delivered and intimated with mildeness and gentleness, soe as it may not be hated afore it be understood, and theyr Professors dispised and rejected." In noticeably similar phraseology the French writer had expressed the same idea: "I do not speak here," he says, "as to which religion is the best (since there is only one religion, one truth, one divine law published by the mouth of God) but if the Prince, who will be assured of the true religion, would attract to it his subjects divided into sects and factions, it is not necessary in my judgment that he should use force, for the more the will of men is forced, the more it is recalcitrant. By following and adhering to the true religion without feint or dissimulation he will turn to himself perhaps the hearts and wills of his subjects without violence or any difficulty. Thus he will not only avoid disturbances and civil wars but he will also lead his subjects who have gone astray to the haven of salvation."

In his historical method as well as in his political theory Spenser shows points in common with Bodin. His concern for antiquities, topography, and race, while thoroughly in the spirit of the time, is also in accord with Bodin's belief in the significance of *milieu,* as set forth in his *Methodus ad facilem historiarum cognitionem,* published in 1566. Necessarily involved in a doctrine of *milieu* is one of relativity; so that we find Spenser and Bodin agreeing in the position that laws and institutions should be carefully adapted in the light of historical knowledge to the special character of the people for whom they are intended. At best, however, both writers argue, our knowledge of history cannot be compared with scientific or religious knowledge. Bodin speaks of an *assensio triplex, probabilis, necessaria, religiosa;* and it is the *assensio probabilis* which in his judgment applies to history. As Irenæus says: "Not certaynly affirming anything, but by conferring of times, languages, monumentes, and such like, I doe hunte out a probabilitye of thinges, which I leave to your judgement to beleve or refuse."

To make assent as probable as possible, the historian, Bodin maintains, should go back to original documents, should carefully collate these, and, with full consideration of philological and geographical evidence, not fail to take into account the learning, prejudice, and religion of the author. Contemporary and native historians and oral tradition are to be viewed with some suspicion. Quite in line with these opinions is the use which Irenæus makes of the Irish bards and chroniclers. He does not, he says, absolutely rely on them; "but unto them besides I add my owne reading; and out of them both togither, with comparison of times, likewise of manners and customes, affinitye of woordes and names, propertyes of natures and uses, resemblances of rytes and ceremonyes, monumentes of churches and tombes, and many other like circumstances, I doe gather a likelihood of trueth." With reference to oral tradition, Irenæus says: "neither is there any certayne hold to be taken of any antiquitye which is receaved by tradition, since all men be lyars and may lye when they will."

It should go without saying that neither Spenser nor Bodin has made a strict application of either the political ideals or the ideal method of historiography which he has advocated. In the *View* Spenser is both tolerant and uncompromisingly ruthless, both critical and credulous. At one point Irenæus can maintain that "regard and moderation ought to be had in tempering, and managing of this stubborne nation of the Irish, to bring them from that delight of licentious barbarisme unto the love of goodness and civilitye"; elsewhere he argues in a similar tone that "the occasion (of their vices) is to be taken away, or a more understanding and shame of the fault to be imprinted. . . . Soe impossible it is to remove any fault, soe generall in a people, with terrour of lawes or most sharpe restrayntes." In contrast with such counsels of tolerance and restraint is the practical recommendation of Irenæus that the Irish should be brought to such an extremity of famine as had already been terribly illustrated in Munster, where the inhabitants looked like anatomies of death, spoke like ghosts crying out of their graves, and ate of dead carrions and of one another. Each reader will make what he can of the principle which seeks to reconcile such *schrecklichkeit* with counsels of tolerance : "The royall power of the Prince ought to stretche it self foorthe in the cheifest strength to the redressing and cutting of of those evills, which I before blamed, and not of the people which are evill. For evill people by good ordinaunces and government may be made goode; but the evill that is of it self evill will never become good."

The contradiction between theory and practice illustrated above extends to Spenser's historical method. As Miss Harper remarks :— "He did not consistently reject such statements as were without a firm foundation of contemporary records. He was credulous of the printed word.

He even, for all we know, accepted the History of the British kings as a veracious account of the past. Certainly he referred to King Arthur and to Gurgunt exactly as he referred, later in the same speech, to King Egfrid and Edgar." The same scholar reminds us that Wilhelm Riedner in his Spenser's *Belesenheit* (Leipzig, 1908) had shown that Spenser's citations from classical authorities in the *View* "are in nearly every case false"; and she adds that "apparently, to Spenser, a poet was quite as good historical authority as a writer of chronicles." Like other antiquarians of his time, like E. K. in his notes on the *Shepheardes Calender,* he exhibits a pedantic, unintelligent interest in such matters as the evidence for a relationship between Irish and Scythians to be found in their similar methods of pasturing cattle, in their wearing of a mantle, their battle cries, etc.; or in such a subject as the origin of the Irish battle cry, "Farrih," which we are asked to believe may derive from "Fargus, Fergus, or Ferragus," one of the first kings of Scotland or from "Pharao," whose daughter Scota, according to an admittedly "senceless fable," led the Egyptians who first settled Ireland.

Far more noteworthy than Spenser's preoccupation with such subjects is his declared interest in Irish poetry. Some poems he had had translated for him, finding that "they savoured of sweete witt and good invention, but skilled not of the goodly ornamentes of Poetrye; yet were they sprinckled with some prety flowers of theyr owne naturall devise, which gave good grace and comliness unto them, the which it is greate pittye to see soe abused, to the gracing of wickedness and vice, which would with good usage serve to beautifye and adorne virtue." It has been suggested that it was Lord Roche's bard Tadhg by whom Spenser was instructed in Irish lore, even though, according to the Articles of Plantation, the undertakers were forbidden "to receive into their habitations, retain or lodge, any Irish rhymers, bards, harpers or such idle persons." However this may be, the passage quoted from the *View* justifies an inquiry into Irish influences on Spenser's poetry.

Since in Irish legend there is a queen of the fairies named Una, Grosart thought that Spenser derived this name from Irish sources. Miss Pauline Henley goes much farther in her book on *Spenser in Ireland*. No doubt, as she concedes, the correspondence between Spenser's verse and Irish bardic compositions in alliteration, assonance, onomatopœa, and internal rhyme is a coincidence, since these features of his poetry can be more plausibly accounted for in other ways; and one might suspect that the same is true of "the picturesque details and forceful similes," which she thinks might have been borrowed from Irish epics and romances. In view of the parallels in the *Odyssey,* the *True History* of Lucian, and the books of travel, one need not insist upon the similarity between the scenery of Sir Guyon's voyage to the Bower of Bliss and that which one sees in sailing from the Kenmore river around the Dingle peninsula to Smerwick Bay; and we may perhaps regard as doubtful any indebtedness of Phædria's island to the Irish Island of Joy. "In the drawing of the Genius of the Porch and the Comely Dame with the wine cup," Miss Henley thinks, "there may also be a Gaelic influence, as the same two figures are to be found in the story of the prophecy revealed to Conn the Hundred Fighter"; and she compares the fight of Timias at the ford with a similar conflict between Ferdiad and Cuchullin, Ferdiad having been threatened with Blame, Blemish, and Disgrace, and Timias actually attacked by Despetto, Decetto, and Defetto.

REFERENCES

Covington, F. F., Jr. *Elizabethan Notions of Ireland.* Texas Review, VI (1921), 222 ff.

Covington, F. F. Jr. *Another View of Spenser's Linguistics.* Studies in Philology, XIX (1922), 244 ff.

Covington, F. F., Jr. *Spenser's Use of Irish History in the "View of the Present State of Ireland."* Texas Studies in English, IV (1924), 5–38.

Draper, J. W. *Spenser's Linguistics in The Present State of Ireland.* Modern Philology, XVII (1919), 471–486.

Falkiner, C. L. *Essays Relating to Ireland.* London, 1909; 26–31.

Greenlaw, Edwin. *The Influence of Machiavelli on Spenser.* Modern Philology, VII (1909), 187 ff.

Greenlaw, Edwin. *Spenser and British Imperialism.* Modern Philology, IX (1912), 347 ff.

Harper, Carrie A. *The Sources of the British Chronicle History in Spenser's Faerie Queene.* Philadelphia, 1910.

Henley, Pauline. *Spenser in Ireland.* Cork and London, 1928.

Jones, H. S. V. *Spenser's Defense of Lord Grey.* University of Illinois Studies in Language and Literature. V, No. 3 (1919).

Merrill, Elizabeth. *The Dialogue in English Literature.* N. Y., 1911; 64 ff.

Padelford, F. M. *The Political, Economic, and Social Views of Spenser.* Journal of English and Germanic Philology, XIV (1915), 412 ff.

Riedner, Wilhelm. *Spenser's Belesenheit.* Leipzig, 1908.

CHAPTER XXXI

LETTERS

THERE are two brief letters from Spenser to Gabriel Harvey which are contained in booklets entered for publication on the Stationers' Register, June 30, 1580 and duly published the same year. The first of the two title-pages reads: *Three Proper, and Wittie, familiar Letters: lately passed between two Universitie men: touching the Earthquake in Aprill last, and our English refourmed Versifying. With the Preface of a Wellwiller to them both.* The second runs: *Two Other, very commendable Letters, of the same mens writing: both touching the foresaid Artificiall Versifying, and certain other Particulars: More lately delivered unto the Printer.* To judge from their title-page, the second two letters, though antedating the others, were to follow them; and indeed this is their position in the possibly unique British Museum copy.

The Preface of the Wellwiller, alluded to above, should be read with care. It was "lately at the fourthe or fifte hande" that he was "made acquainted with the *three Letters following,* by means of a faithfull friend, who with much entreaty had procured the copying of them oute, at *Immeritos* handes." From this it would seem that Harvey had nothing to do with the publication, but that Spenser furthered it to the extent of supplying the copy. Evidently, however, the Wellwiller wishes Harvey better than

Spenser. Somewhat patronizingly he describes Spenser's epistle as "a good familiar and sensible Letter," which "sure liketh me verye well, and gyveth some hope of good mettall in the Author, in whom I knowe myself to be very good partes otherwise." To Harvey's letters he accords much warmer praise: "But shewe me, or *Immerito,* two Englyshe Letters in Printe, in all pointes equall to the other twoo, both for the matter it selfe, and also for the manner of handling, and saye, we never sawe good Englishe Letter in our lives." We are given to understand that what is here printed is not all. There are many others by Harvey "of the same stamp bothe to Courtiers and others, and some of them discoursing uppon matter of great weight and importance wherein he is said, to be sufficient and hable, as in these schollerly pointes of learning." The two letters published are described as "twoo of the rarest, and finest Treaties, as wel for ingenious devising, as also for significant uttering, and clearly conveying of his matter, that ever I read in this Tongue." The Wellwiller will make the best amends he can if the authors think he has done them wrong "in not making them privy to the Publication."

The view of the publication of the letters which we gather from the Wellwiller's Preface is not that either of Thomas Nashe or of the modern critic. In the former's *Strange Newes, Of the intercepting certaine Letters, and a Convoy of Verses, as they were going Privilie to victuall the Low Countries,* it is declared that Harvey was responsible for and Spenser in no sense privy to the undertaking. "Why, why," writes Nashe, "infractissime Pistlepragmos, though *you were yong in yeares, fresh in courage, greene in experience, and over-weaning in conceipt* (we

will refuse nothing that you give us) when you privately
wrote the letters *that afterward* (by no other than your
selfe) *were publiquely divulged;* yet when the bladder is
burst that held you up swimming in selfe love, you must
not be discontented though you sink." In another passage
Nashe wrote: "Signior Immerito (so called because *he was
and is his friend* undeservedly) was counterfeitly brought
in to play a part in that his Enterlude of Epistles that was
hist at, thinking his very name (as the name of *Ned Allen*
on the common stage) was able to make an ill matter good.
I durst on my credit undertake, Spencer was no way privie
to the committing of them to the print. Committing I may
well call it, for in my opinion *G. H.* should not have reapt
so much discredite by being committed to Newgate, as by
committing that misbeleeving prose to the Presse." (Mc-
Kerrow's Nashe, I, 295 ff.) Again, in *Have With you to
Saffron-Walden* Nashe wrote: "His imprisonment in the
Fleete, he affirms, is a lewd supposall (the Hexameter
vearse before prooves it) as also his writing *The Wel-
willers Epistle* in praise of himselfe, before his first four
Letters a yeare ago." To this contemporary opinion we may
add that of Professor G. C. Moore Smith, the editor of
Harvey's *Marginalia.* "No one," he writes, "could believe
then, any more than now, that the publication was without
Harvey's connivance."

Harvey, who found himself in difficulties after the publication of the *Letters,* on account of his criticism of Cambridge and what was supposed to be his satire on the Earl
of Oxford in his *Speculum Tuscanismi,* states his own
position in the third of his *Foure Letters* published in
1592:— "Signor Immerito (for that name will be remem-
bred) was then, and is still, my affectionate friend, one

that could very wel abide Gascoignes Steel glasse, and that stoode equallie indifferent to either part of the state Demonstrative: many communications, and writings may secretlie passe between such, even for an exercise of speech, and stile that are not otherwise convenient to be disclosed: it was the sinister hap of those infortunate Letters, to fall into the left handes of malicious enemies, or undiscreete friends: who adventured to imprint in earnest, that was scribled in jest (for the moody fit was soone over:) and requited their private pleasure with my publike displeasure: oh my inestimable, and infinite displeasure."

The letters are of first-rate biographical interest. From them we learn that Spenser was not indifferent to the vogue at Cambridge and the court of writing English verses in classical meters. In London he has discovered that Harvey is not the only one who is wise with Ascham, an early advocate of classical verse forms in English poetry. Harvey himself is willing to believe that the good angel who has inspired the movement at court is no other than Gabriel; but, in any case, he is glad that Sidney and Dyer are disposed "to helpe forwarde our new famous enterprise for the Exchanging of Barbarous and Balductum Rymes with Artificial Verses," and he thinks that "their livelie example and Practise, wil prevaile a thousand times more in short space, than the dead Advertizement and persuasion of M. Ascham to the same Effecte." Nevertheless, there seems to have been a difference between the rules for "Englishe Versifying" recommended by Harvey and those laid down by Archdeacon Drant, the lawgiver of the Sidney-Dyer group, whom Spenser's University friend with some animus disrespectfully describes as the "gorbellyed" Drant. Where Drant seems to approve a pronunciation for the

sake of the meter at variance with that which strictly ob-
tains, Harvey maintains that metrical requirements should
not be allowed to do violence to the proper accent and
quantity" of English words. The Cambridge reformer,
disposed to minimize these differences, expresses the belief
that his own "Rules and Precepts of Arte wil fal out not
greatly repugnant though peradventure somewhat different."

The Harvey-Spenser correspondence is further of interest because it reveals something of Spenser's relations
with Sidney. In the *Shepheardes Calender* the latter was
celebrated as the "president of Noblesse and of chevelree,"
and, in the Sonnet addressed to the Countess of Pembroke,
Spenser calls him the one

> Who first my muse did lift out of the floor
> To sing his sweet delights in lowly lays.

Again, in the dedication of the *Ruines of Time,* to mention
only a few of many allusions, Spenser speaks of his "entire
love and humble affection" for Sidney, in *Mother Hubberds Tale* he no doubt was thinking of him as he described
his brave courtier, to him he dedicates the *Astrophel,* and
he makes him the hero of his "Legend of Courtesy." To the
evidence of the poetry we should add that of the Letters.
Under date of October, 1579, Spenser writes Harvey that
he has Sidney and Dyer "in some use of familiarity"; they
have "drawn him to their faction"; and he promises to im-
part Harvey's metrical rules to Sidney and Dyer when he
next goes to court. In the same letter, alluding to his expectation of service abroad, he says that he and Sidney
have agreed to correspond during his absence, and the
following passage would seem to imply some degree of

literary friendship:— "I would heartily wish you would either send me the Rules and Precepts of Arte, which you observe in Quantities, or else follow mine that M. Philip Sidney gave me, being the very same which *M. Drant* devised, but enlarged with M. Sidneys own judgement and augmented with my Observation, that we might both accorde and agree in one."

Finally, we might turn to the *Letters* for a fuller understanding of the relations between the two correspondents. We find the evidence here in substantial agreement with what we have learned from the *Calender* and the sonnet addressed to Harvey. Of special significance is the Latin poem in the letter of October, 1579. To Spenser, Harvey is "the greatest Cato of our time," who thinks that he alone is wise who wishes neither to play the fool too much nor to be too wise. *Tuta sed in medio superest via gurgite.* If one is wise, he will pursue nothing too eagerly. He has every advantage who mingles the sweet and the useful. Such is Harvey's way; whereas, in Spenser's case, while the gods long since granted him the sweet, they have never, says the poem, accorded him the useful.

REFERENCES

Berli, Hans. *Gabriel Harvey.* Zurich, 1913.
Long, P. W. *Spenser and The Bishop of Rochester.* Publications of the Modern Language Association, XXXI (1916), 713–35.

CHAPTER XXXII

LANGUAGE AND VERSIFICATION

LANGUAGE

IN fashioning the language of his poetry Spenser came under the influence of both an English tradition and a European theory. The native tradition derives in part from Chaucer through Gower and the English Chaucerians and in some of its developments is well represented in the archaizing style of Malory's *Morte Darthur*. The European theory, which in certain details may be traced back to Aristotle, is perpetuated by Horace, Dante, Vida, Trissino, Muzio, Minturno, and Tasso. In French literature it is developed by the poets of the *Pléiade,* particularly by Ronsard and Du Bellay, and, in English, under a strongly national bias, by Wilson, Cheke, Ascham, and E.K. of the *Shepheardes Calender*.

Aristotle, treating in the *Poetics* the subject of the poet's diction, distinguishes between a mean style, which uses only current or proper words, and the more lofty forms of expression, which in part depend for their effect upon the employment of an unfamiliar vocabulary. In heroic poetry he thought that words of all kinds might properly find a place, and he maintained that clearness freed from the commonplace might be attained by the alteration of words, for example in lengthenings and contractions, and he would even give a poet the right to coin new words. In general Aristotle takes the position that while intent on diversifying his vocabulary a writer should always exercise moderation and observe carefully the principle of decorum.

The lessons of Aristotle are repeated in the *Ars Poetica* of Horace, and Vida, in turn, recommends the moderate use of archaic terms, borrowing from the ancients, and even the coinage of new words. In view of the later practice of the *Pléiade* and Spenser we should note in particular his commendation of compound words. Trissino, while repeating much that was said before, should interest students of Spenser because of his particular recommendation of a rustic language for pastoral poetry. One should also remark the praise by both Trissino and Minturno of the *suave* or smooth sweetness that characterizes notably the style of the English poet. This quality, to quote Miss Pope's paraphrase, "consists first, in the elegance and fecundity of slow, resounding words, next in a conjunction of words which admits no harshness, no break, no rough breathing, no long digression; rather the words must be adapted to the spirit, be like and equal, and so selected from opposites, that numbers may respond to numbers, and like to like." Next in the line of critics dealing with poetic diction is Tasso. Contending with Aristotle for a combination of clearness and elevation he shows how Homer, Virgil, and Dante exercised poetic license in drawing upon many sources for the enrichment of their vocabulary.

Turning from the Italian to the French critics, we should note that Spenser's practice was remarkably in accord with the theories developed in Du Bellay's *La Deffence et Illustration de la Langue Française* and in Ronsard's Preface to the *Françiade*. Both critics were in favor of the enrichment of the vernacular with archaic, dialect, foreign, and newly-coined words. In the *Deffence* Du Bellay especially recommended those hyphenated words which abound in the poetry of Spenser and the *Pléiade,* and he would permit a free shifting of clauses within the sentence and that substitution of one part of speech for another.

In England, criticism was conservative and nationalistic. For example, Thomas Wilson in his *Art of Rhetoric* (1560) inveighs against "oversea language" and "outlandish English," and protests against the affectation of "any straunge or ynkehorne termes." He regards with disapproval the "fine courtier" who "will talke nothing but Chaucer," and those who "so Latin their tongues, that the simple can not but wonder at their talke." Similar views are expressed by John Cheke in his letter to Thomas Hoby published with the latter's translation of Castiglione's *Courtier*. He would keep the mother-tongue "cleane and pure, unmixt and un-mingled with borrowing other tunges." His position is that one should draw upon foreign languages only when the resources of the mother-tongue will not meet his needs. With these views Roger Ascham is in full agreement. Many English writers, he thought, by using strange Latin, French, and Italian words, "do make all things dark and hard." Such writers, E.K. declared in his Preface to the *Shepheardes Calender,* "have made our English tongue a gallimaufray or hodgepodge of al other speches." On the other hand, he complains of those who happening "to here an olde word, albeit very naturall and significant, crye out streightway, that we speak no English, but gibbrish."

It is against the background of critical theory outlined in the above paragraphs that we must project a study of Spenser's language. While influenced by the theories of the

Pléiade, Spenser is also true to the English criticism represented by Wilson, Cheke, Ascham, and E.K. With respect to the proportion of foreign words in his vocabulary, he stands half-way between Shakespeare and Milton. In Shakespeare the foreign element is approximately 10%, in Spenser 14%, and in Milton, 19%. But the foreign words here counted were mostly an integral part of the language and felt to be as thoroughly English as those of Anglo-Saxon derivation. When Spenser consciously undertook to enrich the language of poetry, he acted in full accord with E.K.'s critical doctrine by utilizing dialect, chiefly Northern, or by reviving obsolete words. He was careful to maintain the essentially English character of his idiom.

This idiom of course varies from poem to poem. Manifestly the style of the Moral Eclogues differs from that of the others; and the familiar rhetoric of *Colin Clout* and *Mother Hubberds Tale* is at some remove from the aureate, high-pitched phrasing of the *Ruines of Time* or the *Teares of the Muses*. We are now reminded rather definitely of Chaucer and again of the more consciously or deliberately rhetorical Chaucerians. In the *Shepheardes Calender* the poet indulges in rhetorical as well as metrical experiments. In the Moral Eclogues he is clearly experimenting with dialect and archaic speech with a view to creating the effect of a rustic idiom. The former element is less considerable, less easily localized than was once supposed. It may be vaguely described as prevailingly Northern rather than definitely, as has been suggested, the dialect of either Lancashire or Cambridge. Many of the words once regarded as dialectal are now known to belong to the fund of the literary Middle English vocabulary, with which Spenser seems to have been better acquainted than most of his contemporaries. For example, to the earlier literary language rather than to any contemporary dialect certainly belong such words as *accloieth, couthe,* and *herie,* though in some cases we must remember that many literary Middle English words also existed in the spoken dialects of the sixteenth century. In the use of other dialect words, such as *adawed, chamfred, venteth,* Spenser had been anticipated by previous sixteenth-century authors. After due allowance has been made for the poet's indebtedness to all these sources, we shall find only a relatively short list of words which he certainly borrowed from the spoken dialects of his day. Among these may be placed *busket, crag, dapper, hidder and shidder, ronte, todde,* and *wimble.*

The effect of an older speech Spenser further enhanced by the occasional use of archaic forms. For example, one meets with the verbal ending *-en* as an inflection not only for the past participle and the infinitive but as well for the plurals of both present and preterite. With other writers of the period Spenser shares the endings *-st, -est, -edest, -eth* and a number of the older preterites of both strong and weak verbs, such as *strake, dronck, meint, yold, swolt.* He further varies his diction effectively by a free use of the prefixes *a-, ab-, ac-, af-, de-, dis- en-, for-, un-, to-,* and *y-,* as in *abeare, accourage, enraced, to-worn, ytost;* and he employs frequently both *do* and *can* as auxiliaries. Finally he uses freely older adverbs and connectives, such as *albe, forthy, eath, liever, enaunter.*

The archaic element in Spenser's vocabulary is not as considerable as one has been led to suppose. In the pastorals this element is of course greater than in the poet's other verse. Dr. Roscoe Parker has estimated that "the percentage of archaisms in Spenser's diction ranges from 3.19 in the extreme case of the early moral-allegorical 'February' eclogue of the *Shepheardes Calender* to .81 in the later chivalric *Faerie Queene,* and to 1.10 in the late political-allegorical, *Colin Clouts Come Home Againe."*

From foreign sources Spenser has introduced very few words into the language of the *Calender.* Apparently he was the first to use *crumenall* from the Latin *crumena,* meaning a purse. *Overture,* in the sense of an open space, he adopted from the French, and *stanck* (weary) he derived from the Italian *stanco.* There is a longer list of anomalous inflections and of new derivatives and compounds. *Betight* may be noted as a past participle of *betide, lepped* as the preterite of *leap,* and attention should be called to such forms as *beastliheed, dreeriment, derringdoe,* and *headlesse-hood.*

The hyphenated words in Spenser's vocabulary make by far the largest number of his new compounds. In its beginnings the influence is here Greek, though Spenser was of course more directly affected by the poets of the *Pléiade,* whose verse is liberally sprinkled with such word-formations. It has been shown that Spenser avoided such words in the homely or archaic style of the *Calender, Mother Hubberds Tale, Daphnaïda,* and *Colin Clout;* and that their frequency is much greater in Books I–III of the *Faerie Queene* than in Books IV and VI. The larger proportion of them in V and VII has been regarded as evidence that these parts of the poem were composed earlier than their present position would lead us to suspect. On the other hand, we find the poet freely coining hyphenated compounds in such a late lyric as the *Prothalamion* and they abound, too, in *Amoretti, Epithalamion* and *Muiopotmos.* Seemingly Spenser had come to regard such words as better suited to lyric than narrative poetry.

As to the constitution of the compounds, by far the greater number are verbal adjectives modifying nouns, like *air-cutting,* followed in point of frequency by participles proper, like *well-thewed* and *off-shaking,* double adjectives like *filthy-feculent* and *silver-scaly,* double nouns like *love-lads* and *woman-wight.* There are relatively few compound verbs and even fewer adverbs; examples of the former class are *out-lanced, over-wrestled, thunder-drive,* and of the latter *greedy-wide* and *true-love-wise.*

As noted above, Spenser drew chiefly upon English sources in enriching his vocabulary. In his avoidance of "ynkhorne termes" he fell in with the best critical opinion of the century. His Latinisms are relatively few. His well-known coinage, *blatant,* may be connected with Latin *blaterare,* to babble, but perhaps it should rather be associated with the dialect *blate,* to bellow. Although the influence of French is more obvious, a large proportion of Spenser's French borrowings are drawn, according to the principle of decorum, from the traditional vocabulary of chivalry and courtly love. From Italian he has borrowed little besides his Italian proper names. Examples of common nouns from Italian are *capuccio* and *basciomani.*

VERSIFICATION

The Line

It need hardly be said that the vast majority of Spenser's lines are iambic pentameter. The dimeter is used in "April" and "November"; the trimeter in the *Prothalamion* and *Epithalamion,* the trimeter and tetrameter again in "April," "November," in the ballad stanzas of "March" and "July," and in the "Epigrams" in the *Amoretti* volume. The tetrameter with free syllabication is also employed in the accentual verse of "February," "May," and "September"; the hexameter or Alexandrine, at the close of the Spenserian stanza and of the *Epithalamion* strophe, and at the beginning of the "November" dirge.

Cæsura: The metrical pause known as the cæsura comes ordinarily immediately after the second or third stress. These are cases of the masculine cæsura. The feminine or lyric cæsura usually follows the first unstressed syllable in the third foot; sometimes it follows the first unstressed syllable in the fourth. The concluding Alexandrine of the Spenserian stanza may have two cæsuras.

Masculine Cæsura:

The noble hart, that harbours vertuous thought.

Feminine Cæsura:

Framed of wanton Yvie flouring faire.

Double Cæsura:

A bridge of bras, whose sound heavens thunder seem'd to me.

Enjambement: Spenser secures variety by a frequent employment of run-over lines, illustrating what is technically known as enjambement.

> 'Where ever yet I be, my secret aid
> Shall follow you.' So passing forth she him
> > obaid.

Rhyme

Feminine Rhyme:

> And over al the fields themselves did muster,
> With bils and glayves making a dreadfull luster.

Hovering Rhyme:

> But subtill Archimago, when his guests
> He saw divided into double parts,
> And Una wandring in woods and forrests.

Broken Rhyme. The separation of adjacent rhyming lines by a strong rhetorical pause appears more often in the stanzas than in the couplets of *Mother Hubberds Tale*.

> Did all she might, more pleasing to appeare.
> One day, to worke her to his will more neare,
> He woo'd her thus.

>   felly slewe
> Those warders strange, and all that els he met.
> But th' Ape, still flying, he no where might get.

The Foot

Almost all of Spenser's poetry is written in iambic measures. The anapæst occurs in the Moral Eclogues, in the ballad stanzas of "March" and "July," in "April," in *Epithalamion,* and occasionally elsewhere. The trochee often takes the place of the iambus at the beginning of the line and occasionally after the cæsura:—

(*At beginning*)

Calme was the daye, and through the trembling ayre.

Like the old ruines of a broken towre.

(After cæsura)

When suddenly casting aside his vew.

With pleasant tales (fit for that idle stound).

To complete the foot archaic infinitives and past participles in *-en* are sometimes used, and in weak preterites and past participles the *-ed* is often sounded when in ordinary usage it was silent.

And lastly Justice charged her with breach of lawes.

On the other hand, contractions and, in rare instances, slurring are used to diminish the number of syllables.

The Foxe and th'Ape, disliking of their evill.

The cruell markes of many 'a bloody fielde.

Stanzas

The following stanza-forms are met with in Spenser:—

1. The four-line ballad stanza: 4343. abab. "July." The elegiac quatrains (iambic pentameter, abab): *Colin Clouts Come Home Againe.* Note the irregularities of rhyme at the beginning and end of the poem.
2. The six-line ballad stanza: 443 443. aabaab. "March."
3. The linked pentameter quatrain with alternating rhymes: abab, bcbc etc. "April," "November."
4. The sixain, or six-lined pentameter stanza:
    ababcc—"January," "December."
    abbaba—"October."
    Note. For the sestina of August see p. 69.
5. Seven-line stanza: Rhyme Royal.
    ababbcc. *Ruines of Time, Fowre Hymnes.*

Note what Saintsbury calls the "sonnet-coupled" rhyme royal in the visions at the close of the *Ruines of Time.*

ababcbc. *Daphnaïda.*

6. Eight-line stanza: ababbaba—"June."

Ottava Rima: abababcc—*Virgils Gnat, Muiopotmos.* For the strophe forms of "April," "November," *Epithalamion,* and *Prothalamion,* see pp. 69 f., 70 f., 355, 375 f.

For the sonnet, see p. 346.

The Couplet

In *Mother Hubberds Tale* Spenser has employed the iambic pentameter rhyming in couplets—the heroic couplet.

REFERENCES

Language

Brunner, K. *Die Dialektwörter in Spensers "Shepherd's Calendar."* Archiv f.d. Studium d.n. Spr. u. Lit. CXXXII (1914), 401–4.

Covington, F. F. Jr. *Another View of Spenser's Linguistics.* Studies in Philology, XIX (1922), 244–48.

Draper, J. W. *Spenser's Linguistics in The Present State of Ireland.* Modern Philology, XVII (1919), 471–486.

Draper, J. W. *Glosses to Spenser's "Shepheardes Calender."* Journal of English and Germanic Philology XVIII (1919), 556 ff.

Herford, C. H. Ed. *Shepheards Calendar.* Introduction, IV.

Jones, Richard Foster. *Richard Mulcaster's "View of the English Language."* Washington University Studies, XIII (1926), 267–303.

Padelford, F. M., and Maxwell, W. C., *The Compound Words*

in Spenser's Poetry. Journal of English and Germanic Philology, XXV (1926), 498 ff.

Parker, Roscoe E. *Spenser's Language and the Pastoral Tradition.* Language, I, No. 3 (1925), 80 ff.

Pope, Emma F. *Renaissance Criticism and the Diction of "The Faerie Queene."* Publ. Mod. Lang. Ass. XLI (1926), 575 ff.

Renwick, W. L. *The Critical Origins of Spenser's Diction.* Modern Language Review, XVII (1922), 1–16.

Renwick, W. L. *Mulcaster and Du Bellay.* Modern Language Review, XVII (1922), 282 ff.

Smith, Gregory. Ed. *Elizabethan Critical Essays.* Introduction V, 3.

Versification

Alden, R. M. *English Verse.* 1903.

Bradner, Leicester. *Forerunners of the Spenserian Stanza.* Review of English Studies IV (1928), 207–8.

Erskine, J. *The Elizabethan Lyric.* 1903.

Kaluza, Max. *Englische Metrik in historischer Entwicklung.* Berlin, 1909. 358 ff.

Pope, Emma F. *Critical Background of the Spenserian Stanza.* Modern Philology, XXIV, 31–53.

Saintsbury, Geo. *History of English Prosody.* 1906.

Schipper, Jakob. *Neuenglische Metrik,* 1888.

Schipper, Jakob. *History of English Versification.* 1910.

Shipley, J. T. *Spenserian Prosody: The Couplet Forms.* Studies in Philology, XXI (1924), 594 ff.

Skeat, W. W. *The Origin of the Spenserian Stanza.* Athenæum, May 6, 1893; p. 574.

Stovall, Floyd. *Feminine Rimes in "Faerie Queene."* Journal of English and German Philology, XXVI (1927), 91–95.

Taboureux, Etienne. *The Spenserian Stanza.* Revue de l'Enseignement des langues vivantes, XV (1899), 499–505; XVI (1899), 14–21, 112–118, 163–72.

APPENDIX

The following selected list of poems illustrates Spenser's influence on English poetry from Drayton to Keats:—

Idea: The Shepherd's Garland (1593) by Michael Drayton.
   Nine eclogues in imitation of *The Shepheardes Calender.*
The Affectionate Shepherd and *The Shepherd's Content*
   (1594) by Richard Barnfield.
   The first an imitation of Virgil's *Alexis.* The second contains a lament for Sir Philip Sidney.
Three Pastoral Elegies of Anander, Anetor, and Muridella
   (1602) by William Basse.
   The third elegy includes a lament for Colin. Nine eclogues by Basse were published in 1653. These show unmistakably the influence of *The Shepheardes Calender;* they are classified partly according to the days of the week and partly according to the virtues.
Eclogues (1603) by Edward Fairfax.
   Only two of the original twelve are preserved.
Britannia's Pastorals (1613, 1616, 1652) by William Browne.
   The first song of the second book concludes with a eulogy of Spenser.
The Appolyonists (1627) by Phineas Fletcher.
   A paraphrase of Fletcher's Latin poem the *Locustae* (1627) describing an infernal council, like that in *Paradist Lost,* and recounting the activities of the devils in the world. Several of its allegorical characters similar

to those in the first and second books of *The Faerie Queene;* e. g., Despair, represented as sitting close by Sin at the portal of Hell, and such personifications as Sickness, Languor, and Horror, which resemble those encountered by Sir Guyon on his way to the Cave of Mammon.

The Purple Island (1633) by Phineas Fletcher.

The poem falls into two main parts, the first describing the Island as an allegory of the human body and the second a battle betwen the Vices and the Virtues. Chief sources: House of Alma in *F.Q.* Book II and House of Pride in *F.Q.* Book I.

Christ's Victory and Triumph in Heaven over and after Death (1610) by Giles Fletcher.

Satan described as a hermit leading Christ to the bower of Despair, reminiscent of Archimago and the Red Cross Knight in *F.Q.* Book I. The temptation of the Saviour on the mountain-top to be compared with the Bower of Bliss canto in *F.Q.* Book II.

The Shepherd's Pipe (1614). An anthology containing poems by William Browne, Wither, Brooke, and Davies of Hereford.

The Spenserian pastoral as modified by Drayton.

The fifth eclogue should be compared with Spenser's "October."

The Shepheards Hunting (1615) by George Wither.

Five eclogues, two of which had been previously printed in Browne's *Shepherd's Pipe.* They consist of conversation between Wither himself and three of his friends, Browne, William Ferrar, and Christopher Brooke.

Brittain's Ida (1628).

Imitative of Spenser's Bower of Bliss.

Piscatorie Eglogs (1633) by Phineas Fletcher.

Psyche (1648) by Joseph Beaumont.

The assault of the passions on Psyche in the House of Common Sense is like Spenser's House of Alma episode, and the purgation of Psyche in the Castle of Ecclesia is comparable to Red Cross Knight's discipline in the House of Holiness. Compare, further, the House of Persecution with the Castle of Pride, and note that the persecuted Psyche is, like Una, befriended by a lion.

Comus (1637) by John Milton.

Compare the palace of Comus with its rabble of sexual monsters with the Bower of Bliss in the second book of the *Faerie Queene*. Here and there passages echo Spenser; e. g., the Elder Brother's description of the chaste woman—

> clad in complete steel,
> And like a quiver'd nymph with arrows keen,

is reminiscent of Spenser's description of Belphœbe.

Lycidas (1637) by John Milton.

The ecclesiastical satire in *Lycidas* invites comparison with "May," "July," and "September." Note particularly the similarity between "May," 38 ff. and *Lycidas,* 113 ff. Compare, too, "October," 13 ff. with *Lycidas,* 136 ff.; "November," 163 ff. with *Lycidas,* 165 ff.; and finally "April," 136 ff. with *Lycidas,* 142 ff.

Paradise Lost (1658–1665) and *Paradise Regained* (1665–1667) by John Milton.

Professor Greenlaw has compared suggestively the theme of the "Legend of Guyon" and that of *Paradise Lost*. In each case, he argues, the subjects are the machinations of Satan and the Bower of Bliss. He would equate both

Archimago and Mammon with Satan. The three days temptation of Sir Guyon in the Cave of Mammon is compared with Christ's temptation in *Paradise Regained*. Then Guyon's "adventure" in the Bower of Bliss is brought into comparison with Adam's temptation, Raphael taking the place of the Palmer. It should be remarked that what Raphael insists upon is the virtue of temperance.

An Ode, Humbly Inscribed to the Queen on the Glorious Success of Her Majesty's Arms. Written in Imitation of Spenser's Style (1706) by Matthew Prior.

The poem is written in a ten-lined stanza with the following rhyme arrangement: ab, ab, cd, cd, ee. Professor Phelps describes it as "an extremely important poem, being the prototype of a great many of the Spenserian imitations that followed."

The Alley (1727) by Alexander Pope. Published in the "Miscellanies."

A coarse burlesque of Spenser consisting of six Spenserian stanzas.

The Shepherd's Week (1714) by John Gay.

Gay borrows some of the names of Spenser's shepherds. "As he [Spenser] called his eclogues, the Shepherd's Calender, and divided the same into twelve months, I have chosen (peradventure not over-rashly) to name mine by the days of the week."

The School-Mistress (1737, complete edition 1742) by William Shenstone.

In the subject he selected for Spenserian treatment Shenstone illustrates a typical eighteenth-century attitude toward the elder poet.

The Castle of Indolence (1748) by James Thomson.

Described by Joseph Warton as an "exquisite piece of wild and romantic imagery." It consists of only two cantos.

The Minstrel (1771–1774) by James Beattie.

A very influential Spenserian poem inspired by Bishop Percy's Essay on the Ancient Minstrels, published in his *Reliques of Ancient English Poetry.*

The Waterfall and the Eglantine (1800) and *The Oak and the Broom* (1800) by William Wordsworth.

Compare with these poems the February eclogue.

The White Doe of Rylstone (1815) by William Wordsworth.

This is reminiscent of the story of Una and her lamb.

Imitation of Spenser (1817), *Calidore* (1817), *Specimen of an Induction to a Poem* (1817) by John Keats.

REFERENCES

Böhme, T. Spensers literarisches Nachleben bis zu Shelley. Berlin (Palaestra, XCIII), 1911.

Cory, H. E. *The Golden Age of the Spenserian Pastoral.* Publications of the Modern Language Association, XXV (1910), 241–67.

Cory, H. E. *The Critics of Edmund Spenser.* Berkeley, 1911.

Cory, H. E. *Spenser, Thomson, and Romanticism.* Publications of the Modern Language Association, XXVI (1911), 51–91.

Cory, H. E. *Spenser, the School of the Fletchers, and Milton.* Berkeley, 1912.

INDEX